Causes of Delinquency

Causes of Delinquency

Travis Hirschi

With a new introduction by the author

Transaction Publishers
New Brunswick (U.S.A.) and London (U.K.)

Third printing 2004

New material this edition copyright © 2002 by Transaction Publishers, New Brunswick, New Jersey. Originally published in 1969 by University of California Press.

This book is printed on acid-free paper that meets the American National Standard for Permanence of Paper for Printed Library Materials.

Library of Congress Catalog Number: 2001043719
ISBN: 0-7658-0900-1
Printed in the United States of America

Library of Congress Cataloging-in-Publication Data

Hirschi, Travis.
  Causes of delinquency / Travis Hirschi ; with a new introduction by the author.
      p. cm.
  Includes bibliographical references and index.
  ISBN 0-7658-0900-1 (paper : alk. paper)
    1. Juvenile delinquency. I. Title.

HV9069 .H643 2001
364.36—dc21   2001043719

For Anna, Kendal, Nathan, and Justine

Contents

Introduction to the Transaction Edition

Some ten years after the publication of *Causes of Delinquency*, I was asked by the editors of *Current Contents* to account for the 215 times the book had been cited and its subsequent status as a "Citation Classic." Flattered and disarmed by such attention, I distributed credit for the book's popularity among four of its elements: "the [social control] theory of delinquency it advocates; its findings on the correlates of delinquency; the set of data on which it is based; and ...the methodology it employs." The full account, written in 1980, follows:

> The ideas in the book were common in the literature of sociology and criminology at the time (1964) I decided to order them in some systematic fashion for a dissertation at Berkeley. I had been familiar with these ideas for some time, and had learned to respect them because they had been deemed worthy of explication by David Matza, Irving Piliavin, Erving Goffman, and Jackson Toby, among others.

> The central findings in the book had been reported in the criminological literature over a period of many years. I was familiar with these findings because I had by then been working for several years with Hanan Selvin on a methodological critique of delinquency research.

> My initial plan was simply to put the ideas and the research findings together. With this plan in mind, I went on the job market. I came home from my first trip east convinced there were more important things than regular employment. The ideas I found exciting and obviously consistent with available data had been treated as contrary to fact, passé, and even "appalling." The only way to remedy this situation, it seemed, was to show the ability of the ideas to account for a single body of relevant data.

> Despite the efforts of my dissertation advisor, Charles Y. Glock, I was unable to obtain data for secondary analysis. (In those days, large

scale data sets were rare and investigators perhaps understandably reluctant to release them before they had been thoroughly exploited.) Glock then put me in touch with Alan B. Wilson, whose Richmond Youth Project was just getting underway. Wilson agreed to let me add items to the research instruments in exchange for work on the project. (An NIMH predoctoral fellowship precluded gainful employment and provided large amounts of poverty-induced leisure.) Although I eventually became deputy director of the project, my contributions were mainly clerical (and physical—boxes of questionnaires are heavy) rather than intellectual.

The key to the book is the body of data on which it is based. I know from experience that the ideas could not otherwise have been sharpened sufficiently to impress sociologists. I know that most of the findings were available (though often ignored) before my work was published. I know too that the statistical analysis is not sufficiently sophisticated by itself to attract more than negative attention. It is therefore fitting that many of the citations to my work stem from the fact that it contains a convenient description of the Richmond Youth Project. Thanks to Wilson's generosity, the Richmond data have been available for secondary analysis of delinquency and related issues almost from the day they were transportable. In fact, my work was cited before it appeared in print in an article based on secondary analysis of Richmond data (Hirschi 1980).

With some elaboration, this history may help explain the tone and content of the book as well as its provisional claim to popularity or influence: The book was written in a warm and secure setting for what was assumed to be a basically hostile audience. Its author had spent some time and effort criticizing the work of others on the very topic he now planned to study. He knew in advance the kind of data he would use to test the theory he planned to develop. He also knew, he thought, what he would find in those data. From these circumstances, it is possible to predict the book's occasionally argumentative tone, its preoccupation with alternative interpretations of the data, its frequent use of supportive quotations, its confident hypotheses, and perhaps even the success of the theory it advocates and the failure of popular competing theories. What it does not predict is the subsequent success of the "passé and even 'appalling'" ideas of social control theory.[1]

[1] My 1980 account suggests that I was able to dispel such criticism by deft argument and clever data analysis. This impression is not wholly accurate: "[Hirschi] takes his psychology straight from Thomas Hobbes and seems stuck in the eighteenth century. He seems quite unaware of the great body of psychological research and theory relevant to criminology" (Gibson 1970:452). The same reviewer later

Today, some 30 years after its publication, *Causes of Delinquency* is more frequently cited than ever, but it is not now so easy to lose myself in an understated self-congratulatory account of the origins and content of the book. Control theory has prospered in the interim, but *Causes* no longer stands virtually alone in its defense. The works on which the book was based are now better known and their relevance more widely appreciated; I have since published a sufficient number of articles on control theory to be labeled "the spokesperson of the microsociological perspective" (Adler et al. 1995, 61); dissertations on and formal tests of the theory have appeared "with perhaps unrivaled frequency" (Kempf 1993, 143); and several subsequent books have contributed in important ways to acceptance of the control perspective. These include: Ruth Kornhauser, *Social Sources of Delinquency* (1978 [1984]); Bob Roshier, *Controlling Crime: The Classical Perspective in Criminology* (1989); Michael Gottfredson and Travis Hirschi, *A General Theory of Crime* (1990); and Robert Sampson and John Laub, *Crime in the Making* (1993).

In the hope that the book may be better understood by examining its consequences as well as its origins, let me illustrate and briefly comment on the connections between *Causes of Delinquency* and each of the collections of scholarly work just identified.

Subsequent Books on Control Theory

Kornhauser's work is considered by some to be the greatest book ever written on crime and delinquency. For reasons soon to be clear, I am not inclined to dispute that judgment. Kornhauser did what I was unable to do—champion the claims of social control theory over its major competitors using only published research findings. She was not overly impressed with the exposition of social control theory in *Causes of Delinquency*, but she was eventually *convinced by its data* that her favorite theory, the "strain model" of Merton, Cohen, and Cloward and Ohlin, was wrong. Because she had previously rejected Sutherland's "cultural deviance" theory, social control theory was the only option open to her.

allowed that the results of the Richmond Youth Study had been "rendered nugatory" by the requirement of parental permission. (It is of course likely that the real reason for the success of my argument is that it at last found a receptive audience. The treatment I received the first time I attended the meetings of the American Society of Criminology [1976] was overwhelmingly friendly. So much so that I have had warm feelings toward the ASC and the site of that convention [Tucson] ever since.)

Once she recognized it as a variant of social disorganization theory, Kornhauser saw control theory everywhere and defended it in no uncertain terms against all comers.[2]

Roshier's book is an incisive intellectual history of criminology. He too does something I was unable to do—examine the role of social control theory in the rise of what he calls "postclassical criminology." Roshier may not have been overly impressed by the particular version of control theory he found in *Causes of Delinquency*, but he gave the book credit for filling "important gaps" in classical theory and for "inviting expansion" along classical lines—something he then proceeded to do (1989, 46-49, 67 ff.). Perhaps more significantly, he treated strain and cultural deviance theories as relics of an earlier stage of theoretical evolution.

For purposes of exposition, I should mention Sampson and Laub before Gottfredson and Hirschi, whose book was published three years earlier. Once again we find scholars doing something I was unable to do—in this case analyze a large body of available data using the ideas of social control theory. Like Kornhauser, Sampson and Laub were not impressed with the exposition of social control theory found in *Causes of Delinquency*, but they were impressed (as were other criminologists) by the ability of traditional "informal social control theory" to organize and explain the most important set of data on crime yet collected, especially when they considered that those collecting it had disavowed interest in theories of any kind (Glueck and Glueck, 1950:3-9). At the same time, Sampson and Laub were sharply critical of the self-control version of control theory advanced by Gottfredson and Hirschi.

Gottfredson and Hirschi's self-control theory has attracted considerable research and critical attention, and is a major element in the current "popularity" of control theory. At the same time, as in the example just mentioned, it has contributed to acceptance of *social* control theory by acting as an "undesirable" alternative theory. This has made it possible for me to profit from criticism of my own work. I did not plan this outcome.

In 1979, Michael Gottfredson and I began a collaboration that lasted on an active basis for about ten years. Our first paper was a critique of the Sutherland tradition in criminology from a research or positivist point of

[2] Kornhauser acknowledges the influence of *Causes of Delinquency* in the preface to the paperback edition of her book (Kornhauser 1984, viii). In the dedication of the copy she sent to me, she wrote that the argument in *Causes* was "all that kept this from being a totally wrong-headed book."

view. The stance we took then, and the stance we tried to maintain throughout our collaboration, was that the facts about crime and delinquency should take priority over all other considerations. Sutherland, we argued, had misled the field by his dismissal of the multiple factor approach and by his refusal to grant even provisional validity to non-sociological explanations of crime.

Consistent with this emphasis, our second paper focused on the effects of age on crime. We concluded that the decline in crime with age is one of the "brute facts" of criminology. From there, it was a few short steps (and a good many papers) to *A General Theory of Crime*, which argues that differences in self-control established early in life are highly stable, and account for a large array of criminal, delinquent, deviant, and reckless acts.

Not once during the course of our work together did Gottfredson ask how the position we were taking squared with *Causes of Delinquency*. Nor did I raise such questions. On occasion it may have crossed my mind that I had had a previous life, but it was strictly contrary to our oft-proclaimed position to worry about such things.

If Gottfredson and I felt an obligation to avoid questions about possible reconciliation between social control and self-control theory,[3] others did not. The first reviews of *A General Theory of Crime* wondered about the connection between my old and current views (e.g., Akers 1991), and research comparing their validity followed in short order. The common conclusion of these comparisons seems to be that they reveal serious problems for one or both theories.

It may seem reasonable to ask how the two theories relate to one another, and which better serves some useful purpose. Such questions appear especially reasonable when both theories have been fully formulated and thus cannot claim that their development would be hindered by such concerns. But I cannot help thinking that they are misplaced and their appearance of constructive curiosity ultimately misleading.

> My interpretation is that self-control theory rejects important insights from Hirschi's original formulation of social control and is therefore a less adequate explanation. The adoption of the age-invariance thesis and the assumed stability of self-control beyond early childhood imply that individuals do not have the capacity to change over the life course. Thus, self-control theory completely neglects the impact of wider, structural forces on individuals in later life... (Taylor 2001, 384).

[3] We have tried to explain the role of the age effect in the evolution of our thinking about crime, but we have not attempted to assess the relative merits of the schemes in place at the beginning and end of this process (Hirschi and Gottfredson 2001).

It may be useful to put Taylor's assessment in bald-faced terms: (1) social control theory is better than self-control theory; (2) the major factual premises of self-control theory are wrong; and (3) a major factual implication of self-control theory is also wrong. I think it less likely that she would make such assertions (and less likely that they would be published) were she comparing two theories by two authors. In that situation, the critic does not normally simply declare a winner without examining the claims of the loser. But when one author is on both sides, there is little risk in this exercise. Whatever the position taken on the relative merits of the theories, the critic can claim support from the author's own words. Should the common author prove cantankerous, it can be pointed out that such unreliability is nothing new. Should an uncommon co-author weigh in on the matter, it may be used to remind the reader that this author's views may be discounted because he or she is the likely source of inconsistency in the first place.

So, at issue here is the importance of consistency in theory. Everyone would agree that consistency is a virtue, so much so that inconsistency is prima facie evidence of hidden vice. Indeed, discovery of inconsistency rightfully allows the critic to discount other criteria of theoretical adequacy. Empirical data are of no value because they cannot simultaneously support inconsistent arguments. Pushed a little, even possible inconsistency may raise serious concerns about the claims of a theory.

How, then, could Gottfredson and I pay so little attention to this matter? The answer is this: We believe that consistency *within a theory* is crucial, so crucial that it may require conclusions that one would prefer to do without. At the same time, we believe that consistency *across theories* is no virtue at all. Reconciliation of separate theories of crime is either impossible or unnecessary. If they are the same theory, reconciliation is not required. If they are different theories, they cannot be made the same without doing violence (introducing inconsistency) to one or the other, or both (Hirschi 1979). Social control theory and self-control theory are not unique in this regard. They share important assumptions, but they are not the same theory, and should be judged on their merits, as should some future theory that attempts to encompass them both.

Sources of the Theory

The long-ago reviews of *Causes of Delinquency*, favorable and unfavorable, paid little attention to the sources of social control theory. Those unconvinced by the argument of the book of course had little interest in its intellectual history, and tended to focus on alleged weaknesses in the measures or biases in the sample. As a class, those more favorably inclined mentioned my ties to Durkheim, Hobbes, Reiss, and even Freud, but none mentioned the broad intellectual heritage of control theory and none was concerned about issues of priority. Today, most discussions of the theory summarize works prior to *Causes* to illustrate that "control theories of crime have a long history" or that "there was a rich history of control theories of crime by the mid-1960s"—i.e. before I began to write (Paternoster and Bachman 2001, 73, 77). All of which suggests to me that one contribution of the book was to call attention to the substantial but scattered literature friendly to the control perspective. As the reader will see, I identify and often quote a lengthy list of control theorists—Matza, Nye, Reckless, Toby, Briar, Piliavin, and Reiss—and attribute important elements of the perspective to the likes of Hobbes and Durkheim. To top off the list of donors, I even claim that "the early sociologists in this country" were essentially control theorists. If most authors write their books by ransacking a library, not many are continually reminded of that fact. I am. And I deserve it. Social control theory was not the most popular perspective in the social sciences at the time I wrote, and I thought I needed all the help I could get.

This desire for legitimacy put me in somewhat of a bind. On the one hand, I had to praise famous men. On the other, I had to contribute something of my own. As a result, my version of social control theory is not merely a summary of prior work. I may have been thorough in my efforts to spread responsibility, but I was keenly aware that many of my supporters could not be counted on in a pinch. Many, if not most, had already shown themselves to be disloyal. The test I relied upon to detect unfaithfulness was, of course, inconsistency. To be a full-fledged control theorist, one could not accept assumptions contrary to the theory. Given the times, this was a tall order. Given the times, most criminologists knew that criminal behavior is caused (motivated), that criminals pursue careers in crime, and that cultural variability is virtually without limit. In their usual forms, all of these assumptions are inconsistent with control theory. They are the primary reasons control theory was so hard to sell. Not surprisingly, they are also the major source of discordant elements in the control theories of the time. I was as careful as I could be to avoid all of them.[4]

[4] It may seem strange to suggest that a book titled *Causes of Delinquency* carefully avoided the idea that crime is caused, but—given the tendency of social

The assumption that theories must provide motives (causes) for criminal behavior shows itself in control theories in lists of basic human needs and in a view of human nature "in which man is active, moved to gratify strong wants, and receptive to efforts to socialize him primarily as they relate to the gratification of wants" (Kornhauser 1984, 39). According to Kornhauser, this assumption is common to American social disorganization theorists—from W. I. Thomas through Thrasher and Riess and Nye to Kornhauser herself. She takes me to task for missing this point, for arguing in favor of "constant [and undescribed] motivation to crime across persons" in the face of evidence and a statement by Durkheim to the contrary (1984, 48). Kornhauser is partially correct. I did not clearly see the motivational element in social disorganization theory. When I did see it, I acted properly. For example, I did not include W. I. Thomas as a control theorist for precisely the reason that he analyzed behavior as an attempt to realize his famous "four wishes." I continue to believe that I was correct in rejecting the basic assumption of a competing perspective, and, if anything, I was too timid on this score. In control theory, strong wants are conducive not to crime but to conformity because they tie us to the future and because crime is an inefficient means of realizing one's goals. As would then be expected, the view that crime is need-based or strongly motivated behavior has produced a series of concepts and hypotheses sharply at odds with the facts (Gottfredson and Hirschi 1993).

The idea that crime is a profession, a full-time role, or a way of life was also accepted by more than one scholar otherwise counted as a control theorist. The wish to locate career criminals, types of offenders, or specialists in particular crimes remains as strong today as when *Causes of Delinquency* was written. The motives behind this enterprise, if I may, are clear. Success would justify differential treatment and special handling within the criminal justice system. But the search for qualitative differences among offenders and between offenders and law-abiding citizens remains contrary to basic assumptions of control theory, and claims of discovery of such differences remain, in my view, premature.

The idea that cultures vary in myriad ways in their definitions of criminal and deviant behavior was just beginning to come under attack when I wrote *Causes of Delinquency*. Much to the glee of some of its critics, *Causes* purported to provide its own evidence of the universality of attitudes toward crime, of core values common to all cultures and

scientists to equate causes with motives—such is the case. I address this issue in "Causes and Prevention of Juvenile Delinquency" (1977).

social groups. Interestingly enough, despite the current celebration of multiculturalism in the larger society, mainstream criminology now appears to accept cultural universalism with respect to crime. And I think for good reasons. Here is one of them: Cross-cultural studies of self-reported delinquency routinely find that the causes and correlates of delinquent behavior do not vary from country to country. In other words, the findings of research do not depend on, and are unaffected by, local legal definitions of the behavior in question (Junger-Tas et al 1994). By pointedly ignoring the operations of the criminal justice system, social control theory predicts this result. Still, even control theorists find it hard to resist the seemingly reasonable conclusion that some groups favor crime, and that for people in them lack of social control may be conducive to conformity (e.g., Roshier 1989, 89).

Tests of the Theory

Kempf (1993) identified seventy-one empirical tests of social control theory published between 1970 and 1991, and was able to locate twenty-seven dissertations on the theory completed during the same period. She concludes, I think it fair to say, that the theory has not been challenged by these "tests." Together, they raise many issues and offer much advice, but they tend to see salvation in methodological refinement rather than in rethinking the problem.

What, then, makes social control theory particularly attractive to empirical researchers? LeBlanc (1983, quoted by Kempf 1993, 143-44) answers the question this way: "[A]t the beginning of the 1970's, [Hirschi's theory] was the only theoretical formulation that tried to synthesize in a coherent and complex theoretical plan a great deal of information on the causes of delinquent behavior."

So, the mystery is no mystery at all. My version of social control theory has been so frequently called upon because it guides and justifies research on a broad range of topics, and has few competitors in this regard. Perhaps equally important, it has a special affinity to a well-known, widely practiced research method. It is easily shown that the theory's virtues for research purposes are in its structure as much as in its content. It starts from the straightforward assumption that deviant behavior occurs when the bond of the individual to society is weak or broken. The bond has many potential dimensions or elements. And "society" turns out to encompass a potentially large array of persons, groups, institutions, and even futures states of the individual—e.g. parents, teachers, families, schools, peers, gangs, churches, education, marriage, children. To make things even better for those who would test or use the theory: (1) the strength of each element of the bond to each of the objects is assessed and reported by the individual—making the theory directly amenable to survey research and the large array of statistical devices available for the analysis of survey data; (2) the strength of each element of the bond is a function of characteristics of the individual and of the object in question—making the theory receptive to study of the role of individual differences and various institutional arrangements.

Looked at in this way, what is surprising is not how many researchers have tested the particular theory found in *Causes of Delinquency*, but how few have advanced alternative versions within the control theory framework.

My Career as Spokesperson

Books may tend to lose their force and cogency with age, but the same is true of lists of their alleged shortcomings. I spent long years assessing the validity of some of the major criticisms of the data on which *Causes of Delinquency* is based, and came away with the conclusion that I pretty much had it right in the first place (Hindelang, Hirschi, and Weis 1981). At the same time, much of my subsequent work was devoted to issues raised but not settled in the book. As a result of these efforts, I am not inclined to defend it further against its methodological critics, or to grant the accuracy or wisdom of the lists of deficiencies that have accumulated over the years. I have tried on occasion to force myself to think about fixing it, about bringing it into line with what we think we know now that we did not know then, but in every instance the pen has refused to move.

I think the pen may be on to something. What do we know now that I didn't know then? We know that the police respond to the behavior more than to the status of the offender. (At the same time, racial profiling has become a major policy issue.) We know that alcohol and drug use may well be manifestations rather than causes of delinquency. (But see almost any textbook.) We know that the age effect on delinquency is highly robust, and that differences in delinquency are reasonably stable over the life course. (As the journals swell with contrary theories.) We knew then that our measures of delinquency were suspect, and that our results were dependent on the composition and representativeness of our samples. But there is good evidence and the testimony of *Causes of Delinquency* ("the empirical findings on delinquency fluctuate much less widely than the statements made about them" [p. 243]) that our fears were baseless. Still, we continue to think otherwise and to dismiss perfectly good findings for not very good reasons. All in all, then, *Causes of Delinquency* may stand as a reasonably balanced account of what we knew at the beginning of the research explosion of the last third of the 20th century—an account not too far from what we know at the end of it.

* * *

For some time now, John Laub has been prodding me to acknowledge the true sources of my views about crime and criminology and to propose fresh ways of resolving important issues in the field. This extended interview will become the introduction to a collection of my papers John is editing. A recurrent theme of our discussion has, of course, been the connection between social control and self-control theory, and I am afraid I may have taken more than one position on this issue. Nevertheless, I remain convinced that the befuddlement of a theorist, however profound, says nothing about the validity of his or her theories. As a not incidental byproduct of this discussion, we concluded that it was important to see *Causes of Delinquency* once again in print. John has taken the lead in this effort. I am grateful to him for that as well as for his good-natured insistence that I take seriously some of my long-standing velleities.

I am also grateful to Irving Louis Horowitz for his unfailing support. I can count many things I would not have done without it.

Travis Hirschi
March 2001

References

Adler, Freda, Gerhard O. W. Mueller, and William S. Laufer. 1995. *Criminology*. New York: McGraw-Hill.

Akers, Ronald. 1991. "Self-Control as a General Theory of Crime." *Journal of Quantitative Criminology* 7:201-211.

Gibson, H. B. 1970. Review of *Causes of Delinquency*. *Sociological Review* 18:452-453.

Glueck, Sheldon, and Eleanor Glueck. 1950. *Unraveling Juvenile Delinquency*. Cambridge: Harvard University Press.

Gottfredson, Michael, and Travis Hirschi. 1990. *A General Theory of Crime.* Stanford: Stanford University Press.

_____. 1993. "A Control Theory Interpretation of Psychological Research on Aggression." In *Aggression and Violence: Social Interactionist Perspectives,* ed. R. B. Felson and J. T. Tedeschi, 47-68. Washington, DC: APA Monographs.

Hindelang, Michael, Travis Hirschi, and Joseph Weis. 1981. *Measuring Delinquency.* Beverly Hills: Sage.

Hirschi, Travis. 1977. "Causes and Prevention of Juvenile Delinquency." *Sociological Inquiry* 47:322-41.

_____.1979. "Separate and Unequal is Better." *Journal of Research in Crime and Delinquency* 16:34-38.

_____.1980. "This Week's Citation Classic." *Current Contents* 12-38:16.

Hirschi, Travis, and Michael Gottfredson. 1983. "Age and the Explanation of Crime." *American Journal of Sociology* 89:552-84.

_____. 2001. "Self Control Theory." In *Explaining Criminals and Crime,* ed. Raymond Paternoster and Ronet Bachman, 81-96. Los Angeles: Roxbury.

Junger-Tas, Josine et al. 1994. *Delinquent Behavior Among Young People in the Western World.* New York: Kugler Publications.

Kempf, Kimberly. 1993. "The Empirical Status of Hirschi's Control Theory." In *New Directions in Criminological Theory,* volume 4, ed. Freda Adler and William S. Laufer, 143-185. New Brunswick: Transaction Publishers.

Kornhauser, Ruth. 1984 [1978]. *Social Sources of Delinquency.* Chicago: University of Chicago Press.

LeBlanc, Marc. 1983. "Delinquency as an Epiphenomenon of Adolescence." In *Current Issues in Juvenile Justice,* ed. R. Corrado, M. LeBlanc, and J. Tre'panier. Toronto: Butterworths.

Paternoster, Raymond, and Ronet Bachman. 2001. *Explaining Criminals and Crime.* Los Angeles: Roxbury.

Roshier, Bob. 1989. *Controlling Crime: The Classical Perspective in Criminology.* Chicago: Lyceum.

Taylor, Claire. 2001. "The Relationship between Social and Self-control: Tracing Hirschi's Criminological Career." *Theoretical Criminology* 5:369-88.

Preface

In this book I attempt to state and test a theory of delinquency. The theory I advocate sees in the delinquent a person relatively free of the intimate attachments, the aspirations, and the moral beliefs that bind most people to a life within the law. In prominent alternative theories, the delinquent appears either as a frustrated striver forced into delinquency by his acceptance of the goals common to us all, or as an innocent foreigner attempting to obey the rules of a society that is not in position to make the law or to define conduct as good or evil. Throughout the book, I stress the incompatibility of these images of the delinquent and the contrasting predictions to which they lead us.

Although this study is based on a large body of data collected with delinquency as a major focus of attention, I have tried to rely upon earlier investigations and to emphasize the extent to which the present findings are consistent with them. This consistency is, to my mind, remarkable. It is also a source of some difficulty. As anyone who has tried it knows, it is easier to construct theories "twenty years ahead of their time" than theories grounded on and consistent with data currently available. But the day we could pit one study of delinquency against another and then forget them both is gone. We are no longer free to construct the factual world as we construct our explanations of it. As a consequence, our theories do not have the elegance and simplicity of those of an earlier period. I take consolation in the certain hope that they are somehow nearer the truth.

Seattle, Washington
October 1968

Acknowledgments

The data upon which this study is based were collected as part of the Richmond Youth Project at the Survey Research Center, University of California, Berkeley, with support from a research grant from the National Institute of Mental Health (NH-00970).

For reasons they will understand, I should like to thank Charles Y. Glock, Irving Piliavin, David Matza, James F. Short, Jr., Debora Dean Kerkof, Rodney Stark, Robert Wenkert, Glen Elder, Beulah Reddaway, and, especially, Alan B. Wilson.

"But the philosopher doesn't admit these relationships. Considering but himself alone, only to himself does he account for everything; and he prevails by his own strength. He has recourse to those fine systems of humanity and beneficence only at times for policy's sake."

"Such a man is a monster!" Justine said.

"Such a man is a man of nature."

DeSade, Justine.

Chapter I

Perspectives on Delinquency

Three fundamental perspectives on delinquency and deviant behavior dominate the current scene. According to *strain* or motivational theories, legitimate desires that conformity cannot satisfy force a person into deviance.[1] According to *control* or bond theories, a person is free to commit delinquent acts because his ties to the conventional order have somehow been broken.[2] According to *cultural deviance* theories, the deviant conforms to a set of standards not accepted by a larger or more powerful society.[3] Although most current theories of crime and delinquency contain elements of at least two and occasionally all three of these perspectives,

[1] The purest example of a strain theory, contaminated only rarely by assumptions appropriate to a control theory, is found in Merton's "Social Structure and Anomie" (Robert K. Merton, *Social Theory and Social Structure* [New York: The Free Press, 1957], pp. 131–160). One characteristic of strain theory is that the motivation to crime overcomes or eliminates restraints—such as considerations of morality (see also Talcott Parsons, *The Social System* [New York: The Free Press, 1951], pp. 249–325). Because Merton traces his intellectual history to Durkheim, strain theories are often called "anomie" theories (see Richard A. Cloward and Lloyd E. Ohlin, *Delinquency and Opportunity* [New York: The Free Press, 1960], especially pp. 77–143). Actually, Durkheim's theory is one of the purest examples of a control theory: both anomie and egoism are conditions of "deregulation," and the "aberrant" behavior that follows is an automatic consequence of such deregulation.

[2] Control theories take many forms, but all of the works by control theorists listed below explicitly adopt the assumption that I take as essential to this perspective. David Matza, *Delinquency and Drift* (New York: Wiley, 1964). F. Ivan Nye, *Family Relationships and Delinquent Behavior* (New York: Wiley, 1958). Walter C. Reckless, *The Crime Problem*, 4th ed. (New York: Appleton-Century-Crofts, 1967), Ch. 22. See also Jackson Toby, "Hoodlum or Businessman: An American Dilemma," *The Jews*, ed. Marshall Sklare (New York: The Free Press, 1958), pp. 542–550, and Albert J. Reiss, Jr., "Delinquency as the Failure of Personal and Social Controls," *American Sociological Review*, XVI (1951), 196–207.

[3] I take the term "cultural deviance" from a paper by Ruth Kornhauser, "Theoretical Issues in the Sociological Study of Juvenile Delinquency," mimeographed, Center for the Study of Law and Society, Berkeley, 1963. Other terms for theories of this type are "cultural conflict," "transmission," "subcultural," and "differential association." The most influential theory of cultural deviance is Sutherland's theory of differential association (see Edwin H. Sutherland and Donald R. Cressey, *Principles of Criminology*, 7th ed. [Philadelphia: Lippincott, 1966], pp. 77–83). See also Walter B. Miller, "Lower

reconciliation of their assumptions is very difficult.[4] If, as the control theorist assumes, the ties of many persons to the conventional order may be weak or virtually nonexistent, the strain theorist, in accounting for their deviance, builds into his explanation pressure that is unnecessary. If, on the other hand, it is reasonable to assume with the strain theorist that everyone is at some point strongly tied to *the* conventional system, then it is unreasonable to assume that many are not (control theories), or that many are tied to different "conventional" systems (cultural deviance theories).

In the present study I analyze a large body of data on delinquency collected in Western Contra Costa County, California, contrasting throughout the assumptions of the strain, control, and cultural deviance theories. I begin by outlining the assumptions of these theories and discussing the logical and empirical difficulties attributed to each of them. I then draw from many sources an outline of *social control* theory, the theory that informs the subsequent analysis and which is advocated here.

Strain Theories

Strain theories are the historical result of good answers to a bad question.[5] The question was Hobbes's: "Why do men obey

Class Culture as a Generating Milieu of Gang Delinquency," *The Journal of Social Issues*, XIV (1958), 5–19.

[4] The most forthright attempt to construct a theory combining assumptions from two of these perspectives is Cloward and Ohlin's synthesis of strain and cultural deviance theories (*Delinquency and Opportunity*). Kornhauser concludes that they have "constructed theories of subcultural delinquency that are congruent with social disorganization [strain] theories but unacceptable to cultural transmission theorists" ("Theoretical Issues," Part III, p. 4). My own analysis had led to the conclusion that the Cloward–Ohlin synthesis was unacceptable to both strain and cultural deviance theorists. In any event, the difficulties are clearer in Richard A. Cloward's "Illegitimate Means, Anomie, and Deviant Behavior," *American Sociological Review*, XXIV (1959), 164–176.

[5] For the opposite and generally accepted view, see Talcott Parsons, *The Structure of Social Action* (New York: The Free Press, 1949), pp. 89–94, and Dennis H. Wrong, "The Oversocialized Conception of Man in Modern Sociology," *American Sociological Review*, XXVI (1961), 183–193. The question is bad because it assumes that something clearly variable is in fact constant. In their attempts to get out of this difficulty, sociologists are forced to pose the opposite question, which leads to the "interminable dialogue" which Wrong notes and approves of. Actually, of course, the problem of conformity and the problem of deviance are the same problem, and questions concerning conformity and deviance should be posed in such a manner that both problems can be solved at once.

the rules of society?" Although the Hobbesian question is granted a central place in the history of sociological theory, few have accepted the Hobbesian answer: "Of all passions, that which inclineth men least to break the laws, is fear. Nay, excepting some generous natures, it is the only thing, when there is appearance of profit or pleasure by breaking the laws, that makes men keep them." [6] It is not so, the sociologist argued: there is more to conformity than fear. Man has an "attitude of respect" toward the rules of society; he "internalizes the norms." Since man has a conscience, he is not free simply to calculate the costs of illegal or deviant behavior. He feels *morally* obligated to conform, whether or not it is to his advantage to do so.[7] As if this were not enough to show that Hobbes was wrong, the sociologist adduced yet another powerful source of conformity: "People are . . . profoundly sensitive to the expectations of others." [8] Now, since others almost by definition expect one to conform, deviation can occur only at great cost to the deviator.

Having thus established that man is a moral animal who desires to obey the rules, the sociologist was then faced with the problem of explaining his deviance. Clearly, if men desire to conform, they must be under great pressure before they will resort to deviance. In the classic strain theories, this pressure is provided by *legitimate* desires.[9] A man desires success, for example, as everyone tells him he should, but he cannot attain success conforming to the rules; consequently, in desperation, he turns to deviant behavior or crime to attain that which he considers rightfully his. The theoretical assumption that man is moral and the empirical fact that he violates rules in which he believes are thus made consistent.

Examples of this perspective are numerous:

[6] Thomas Hobbes, *Leviathan* (Oxford: Basil Blackwell, 1957), p. 195.

[7] Parsons, *Structure*, especially pp. 378–390.

[8] Francis X. Sutton et al., *The American Business Creed* (Cambridge, Mass.: Harvard University Press, 1956), p. 264, quoted by Wrong, "The Oversocialized Conception," p. 188.

[9] There was a more or less conscious attempt in one period of American sociology to avoid the evil-causes-evil "fallacy." Vices were consequently traced to prior virtues or to virtuous institutions: for example, crime to ambition, prostitution to marriage. The most sophisticated spokesman for this good-causes-evil view is Albert K. Cohen (see, for example, his "Multiple Factor Approaches" in Marvin E. Wolfgang et al., eds., *The Sociology of Crime and Delinquency* [New York: Wiley, 1962], pp. 77–80).

. . . a cardinal American virtue, "ambition," promotes a cardinal American vice, "deviant behavior." [10]

We suggest that many lower-class adolescents experience desperation born of the certainty that their position in the economic structure is relatively fixed and immutable—a desperation made all the more poignant by their exposure to a cultural ideology in which failure to orient oneself upward is regarded as a moral defect and failure to become mobile as proof of it.[11]

Although the strain model has been applied to deviant acts that appear to be the result of cold calculation (the "decision" to become a professional criminal), it has been particularly appealing as an explanation of acts that are characterized by apparent irrationality or intense emotion (such as suicide and malicious and/or "pointless" destruction of property). Since the strain theorist uses such concepts as "discontent," "frustration," or "deprivation" as part of his explanation of deviant acts, he can easily transfer some of the emotion producing the act to the act itself. This virtue of strain theory is at the same time a source of difficulty.

Criticisms of Strain Theory

The strain theorist must provide motivation to delinquency sufficient to account for the neutralization of moral constraints. Once he builds motivation as powerful as this into his explanatory system, he usually has a plausible explanation of delinquency. "Intense frustration" would seem to provide sufficient motivational energy to account for "delinquency." In fact, given the seriousness of most delinquent acts, it provides a little too much pressure; and during the days, weeks, or months that the intensely frustrated boy is conforming to conventional expectations, its dormancy is hard to explain.

The fact that most delinquent boys eventually become law-abiding adults is also a source of embarrassment to the strain theorist. The conditions he builds into his model normally do not change during adolescence or, for that matter, at the attainment of adulthood. As the strain theorist himself contends, the lower-class boy's position in the economic structure is relatively fixed. His

[10] Merton, *Social Theory*, p. 146.
[11] Cloward and Ohlin, *Delinquency and Opportunity*, pp. 106–107.

eventual reform, attested to by many empirical studies,[12] thus cannot be explained by changes in the conditions that initially forced him into delinquency.[13]

Delinquency is not confined to the lower classes. In order to get the pressure he needs, the strain theorist usually creates a perfect relation between social class and delinquency.[14] This relation *is* "created": the strain theorist is interested in explaining only *lower-class delinquency.*[15] Since there is no lower-class delinquency in the middle classes, the strain theorist may ask: What is it about the lower-class situation that produces delinquency? If he ever feels called upon to explain middle-class delinquency, the strain theorist has two options: he can argue that apparently middle-class boys committing delinquent acts are "really" lower-class boys;[16] or he can reverse his original procedure and ask:

[12] Much of this literature is summarized and critically evaluated in Barbara Wootton, *Social Science and Social Pathology* (New York: Macmillan, 1959), pp. 157–172. Actually, one may derive contradictory statements from research on "reform." The statement in the text (most delinquent boys eventually become law-abiding adults) is true, but so, too, is the statement that most delinquent boys will be arrested for crimes as adults. The reconciliation of these statements is simple: the first relies upon a broader definition of delinquency than does the latter. To be meaningful, then, such statements must specify fairly carefully the degree of delinquency entailed. Follow-up studies of boys appearing in juvenile court suggest that a majority will be arrested for crimes as adults (see Henry D. McKay, "Report on the Criminal Careers of Male Delinquents in Chicago," *Juvenile Delinquency and Youth Crime*, Report of The President's Commission on Law Enforcement and Administration of Justice [Washington: USGPO, 1067], pp. 107–113, and Sheldon and Eleanor Glueck, *Juvenile Delinquents Grown Up* [New York: The Commonwealth Fund, 1940]. Follow-up studies of boys picked up by the police would show that the vast majority will not be arrested for crimes as adults (see Matza, *Delinquency and Drift,* pp. 22–26, nn. 30, 31).

Since strain theories attempt to explain the behavior of more or less serious offenders, the fact that the "great majority" of delinquent boys become law-abiding adults is not, strictly speaking, evidence against these theories. In the end, however, this criticism does not depend on a shift in the definition of delinquency. The fact is that strain theory has difficulty with "maturational reform" regardless of the proportion actually reforming.

[13] The importance of maturational reform as a problem for most theories of delinquency is abundantly documented in Matza, *Delinquency and Drift,* pp. 22–26.

[14] A perfect ecological correlation and/or a perfect individual relation as defined by such measures as Yule's Q. In short, low social class is a necessary but not sufficient condition for delinquency, as delinquency is defined.

[15] Cloward and Ohlin, *Delinquency and Opportunity,* pp. 27–30; Albert K. Cohen, *Delinquent Boys* (New York: The Free Press, 1955), pp. 36–44.

[16] Cohen, *Delinquent Boys,* pp. 157–161; Robert H. Bohlke, "Social Mobility, Stratification Inconsistency and Middle Class Delinquency," *Social Problems,* VIII (1961), 351–363.

what is it about the middle-class situation that produces (middle-class) delinquency? [17]

Every theorist discusses the actual class distribution of delinquency and attempts to base his decision to restrict his explanation to the lower class on an evaluation of available evidence. Implicit in such an effort is a criterion for deciding whether the relation between social class and delinquency is sufficiently strong to justify a class theory of delinquency. What is this criterion? How strong a relation between social class and delinquency is required to justify a class theory of delinquency?

The mere raising of these questions emphasizes the shakiness of the factual and logical foundations upon which strain theory is erected, since it is common among strain theorists themselves to question the correlation between class and crime.[18] Indeed, recent delinquency research has tended to support this skepticism and more and more to undermine any theory that takes social class as the starting point for an explanation of juvenile delinquency.[19]

High aspirations are not conducive to delinquency. All strain theories generate pressure to delinquency from a *discrepancy* between aspirations and expectations. In order directly to test a strain theory, it is thus necessary to measure at least two independent variables simultaneously. (In Robert K. Merton's original theory, aspirations were assumed to be uniformly high within American society, and a discrepancy could thus be inferred directly from the realistically low expectations of segments of the population. However, subsequent research has undercut the assumption that all Americans place high and equal value on success, as Merton defined it.) [20] The need to measure two independent

---

[17] Cohen, *Delinquent Boys*, pp. 162–169 (Cohen exercises both options); Ralph W. England, Jr., "A Theory of Middle Class Juvenile Delinquency," *Readings in Juvenile Delinquency*, ed. Ruth Shonle Cavan (Philadelphia: Lippincott, 1964), pp. 66–75.

[18] See Merton, *Social Theory*, pp. 141–145, and Cloward, "Illegitimate Means," p. 174.

[19] This literature is summarized and discussed in Chapter IV.

[20] Herbert H. Hyman, "The Value Systems of Different Classes," *Class, Status and Power*, ed. Reinhard Bendix and Seymour Martin Lipset (New York: The Free Press, 1953), pp. 426–442. Hyman shows that lower-class persons are less likely to have high aspirations. In a reply to Hyman, Merton argues (*Social Theory*, pp. 170–176) that the problem is one of absolute frequencies rather than proportions. Actually the problem is one of correlation: Are lower-class persons with high aspirations more likely to become criminal than lower-class persons with low aspirations?

variables at once has tended to shield strain theory from potentially falsifying evidence: for example, the finding that legitimate aspirations are negatively related to delinquency could be countered by the argument that the relation would become positive if expectations were held constant.[21] At the same time, much indirect evidence that the desires upon which the strain theorist relies were at work has been provided by research which shows relations between delinquency and factors that presumably impede the realization of these desires, such as school failure. In fact, on the basis of this indirect evidence, strain theories appear to have substantial empirical support, and research articles in which one of them provides the interpretive framework appear regularly.[22]

Nevertheless, there is some direct evidence that the relation between aspirations and delinquency does not reverse when expectations are held constant,[23] that many delinquents are not deprived in an objective sense,[24] and that many delinquents do not *feel* deprived in the ways suggested by strain theorists.[25]

Therefore, I tentatively reject strain theory on the ground

---

[21] Kornhauser, "Theoretical Issues," Part I, pp. 21–22.

[22] For example, Erdman B. Palmore and Phillip E. Hammond, "Interacting Factors in Juvenile Delinquency," *American Sociological Review*, XXIX (1964), 848–854; Delbert S. Elliott, "Delinquency, School Attendance and Dropout," *Social Problems*, XIII (1966), 307–314. Palmore and Hammond rely on Cloward and Ohlin's theory, and Elliott relies on Cohen's.

[23] James F. Short, Jr., "Gang Delinquency and Anomie," *Anomie and Deviant Behavior*, ed. Marshall B. Clinard (New York: The Free Press, 1964), pp. 105–115. As far as I can determine, there is no good evidence to the contrary. Two studies apparently to the contrary are Arthur L. Stinchcombe, *Rebellion in a High School* (Chicago: Quadrangle, 1964), and Irving Spergel, *Racketville, Slumtown, Haulburg* (Chicago: University of Chicago Press, 1964). In Stinchcombe's study, the hypothesis that "whenever the goals of success are strongly internalized but inaccessible, expressive alienation results" is the subject of much analysis. I think it fair to say that this hypothesis explains very little of the "expressive alienation" in Stinchcombe's sample, and that the links between concepts and indicators with respect to this hypothesis are tenuous. Stinchcombe acknowledges the shakiness of his hypothesis and remains faithful to it only because he feels no alternative hypothesis is available.

Spergel's study is based on comparisons of three groups, each consisting of ten boys. Although his data often conform to minutely detailed hypotheses derived from strain theory, they are in effect ecological data since variation on delinquency within the groups is consistently ignored.

[24] Larry Karacki and Jackson Toby, "The Uncommitted Adolescent: Candidate for Gang Socialization," *Sociological Inquiry*, XXXII (1962), 203–215.

[25] Albert J. Reiss, Jr., and A. Lewis Rhodes, "Status Deprivation and Delinquent Behavior," *The Sociological Quarterly*, IV (1963), 135–149.

that it is inadequate and misleading. It suggests that delinquency
is a relatively permanent attribute of the person and/or a regularly
occurring event; it suggests that delinquency is largely restricted to
a single social class; and it suggests that persons accepting legitimate goals are, as a result of this acceptance, more likely to commit delinquent acts. Much of the discussion and data which follow
will bear on my position that these suggestions are inadequate and
misleading.

Control Theories

If strain theories may be traced to answers to Hobbes's question, control theories may be traced to the question itself. Strain
theories assume that the Hobbesian question has been answered,
that the important question is, "Why do men *not* obey the rules
of society?" Conformity is taken for granted; deviance is problematic. In control theories, the Hobbesian question has never
been adequately answered. The question remains, "Why *do* men
obey the rules of society?" Deviance is taken for granted; conformity must be explained.[26]

In strain theory, man is a moral animal. His morality accounts
for the pressure that is built into the model. If morality is removed, however, if man is seen as an amoral animal, then tremen-
dous pressure is unnecessary in accounting for his deviance. It is
just such a removal of the moral roadblock that explains the deem-

---

[26] Cohen's oft-quoted statement that "a theory of deviant behavior not only
must account for the occurrence of deviant behavior, it must also account for
its failure to occur" is followed by the statement that "the explanation of one
necessarily *implies* the explanation of the other." A sociologist trained to
think in terms of variables is likely to translate the latter statement as "the
explanation of deviance *has to be* an explanation of conformity"—as Stinchcombe in fact translates it. But then the statement is no longer true. For, in
fact, many present-day explanations of conformity make it very difficult to
explain deviance, although, as Cohen rightly suggests and as I have tried to
show in the preceding section, these theories of conformity do have profound
implications for the theories of deviance that accompany them. See Albert K.
Cohen, "The Study of Social Disorganization and Deviant Behavior," *Sociology Today*, ed. Robert K. Merton et al. (New York: Basic Books, 1959), p.
463, and Stinchcombe, *Rebellion*, p. 4. (Emphasis in both statements supplied.)

This contrast in what is taken for granted has been noted frequently in the
literature. See, for example, Howard S. Becker, *Outsiders* (New York: The
Free Press, 1963), pp. 26–27, and David J. Bordua, "Sociological Perspectives," *Social Deviancy Among Youth*, ed. William W. Wattenberg (Chicago: University of Chicago Press, 1966), pp. 84–85.

phasis on motivation that is characteristic of control theory: "It is our position, therefore, that in general behavior prescribed as delinquent or criminal need not be explained in any positive sense, since it usually results in quicker and easier achievement of goals than the normative behavior." [27]

It is oversimplification to say, however, that strain theory assumes a moral man while control theory assumes an amoral man. Control theory merely assumes variation in morality: for some men, considerations of morality are important; for others, they are not. Because his perspective allows him to free some men from moral sensitivities, the control theorist is likely to shift to a second line of social control—to the rational, calculational component in conformity and deviation. This emphasis on calculation is reflected in a recent proposal by theorists operating from within this perspective: "The idea of paying boys to conform is sufficiently intriguing to merit study and experimentation." [28]

The criticisms of control theory stemming from these and related assumptions are discussed in the following chapter, where a control theory of delinquency is presented in greater detail.

Theories of Cultural Deviance

A third set of theories assumes that men are incapable of committing "deviant" acts. A person may indeed commit acts deviant by the standards of, say, middle-class society, but he cannot commit acts deviant by his own standards. In other words, theorists from this school see deviant behavior as *conformity* to a set of standards not accepted by a larger (that is, more powerful) society. "If the community standards are positive but not according to accepted codes of conventional society, behavior will accordingly be contrary to standards of the larger society." [29]

Obviously, if "deviant behavior" is simply *behavior* frowned upon by outsiders and not by insiders, it is unnecessary to posit any special motivational force or strain to account for it. A person simply learns to become a "criminal" in much the same way he

[27] Nye, *Family Relationships*, p. 5.
[28] Scott Briar and Irving Piliavin, "Delinquency, Situational Inducements, and Commitment to Conformity," *Social Problems*, XIII (1965), 45.
[29] Clifford R. Shaw et al., *Delinquency Areas* (Chicago: University of Chicago Press, 1929), p. 6.

learns to play a violin or develops a taste for peanut butter. "A person becomes delinquent because of an excess of definitions favorable to violation of law over definitions unfavorable to violation of law." [30]

The cultural deviance theorist rejects a fundamental assumption of strain theory. But, since he has no language with which to express his rejection, the cultural deviance theorist attacks this assumption indirectly. Edwin H. Sutherland has written: "The attempts by many scholars to explain criminal behavior by general drives and values, such as . . . striving for social status, [and] the money motive . . . , have been and must continue to be futile since they explain lawful behavior as completely as they explain criminal behavior." [31] The strain theorist would grant that values common to all men cannot directly explain the criminal actions of some of them. These common values take on significance within his theory because he assumes that all men are not equally capable of realizing them. They are irrelevant to the cultural deviance theorist because he has no way of describing failure to attain them. In his world, failure and frustration have no place.[32]

The control theory assumption that crime is an amoral act is dismissed by the cultural deviance theorist as middle-class nonsense. In fact, since "criminal behavior is learned in interaction with other persons," principally "within intimate personal groups," [33] the idea implicit in control theory that the criminal is cut off from his fellows is explicitly repudiated. Indeed, the cultural deviance theorist often suggests that the delinquent is unusually "sociable" and "gregarious." [34]

[30] The Sutherland Papers, ed. Albert K. Cohen et al. (Bloomington: Indiana University Press, 1956), p. 9.

[31] Sutherland and Cressey, Principles of Criminology, p. 81.

[32] For what to my mind is a truly devastating critique of theories of cultural deviance, see Kornhauser, "Theoretical Issues," Part III. As Kornhauser notes, theories of cultural deviance do not distinguish between culture and social structure. They are thus incapable of making statements about discrepancies between what men desire and what they have, if, in fact, these theories recognize the possibility of such discrepancies. If strain theories assume a moral man, and control theories an amoral man, cultural deviance theories assume a hypermoral man. In a world where sin is impossible, the upright man hardly deserves congratulations, however.

[33] Sutherland and Cressey, Principles of Criminology, p. 81.

[34] Ibid., p. 82. See also Cohen, Delinquent Boys, pp. 105–107. In the end, of course, the criminal ends up just a little more moral than the law-abiding citizen because his actions are based on considerations of social solidarity rather than personal achievement.

Criticisms of Cultural Deviance Theory

Cultural deviance theory has been heavily criticized,[35] yet it remains one of the most widely used perspectives in research and theory on crime and delinquency.[36] The impact of this criticism is suggested by a recent statement of one of the proponents of the theory: "By comparison with its principal competitors . . . , differential association stands fairly secure."[37] What is the basis of this security?

Perhaps the outstanding event in the intellectual history of theories of cultural deviance was not a decision about the nature of man, but a rather ordinary-appearing decision about the nature of scientific explanation: "I reached the general conclusion that a concrete condition cannot be a cause of crime, and that the only way to get a causal explanation of criminal behavior is by abstracting from the varying concrete conditions things which are universally associated with crime."[38] Sutherland decided that every case

[35] For a list of criticisms of differential association (which, by someone else's count, contains seventy items) and a reply to these criticisms, see Donald R. Cressey, "Epidemiology and Individual Conduct: A Case from Criminology," *The Pacific Sociological Review*, III (1960), 37–54.

[36] Of the theoretical works cited previously, Cohen's *Delinquent Boys* and Cloward and Ohlin's *Delinquency and Opportunity* are heavily influenced by the cultural deviance perspective. Several attempts to refine Sutherland's theory have appeared. For a good example, see Robert L. Burgess and Ronald L. Akers, "A Differential Association-Reinforcement Theory of Criminal Behavior," *Social Problems*, XIV (1966), 128–147. Research on differential association has been mainly concerned with such things as relating the number of delinquent friends to delinquency—see, for example, Harwin L. Voss, "Differential Association and Delinquent Behavior: A Replication," *Social Problems*, XII (1964), 78–85.

[37] Daniel Glaser, "The Differential-Association Theory of Crime," *Human Behavior and Social Processes*, ed. Arnold M. Rose (Boston: Houghton Mifflin, 1962), p. 439. The competitors in this case are "the multiple factor theory" and "absence-of-control theories analogous to the psychoanalytic model." The multiple factor approach is a favorite whipping boy of cultural deviance theorists, even though there should be no inconsistency between the two approaches. In his discussion Glaser grants control theories the ability to explain such things as "temper tantrums."

[38] *The Sutherland Papers*, p. 19. Hanan C. Selvin and I have shown that the view that "only concepts can be causes" leads to misinterpretation of empirical results and ultimately to the view that the quest for causes is futile. We would not argue that the solution is to treat indicators as causal explanations of crime. The issue is generated by confusion concerning the relation between facts and theory. Thus, for example, Sutherland's statement *should* read: I realized that while concrete conditions are the *causes* of crime, the only way to get a causal *explanation* of crime is by abstracting from the vary-

of crime should be explained by the theory he proposed to construct; he thus appears to have relied upon the well-known method of analytic induction.[39]

Analytic induction proceeds by reformulating the hypothesis and/or redefining the phenomenon to be explained each time a deviant case is encountered. The ability to redefine the phenomenon may trick the user of analytic induction into merely defining that which he was to have explained.[40] Yet, to my knowledge, Sutherland never felt called upon to redefine crime. Crime began and remained simply "violation of the law." Instead, he reformulated his hypotheses until they were compatible with all known facts about crime. Hypotheses encompassing the cannibalism of the Donner Party, the murder of one newspaper editor by another, and a slum boy stealing a bike, are of necessity highly abstract. Given the inferential distance between the concepts of such hypotheses and concrete events, it is not surprising that the theory of

ing concrete conditions things that are universally associated with crime. See our *Delinquency Research* (New York: The Free Press, 1967), pp. 130–133, 177–183.

[39] Sutherland acknowledges the influence of Lindesmith, one of the first users of analytic induction (*The Sutherland Papers*, pp. 17–18). The paper most frequently cited by users of this method is by Ralph H. Turner, "The Quest for Universals in Sociological Research," *American Sociological Review*, XVIII (1953), 604–611. Although users of analytic induction have been invariably contemptuous of quantitative—that is, probabilistic—research, Turner does not see the two as incompatible or antithetical. He argues, in fact, that by themselves theories derived from analytic induction are inadequate.

[40] Thus Becker summarizes the results of his study of marihuana use with a series of tautologies, undoubtedly produced by his emendation of "marihuana use" to "marihuana use for pleasure." He says, for example: "A person, then, cannot begin to use marihuana for pleasure, or continue its use for pleasure, unless he learns to define its effects as enjoyable, unless it becomes and remains an object he conceives as capable of producing pleasure." (Becker says at the beginning of his paper that the qualifier "for pleasure" was added to emphasize that the use of marihuana does not produce addiction, that it is "noncompulsive and casual," and to eliminate "those few cases in which marihuana is used for its prestige value only." Becker thus suggests that neither the hypothesis nor the definition was altered by research. Such an hypothesis, it should be pointed out, could not conceivably be altered by research, whether or not the substance involved was addictive.) Becker's "research finding" is true. There is no way to dispute such a statement on empirical grounds. Is the statement also useful? Does it allow us to predict that jazz musicians or truck drivers would be more likely to use marihuana? Does it help us make sense of what we observe in the world? Suppose it were found that jazz musicians are more likely than truck drivers to use marihuana for pleasure. Would it help in understanding this difference to know that those who use marihuana for pleasure enjoy it? See *Outsiders*, pp. 41–58.

differential association is virtually nonfalsifiable. (It is also not surprising that empirical predictions derived from the theory tend to be trivial.) [41]

Once the meanings of the concepts in Sutherland's theory are to some extent specified, the issue immediately shifts from one of falsifiability to one of truth or falsity. For example, if the "definitions favorable to violation of law" upon which the theory rests are taken to be definitions that *free* the actor to commit delinquent acts, the theory is falsifiable (and the distinction between Sutherland's theory and social control theory is easily lost).[42] On the other hand, if the definitions favorable to violation of law are taken to be definitions that *require* delinquent behavior, the theory is again falsifiable (and, according to many critics and researchers, false).[43]

Because of the generality and complexity of cultural deviance theories, I hesitate to assert either that they are inconsistent with control theory or that they are in general false.[44] It is clear, however, that predictions derived from control theory will differ markedly from those deriving from particular cultural deviance theories. I shall therefore examine these cases in some detail and return to a general comparison of control and cultural deviance theory only after the analysis is essentially complete.

[41] Glaser shows that one can derive from the theory of differential association such predictions as: residence in a high delinquency area will be associated with arrest rates (*Human Behavior*, ed. Rose, pp. 434–435).

[42] Gresham M. Sykes and David Matza, "Techniques of Neutralization: A Theory of Delinquency," *American Sociological Review*, XXII (1957), 664–670. See also Burgess and Akers, "A Differential Association-Reinforcement Theory," pp. 142–143.

[43] James F. Short, Jr., and Fred L. Strodtbeck, *Group Process and Gang Delinquency* (Chicago: University of Chicago Press, 1965), Chapter 3; Kornhauser, "Theoretical Issues," Part III, pp. 36–51.

[44] My timidity with respect to the evidence against cultural deviance theories results from the following consideration: the survey studies showing little or no difference from one group to another with respect to crime-related values also show variation within the groups. Certainly the first fact requires modification, perhaps fatal modification, of cultural deviance theories. At the same time, it is difficult to conceive of the values measured being unrelated to crime at the individual level. If they are related, the arguments against cultural deviance theory are not as compelling as its critics take them to be. And criminological research has for too long based its theories on ecological data.

Chapter II
A Control Theory of Delinquency

"The more weakened the groups to which [the individual] belongs, the less he depends on them, the more he consequently depends only on himself and recognizes no other rules of conduct than what are founded on his private interests." [1]

Control theories assume that delinquent acts result when an individual's bond to society is weak or broken. Since these theories embrace two highly complex concepts, the *bond* of the individual to *society*, it is not surprising that they have at one time or another formed the basis of explanations of most forms of aberrant or unusual behavior. It is also not surprising that control theories have described the elements of the bond to society in many ways, and that they have focused on a variety of units as the point of control.

I begin with a classification and description of the elements of the bond to conventional society. I try to show how each of these elements is related to delinquent behavior and how they are related to each other. I then turn to the question of specifying the unit to which the person is presumably more or less tied, and to the question of the adequacy of the motivational force built into the explanation of delinquent behavior.

Elements of the Bond

Attachment

In explaining conforming behavior, sociologists justly emphasize sensitivity to the opinion of others.[2] Unfortunately, as sug-

[1] Emile Durkheim, *Suicide*, trans. John A. Spaulding and George Simpson (New York: The Free Press, 1951), p. 209.
[2] Books have been written on the increasing importance of interpersonal sensitivity in modern life. According to this view, controls from within have become less important than controls from without in producing conformity. Whether or not this observation is true as a description of historical trends, it is true that interpersonal sensitivity has become more important in explain-

gested in the preceding chapter, they tend to suggest that man *is* sensitive to the opinion of others and thus exclude sensitivity from their explanations of deviant behavior. In explaining deviant behavior, psychologists, in contrast, emphasize insensitivity to the opinion of others.[3] Unfortunately, they too tend to ignore variation, and, in addition, they tend to tie sensitivity inextricably to other variables, to make it part of a syndrome or "type," and thus seriously to reduce its value as an explanatory concept. The psychopath is characterized only in part by "deficient attachment to or affection for others, a failure to respond to the ordinary motivations founded in respect or regard for one's fellows"; [4] he is also characterized by such things as "excessive aggressiveness," "lack of superego control," and "an infantile level of response." [5] Unfortunately, too, the behavior that psychopathy is used to explain often becomes part of the *definition* of psychopathy. As a result, in Barbara Wootton's words: "[The psychopath] is . . . *par excellence*, and without shame or qualification, the model of the circular process by which mental abnormality is inferred from anti-social behavior while anti-social behavior is explained by mental abnormality." [6]

The problems of diagnosis, tautology, and name-calling are avoided if the dimensions of psychopathy are treated as causally and therefore problematically interrelated, rather than as logically and therefore necessarily bound to each other. In fact, it can be argued that all of the characteristics attributed to the psychopath follow from, are effects of, his lack of attachment to others. To say

ing conformity. Although logically it should also have become more important in explaining nonconformity, the opposite has been the case, once again showing that Cohen's observation that an explanation of conformity should be an explanation of deviance cannot be translated as "an explanation of conformity has to be an explanation of deviance." For the view that interpersonal sensitivity currently plays a greater role than formerly in producing conformity, see William J. Goode, "Norm Commitment and Conformity to Role-Status Obligations," *American Journal of Sociology*, LXVI (1960), 246–258. And, of course, also see David Riesman, Nathan Glazer, and Reuel Denney, *The Lonely Crowd* (Garden City, New York: Doubleday, 1950), especially Part I.

[3] The literature on psychopathy is voluminous. See William McCord and Joan McCord, *The Psychopath* (Princeton: D. Van Nostrand, 1964).

[4] John M. Martin and Joseph P. Fitzpatrick, *Delinquent Behavior* (New York: Random House, 1964), p. 130.

[5] *Ibid.* For additional properties of the psychopath, see McCord and McCord, *The Psychopath*, pp. 1–22.

[6] Barbara Wootton, *Social Science and Social Pathology* (New York: Macmillan, 1959), p. 250.

that to lack attachment to others is to be free from moral restraints is to use lack of attachment to explain the guiltlessness of the psychopath, the fact that he apparently has no conscience or superego. In this view, lack of attachment to others is not merely a symptom of psychopathy, it *is* psychopathy; lack of conscience is just another way of saying the same thing; and the violation of norms is (or may be) a consequence.

For that matter, given that man is an animal, "impulsivity" and "aggressiveness" can also be seen as natural consequences of freedom from moral restraints. However, since the view of man as endowed with natural propensities and capacities like other animals is peculiarly unpalatable to sociologists, we need not fall back on such a view to explain the amoral man's aggressiveness.[7] The process of becoming alienated from others often involves or is based on active interpersonal conflict. Such conflict could easily supply a reservoir of *socially derived* hostility sufficient to account for the aggressiveness of those whose attachments to others have been weakened.

Durkheim said it many years ago: "We are moral beings to the extent that we are social beings." [8] This may be interpreted to mean that we are moral beings to the extent that we have "internalized the norms" of society. But what does it mean to say that a person has internalized the norms of society? The norms of society are by definition shared by the members of society. To violate a norm is, therefore, to act contrary to the wishes and expectations of other people. If a person does not care about the wishes and expectations of other people—that is, if he is insensitive to the opinion of others—then he is to that extent not bound by the norms. He is free to deviate.

The essence of internalization of norms, conscience, or superego thus lies in the attachment of the individual to others.[9] This

[7] "The logical untenability [of the position that there are forces in man 'resistant to socialization'] was ably demonstrated by Parsons over 30 years ago, and it is widely recognized that the position is empirically unsound because it assumes [!] some universal biological drive system distinctly separate from socialization and social context—a basic and intransigent human nature" (Judith Blake and Kingsley Davis, "Norms, Values, and Sanctions," *Handbook of Modern Sociology*, ed. Robert E. L. Faris [Chicago: Rand McNally, 1964], p. 471).

[8] Emile Durkheim, *Moral Education*, trans. Everett K. Wilson and Herman Schnurer (New York: The Free Press, 1961), p. 64.

[9] Although attachment alone does not exhaust the meaning of internaliza-

view has several advantages over the concept of internalization. For one, explanations of deviant behavior based on attachment do not beg the question, since the extent to which a person is attached to others can be measured independently of his deviant behavior. Furthermore, change or variation in behavior is explainable in a way that it is not when notions of internalization or superego are used. For example, the divorced man is more likely after divorce to commit a number of deviant acts, such as suicide or forgery. If we explain these acts by reference to the superego (or internal control), we are forced to say that the man "lost his conscience" when he got a divorce; and, of course, if he remarries, we have to conclude that he gets his conscience back.

This dimension of the bond to conventional society is encountered in most social control-oriented research and theory. F. Ivan Nye's "internal control" and "indirect control" refer to the same element, although we avoid the problem of explaining changes over time by locating the "conscience" in the bond to others rather than making it part of the personality.[10] Attachment to others is just one aspect of Albert J. Reiss's "personal controls"; we avoid his problems of tautological empirical *observations* by making the relationship between attachment and delinquency problematic rather than definitional.[11] Finally, Scott Briar and Irving Piliavin's "commitment" or "stake in conformity" subsumes attachment, as their discussion illustrates, although the terms they use are more closely associated with the next element to be discussed.[12]

tion, attachments and beliefs combined would appear to leave only a small residue of "internal control" not susceptible in principle to direct measurement.

[10] F. Ivan Nye, *Family Relationships and Delinquent Behavior* (New York: Wiley, 1958), pp. 5-7.

[11] Albert J. Reiss, Jr., "Delinquency as the Failure of Personal and Social Controls," *American Sociological Review*, XVI (1951), 196–207. For example, "Our observations show . . . that delinquent recidivists are less often persons with mature ego ideals or nondelinquent social roles" (p. 204).

[12] Scott Briar and Irving Piliavin, "Delinquency, Situational Inducements, and Commitment to Conformity," *Social Problems*, XIII (1965), 41–42. The concept "stake in conformity" was introduced by Jackson Toby in his "Social Disorganization and Stake in Conformity: Complementary Factors in the Predatory Behavior of Hoodlums," *Journal of Criminal Law, Criminology and Police Science*, XLVIII (1957), 12–17. See also his "Hoodlum or Business Man: An American Dilemma," *The Jews*, ed. Marshall Sklare (New York: The Free Press, 1958), pp. 542–550. Throughout the text, I occasionally use "stake in conformity" in speaking in general of the strength of the

Commitment

"Of all passions, that which inclineth men least to break the laws, is fear. Nay, excepting some generous natures, it is the only thing, when there is the appearance of profit or pleasure by breaking the laws, that makes men keep them." [13] Few would deny that men on occasion obey the rules simply from fear of the consequences. This rational component in conformity we label commitment. What does it mean to say that a person is committed to conformity? In Howard S. Becker's formulation it means the following:

> First, the individual is in a position in which his decision with regard to some particular line of action has consequences for other interests and activities not necessarily [directly] related to it. Second, he has placed himself in that position by his own prior actions. A third element is present though so obvious as not to be apparent: the committed person must be aware [of these other interests] and must recognize that his decision in this case will have ramifications beyond it.[14]

The idea, then, is that the person invests time, energy, himself, in a certain line of activity—say, getting an education, building up a business, acquiring a reputation for virtue. When or whenever he considers deviant behavior, he must consider the costs of this deviant behavior, the risk he runs of losing the investment he has made in conventional behavior.

If attachment to others is the sociological counterpart of the superego or conscience, commitment is the counterpart of the ego or common sense. To the person committed to conventional lines of action, risking one to ten years in prison for a ten-dollar holdup is stupidity, because to the committed person the costs and risks obviously exceed ten dollars in value. (To the psychoanalyst, such an act exhibits failure to be governed by the "reality-principle.") In the sociological control theory, it can be and is generally assumed that the decision to commit a criminal act may well be rationally determined—that the actor's decision was not irrational

bond to conventional society. So used, the concept is somewhat broader than is true for either Toby or Briar and Piliavin, where the concept is roughly equivalent to what is here called "commitment."

[13] Thomas Hobbes, *Leviathan* (Oxford: Basil Blackwell, 1957), p. 195.

[14] Howard S. Becker, "Notes on the Concept of Commitment," *American Journal of Sociology* LXVI (1960), pp. -6

given the risks and costs he faces. Of course, as Becker points out, if the actor is capable of in some sense calculating the costs of a line of action, he is also capable of calculational errors: ignorance and error return, in the control theory, as possible explanations of deviant behavior.

The concept of commitment assumes that the organization of society is such that the interests of most persons would be endangered if they were to engage in criminal acts. Most people, simply by the process of living in an organized society, acquire goods, reputations, prospects that they do not want to risk losing. These accumulations are society's insurance that they will abide by the rules. Many hypotheses about the antecedents of delinquent behavior are based on this premise. For example, Arthur L. Stinchcombe's hypothesis that "high school rebellion . . . occurs when future status is not clearly related to present performance" [15] suggests that one is committed to conformity not only by what one has but also by what one hopes to obtain. Thus "ambition" and/or "aspiration" play an important role in producing conformity. The person becomes committed to a conventional line of action, and he is therefore committed to conformity.

Most lines of action in a society are of course conventional. The clearest examples are educational and occupational careers. Actions thought to jeopardize one's chances in these areas are presumably avoided. Interestingly enough, even nonconventional commitments may operate to produce conventional conformity. We are told, at least, that boys aspiring to careers in the rackets or professional thievery are judged by their "honesty" and "reliability"—traits traditionally in demand among seekers of office boys.[16]

Involvement

Many persons undoubtedly owe a life of virtue to a lack of opportunity to do otherwise. Time and energy are inherently limited: "Not that I would not, if I could, be both handsome and fat

---

[15] Arthur L. Stinchcombe, *Rebellion in a High School* (Chicago: Quadrangle, 1964), p. 5.

[16] Richard A. Cloward and Lloyd E. Ohlin, *Delinquency and Opportunity* (New York: The Free Press, 1960), p. 147, quoting Edwin H. Sutherland, ed., *The Professional Thief* (Chicago: University of Chicago Press, 1937), pp. 211–213.

and well dressed, and a great athlete, and make a million a year, be a wit, a bon vivant, and a lady killer, as well as a philosopher, a philanthropist, a statesman, warrior, and African explorer, as well as a 'tone-poet' and saint. But the thing is simply impossible." [17] The things that William James here says he would like to be or do are all, I suppose, within the realm of conventionality, but if he were to include illicit actions he would still have to eliminate some of them as simply impossible.

Involvement or engrossment in conventional activities is thus often part of a control theory. The assumption, widely shared, is that a person may be simply too busy doing conventional things to find time to engage in deviant behavior. The person involved in conventional activities is tied to appointments, deadlines, working hours, plans, and the like, so the opportunity to commit deviant acts rarely arises. To the extent that he is engrossed in conventional activities, he cannot even think about deviant acts, let alone act out his inclinations.[18]

This line of reasoning is responsible for the stress placed on recreational facilities in many programs to reduce delinquency, for much of the concern with the high school dropout, and for the idea that boys should be drafted into the Army to keep them out of trouble. So obvious and persuasive is the idea that involvement in conventional activities is a major deterrent to delinquency that it was accepted even by Sutherland: "In the general area of juvenile delinquency it is probable that the most significant difference between juveniles who engage in delinquency and those who do not is that the latter are provided abundant opportunities of a conventional type for satisfying their recreational interests, while the former lack those opportunities or facilities." [19]

The view that "idle hands are the devil's workshop" has received more sophisticated treatment in recent sociological writings on delinquency. David Matza and Gresham M. Sykes, for example, suggest that delinquents have the values of a leisure class, the same values ascribed by Veblen to *the* leisure class: a search for

[17] William James, *Psychology* (Cleveland: World Publishing Co., 1948), p. 186.

[18] Few activities appear to be so engrossing that they rule out contemplation of alternative lines of behavior, at least if estimates of the amount of time men spend plotting sexual deviations have any validity.

[19] *The Sutherland Papers*, ed. Albert K. Cohen et al. (Bloomington: Indiana University Press, 1956), p. 37.

kicks, disdain of work, a desire for the big score, and acceptance of aggressive toughness as proof of masculinity.[20] Matza and Sykes explain delinquency by reference to this system of values, but they note that adolescents at all class levels are "to some extent" members of a leisure class, that they "move in a limbo between earlier parental domination and future integration with the social structure through the bonds of work and marriage." [21] In the end, then, the leisure of the adolescent produces a set of values, which, in turn, leads to delinquency.

Belief

Unlike the cultural deviance theory, the control theory assumes the existence of a common value system within the society or group whose norms are being violated. If the deviant is committed to a value system different from that of conventional society, there is, within the context of the theory, nothing to explain. The question is, "Why does a man violate the rules in which he believes?" It is not, "Why do men differ in their beliefs about what constitutes good and desirable conduct?" The person is assumed to have been socialized (perhaps imperfectly) into the group whose rules he is violating; deviance is not a question of one group imposing its rules on the members of another group. In other words, we not only assume the deviant *has* believed the rules, we assume he believes the rules even as he violates them.

How can a person believe it is wrong to steal at the same time he is stealing? In the strain theory, this is not a difficult problem. (In fact, as suggested in the previous chapter, the strain theory was devised specifically to deal with this question.) The motivation to deviance adduced by the strain theorist is so strong that we can well understand the deviant act even assuming the deviator believes strongly that it is wrong.[22] However, given the control theory's assumptions about motivation, if both the deviant and the

---

[20] David Matza and Gresham M. Sykes, "Juvenile Delinquency and Subterranean Values," *American Sociological Review*, XXVI (1961), 712–719.

[21] *Ibid.*, p. 718.

[22] The starving man stealing the loaf of bread is the image evoked by most strain theories. In this image, the starving man's belief in the wrongness of his act is clearly not something that must be explained away. It can be assumed to be present without causing embarrassment to the explanation.

nondeviant believe the deviant act is wrong, how do we account for the fact that one commits it and the other does not?

Control theories have taken two approaches to this problem. In one approach, beliefs are treated as mere words that mean little or nothing if the other forms of control are missing. "Semantic dementia," the dissociation between rational faculties and emotional control which is said to be characteristic of the psychopath, illustrates this way of handling the problem.[23] In short, beliefs, at least insofar as they are expressed in words, drop out of the picture; since they do not differentiate between deviants and nondeviants, they are in the same class as "language" or any other characteristic common to all members of the group. Since they represent no real obstacle to the commission of delinquent acts, nothing need be said about how they are handled by those committing such acts. The control theories that do not mention beliefs (or values), and many do not, may be assumed to take this approach to the problem.

The second approach argues that the deviant rationalizes his behavior so that he can at once violate the rule and maintain his belief in it. Donald R. Cressey has advanced this argument with respect to embezzlement,[24] and Sykes and Matza have advanced it with respect to delinquency.[25] In both Cressey's and Sykes and Matza's treatments, these rationalizations (Cressey calls them "verbalizations," Sykes and Matza term them "techniques of neutralization") occur prior to the commission of the deviant act. If the neutralization is successful, the person is free to commit the act(s) in question. Both in Cressey and in Sykes and Matza, the strain that prompts the effort at neutralization also provides the motive force that results in the subsequent deviant act. Their theories are thus, in this sense, strain theories. Neutralization is difficult to handle within the context of a theory that adheres closely to control theory assumptions, because in the control theory there is no special motivational force to account for the neutralization. This difficulty is especially noticeable in Matza's later

[23] McCord and McCord, The Psychopath, pp. 12–15.
[24] Donald R. Cressey, Other People's Money (New York: The Free Press, 1953).
[25] Gresham M. Sykes and David Matza, "Techniques of Neutralization: A Theory of Delinquency," American Sociological Review, XXII (1957), 664–670.

treatment of this topic, where the motivational component, the "will to delinquency" appears *after* the moral vacuum has been created by the techniques of neutralization.[26] The question thus becomes: Why neutralize?

In attempting to solve a strain theory problem with control theory tools, the control theorist is thus led into a trap. He cannot answer the crucial question. The concept of neutralization assumes the existence of moral obstacles to the commission of deviant acts. In order plausibly to account for a deviant act, it is necessary to generate motivation to deviance that is at least equivalent in force to the resistance provided by these moral obstacles. However, if the moral obstacles are removed, neutralization and special motivation are no longer required. We therefore follow the implicit logic of control theory and remove these moral obstacles by hypothesis. Many persons do not have an attitude of respect toward the rules of society; many persons feel no moral obligation to conform regardless of personal advantage. Insofar as the values and beliefs of these persons are consistent with their feelings, and there should be a tendency toward consistency, neutralization is unnecessary; it has already occurred.

Does this merely push the question back a step and at the same time produce conflict with the assumption of a common value system? I think not. In the first place, we do not assume, as does Cressey, that neutralization occurs in order to make a specific criminal act possible.[27] We do not assume, as do Sykes and Matza, that neutralization occurs to make many delinquent acts possible. We do not assume, in other words, that the person constructs a system of rationalizations in order to justify commission of acts he *wants* to commit. We assume, in contrast, that the beliefs that free a man to commit deviant acts are *unmotivated* in the sense that he does not construct or adopt them in order to facilitate the attainment of illicit ends. In the second place, we do

[26] David Matza, *Delinquency and Drift* (New York: Wiley, 1964), pp. 181–191.

[27] In asserting that Cressey's assumption is invalid with respect to delinquency, I do not wish to suggest that it is invalid for the question of embezzlement, where the problem faced by the deviator is fairly specific and he can reasonably be assumed to be an upstanding citizen. (Although even here the fact that the embezzler's nonshareable financial problem often results from some sort of hanky-panky suggests that "verbalizations" may be less necessary than might otherwise be assumed.)

not assume, as does Matza, that "delinquents concur in the conventional assessment of delinquency." [28] We assume, in contrast, that there is *variation* in the extent to which people believe they should obey the rules of society, and, furthermore, that the less a person believes he should obey the rules, the more likely he is to violate them.[29]

In chronological order, then, a person's beliefs in the moral validity of norms are, for no teleological reason, weakened. The probability that he will commit delinquent acts is therefore increased. When and if he commits a delinquent act, we may justifiably use the weakness of his beliefs in explaining it, but no special motivation is required to explain either the weakness of his beliefs or, perhaps, his delinquent act.

The keystone of this argument is of course the assumption that there is variation in belief in the moral validity of social rules. This assumption is amenable to direct empirical test and can thus survive at least until its first confrontation with data. For the present, we must return to the idea of a common value system with which this section was begun.

The idea of a common (or, perhaps better, a single) value system is consistent with the fact, or presumption, of variation in the strength of moral beliefs. We have not suggested that delinquency is based on beliefs counter to conventional morality; we have not suggested that delinquents do not believe delinquent acts are wrong. They may well believe these acts are wrong, but the meaning and efficacy of such beliefs are contingent upon other beliefs and, indeed, on the strength of other ties to the conventional order.[30]

[28] *Delinquency and Drift*, p. 43.
[29] This assumption is not, I think, contradicted by the evidence presented by Matza against the existence of a delinquent subculture. In comparing the attitudes and actions of delinquents with the picture painted by delinquent subculture theorists, Matza emphasizes—and perhaps exaggerates—the extent to which delinquents are tied to the conventional order. In implicitly comparing delinquents with a supermoral man, I emphasize—and perhaps exaggerate—the extent to which they are not tied to the conventional order.
[30] The position taken here is therefore somewhere between the "semantic dementia" and the "neutralization" positions. Assuming variation, the delinquent is, at the extremes, freer than the neutralization argument assumes. Although the possibility of wide discrepancy between what the delinquent professes and what he practices still exists, it is presumably much rarer than is suggested by studies of articulate "psychopaths."

Relations Among the Elements

In general, the more closely a person is tied to conventional society in any of these ways, the more closely he is likely to be tied in the other ways. The person who is attached to conventional people is, for example, more likely to be involved in conventional activities and to accept conventional notions of desirable conduct. Of the six possible combinations of elements, three seem particularly important and will therefore be discussed in some detail.

Attachment and Commitment

It is frequently suggested that attachment and commitment (as the terms are used here) tend to vary inversely. Thus, according to delinquency research, one of the lower-class adolescent's "problems" is that he is unable to sever ties to parents and peers, ties that prevent him from devoting sufficient time and energy to educational and occupational aspirations. His attachments are thus seen as getting in the way of conventional commitments.[31] According to stratification research, the lower-class boy who breaks free from these attachments is more likely to be upwardly mobile.[32] Both research traditions thus suggest that those bound to *conformity* for instrumental reasons are less likely to be bound to conformity by emotional ties to conventional others. If the unattached compensate for lack of attachment by commitment to achievement, and if the uncommitted make up for their lack of commitment by becoming more attached to persons, we could conclude that neither attachment nor commitment will be related to delinquency.

[31] The idea that the middle-class boy is less closely tied than the lower-class boy to his peers has been widely adopted in the literature on delinquency. The middle-class boy's "cold and rational" relations with his peers are in sharp contrast with the "spontaneous and warm" relations of the lower-class boy. See, for example, Albert K. Cohen, *Delinquent Boys* (New York: The Free Press, 1955), pp. 102–109.

[32] The evidence in favor of this proposition is summarized in Seymour M. Lipset and Reinhard Bendix, *Social Mobility in Industrial Society* (Berkeley: University of California Press, 1959), especially pp. 249–259. For example: "These [business leaders] show strong traits of independence, they are characterized by an inability to form intimate relations and are consequently often socially isolated men" (p. 251).

Actually, despite the evidence apparently to the contrary, I think it safe to assume that attachment to conventional others and commitment to achievement tend to vary together. The common finding that middle-class boys are likely to choose instrumental values over those of family and friendship while the reverse is true of lower-class boys cannot, I think, be properly interpreted as meaning that middle-class boys are less attached than lower-class boys to their parents and peers. The zero-sum methodological model that produces such findings is highly likely to be misleading.[33] Also, although many of the characteristics of the upwardly mobile alluded to by Seymour M. Lipset and Reinhard Bendix could be accounted for as consequences rather than causes of mobility, a methodological critique of these studies is not necessary to conclude that we may expect to find a positive relation between attachment and commitment in the data to be presented here. The present study and the one study Lipset and Bendix cite as disagreeing with their general conclusion that the upwardly mobile come from homes in which interpersonal relations were unsatisfactory are both based on high school samples.[34] As Lipset and Bendix note, such studies necessarily focus on aspirations rather than actual mobility. For the present, it seems, we must choose between studies based on hopes for the occupational future and those based on construction or reconstruction of the familial past. Interestingly enough, the former are at least as likely to be valid as the latter.

Commitment and Involvement

Delinquent acts are events. They occur at specific points in space and time. For a delinquent act to occur, it is necessary, as is true of all events, for a series of causal chains to converge at a given moment in time. Events are difficult to predict, and specification of some of the conditions necessary for them to occur often leaves a large residue of indeterminacy. For example, to say that a boy is free of bonds to conventional society is not to say that he will necessarily commit delinquent acts; he may and he may not. All we can say with certainty is that he is *more likely* to commit

[33] Relations between measures of attachment and commitment are examined in Chapter VIII.
[34] *Social Mobility*, p. 253.

delinquent acts than the boy strongly tied to conventional society.

It is tempting to make a virtue of this defect and espouse "probabilistic theory," since it, and it alone, is consistent with "the facts." [35] Nevertheless, this temptation should be resisted. The primary virtue of control theory is not that it relies on conditions that make delinquency possible while other theories rely on conditions that make delinquency necessary. On the contrary, with respect to their logical framework, these theories are superior to control theory, and, if they were as adequate empirically as control theory, we should not hesitate to advocate their adoption in preference to control theory.

But they are not as adequate, and we must therefore seek to reduce the indeterminacy within control theory. One area of possible development is with respect to the link between elements of the bond affecting the probability that one will yield to temptation and those affecting the probability that one will be exposed to temptation.

The most obvious link in this connection is between educational and occupational aspirations (commitment) and involvement in conventional activities. We can attempt to show how commitment limits one's opportunities to commit delinquent acts and thus get away from the assumption implicit in many control theories that such opportunities are simply randomly distributed through the population in question.

Attachment and Belief

That there is a more or less straightforward connection between attachment to others and belief in the moral validity of rules appears evident. The link we accept here and which we shall attempt to document is described by Jean Piaget:

> It is not the obligatory character of the rule laid down by an individual that makes us respect this individual, it is the respect we feel for the individual that makes us regard as obligatory the rule he lays down. The appearance of the sense of duty in a child thus admits of the simplest explanation, namely that he receives commands from older children (in play) and from

[35] Brair and Piliavin, "Situational Involvements," p. 45.

adults (in life), and that he respects older children and parents.[36]

In short, "respect is the source of law." [37] Insofar as the child respects (loves and fears) his parents, and adults in general, he will accept their rules. Conversely, insofar as this respect is undermined, the rules will tend to lose their obligatory character. It is assumed that belief in the obligatory character of rules will to some extent maintain its efficacy in producing conformity even if the respect which brought it into being no longer exists. It is also assumed that attachment may produce conformity even in the face of beliefs favorable to nonconformity. In short, these two sources of moral behavior, although highly and complexly related, are assumed to have an independent effect that justifies their separation.

The Bond to What?

Control theorists sometimes suggest that attachment to any object outside one's self, whether it be the home town, the starry heavens, or the family dog, promotes moral behavior.[38] Although it seems obvious that some objects are more important than others and that the important objects must be identified if the elements of the bond are to produce the consequences suggested by the theory, a priori rankings of the objects of attachment have proved peculiarly unsatisfactory. Durkheim, for example, concludes that the three groups to whom attachment is most important in producing morality are the family, the nation, and humanity. He further concludes that, of these, the nation is most important.[39] All of which, given much contemporary thinking on the virtues of patriotism,[40] illustrates rather well the difficulty posed by such questions as: Which is more important in the control of delinquency, the father or the mother, the family or the school?

[36] Jean Piaget, *The Moral Judgment of the Child,* trans. Marjorie Gabain (New York: The Free Press, n.d.), p. 101.
[37] *Ibid.,* p. 379.
[38] Durkheim, *Moral Education,* p. 83.
[39] *Ibid.,* pp. 73-79.
[40] In the end, Durkheim distinguishes between a patriotism that leads to concern for domestic problems and one that emphasizes foreign relations (especially that variety which puts "national sentiment in conflict with commitments of mankind").

Although delinquency theory in general has taken a stand on many questions about the relative importance of institutions (for example, that the school is more important than the family), control theory has remained decidedly eclectic, partly because each element of the bond directs attention to different institutions. For these reasons, I shall treat specification of the units of attachment as a problem in the empirical interpretation of control theory, and not attempt at this point to say which should be more or less important.

Where Is the Motivation?

The most disconcerting question the control theorist faces goes something like this: "Yes, but *why* do they do it?" In the good old days, the control theorist could simply strip away the "veneer of civilization" and expose man's "animal impulses" for all to see. These impulses appeared to him (and apparently to his audience) to provide a plausible account of the motivation to crime and delinquency. His argument was *not* that delinquents and criminals alone are animals, but that we are all animals, and thus all naturally capable of committing criminal acts. It took no great study to reveal that children, chickens, and dogs occasionally assault and steal from their fellow creatures; that children, chickens, and dogs also behave for relatively long periods in a perfectly moral manner. Of course the acts of chickens and dogs are not "assault" or "theft," and such behavior is not "moral"; it is simply the behavior of a chicken or a dog. The chicken stealing corn from his neighbor knows nothing of the moral law; he does not *want* to violate rules; he wants merely to eat corn. The dog maliciously destroying a pillow or feloniously assaulting another dog is the moral equal of the chicken. No motivation to deviance is required to explain his acts. So, too, no special motivation to crime within the human animal was required to explain his criminal acts.

Times changed. It was no longer fashionable (within sociology, at least) to refer to animal impulses. The control theorist tended more and more to deemphasize the motivational component of his theory. He might refer in the beginning to "universal human needs," or some such, but the driving force behind crime and delinquency was rarely alluded to. At the same time, his explanations of crime and delinquency increasingly left the reader uneasy. What, the reader asked, is the control theorist assuming? Albert K. Cohen and James F. Short answer the question this way:

> . . . it is important to point out one important limitation of both types of theory. They [culture conflict and social disorganization theories] are both *control* theories in the sense that they explain delinquency in terms of the *absence* of effective controls. They appear, therefore, to imply a model of motivation that assumes that the impulse to delinquency is an inherent characteristic of young people and does not itself need to be explained; it is something that erupts when the lid—i.e., internalized cultural restraints or external authority—is off.[41]

There are several possible and I think reasonable reactions to this criticism. One reaction is simply to acknowledge the assumption, to grant that one is assuming what control theorists have always assumed about the motivation to crime—that it is constant across persons (at least within the system in question): "There is no reason to assume that only those who finally commit a deviant act usually have the impulse to do so. It is much more likely that most people experience deviant impulses frequently. At least in fantasy, people are much more deviant than they appear."[42] There is certainly nothing wrong with *making* such an assumption. We are free to assume anything we wish to assume; the truth of our theory is presumably subject to empirical test.[43]

A second reaction, involving perhaps something of a quibble, is to defend the logic of control theory and to deny the alleged assumption. We can say the fact that control theory suggests the absence of something causes delinquency is not a proper criticism, since negative relations have as much claim to scientific acceptability as do positive relations.[44] We can also say that the present

[41] See their "Juvenile Delinquency," in Contemporary Social Problems, ed. Robert K. Merton and Robert A. Nisbet (New York: Harcourt, Brace and World, 1961), p. 106.

[42] Howard S. Becker, Outsiders (New York: The Free Press, 1963), p. 26. See also Kate Friedlander, The Psycho-Analytic Approach to Juvenile Delinquency (New York: International Universities Press, 1947), p. 7.

[43] Cf. Albert K. Cohen, Deviance and Control (Englewood Cliffs, N.J.: Prentice-Hall, 1966), pp. 59–62.

[44] I have frequently heard the statement "it's an absence of something explanation" used as an apparently damning criticism of a sociological theory.

theory does not impute an inherent impulse *to delinquency* to anyone.[45] That, on the contrary, it denies the necessity of such an imputation: "The desires, and other passions of man, are in themselves no sin. No more are the actions, that proceed from those passions, till they know a law that forbids them." [46]

A third reaction is to accept the criticism as valid, to grant that a complete explanation of delinquency would provide the necessary impetus, and proceed to construct an explanation of motivation consistent with control theory. Briar and Piliavin provide situational motivation: "We assume these acts are prompted by short-term situationally induced desires experienced by all boys to obtain valued goods, to portray courage in the presence of, or be loyal to peers, to strike out at someone who is disliked, or simply to 'get kicks.' " [47] Matza, too, agrees that delinquency cannot be explained simply by removal of controls:

> Delinquency is only epiphenomenally action. . . . [It] is essentially infraction. It is rule-breaking behavior performed by juveniles aware that they are violating the law and of the nature of their deed, and made permissible by the neutralization of infractious [!] elements. Thus, Cohen and Short are fundamentally right when they insist that social control theory is incom-

While the origins of this view are unknown to me, the fact that such a statement appears to have some claim to plausibility suggests one of the sources of uneasiness in the face of a control theory.

[45] The popular "it's-an-id-argument" dismissal of explanations of deviant behavior assumes that the founding fathers of sociology somehow proved that the blood of man is neither warm nor red, but spiritual. The intellectual trap springs shut on the counterassumption that innate aggressive-destructive impulses course through the veins, as it should. The solution is not to accept both views, but to accept neither.

[46] Thomas Hobbes, *Leviathan*, p. 83. Given the history of the sociological response to Hobbes, it is instructive to compare Hobbes' picture of the motivation behind the deviant act with that painted by Talcott Parsons. According to Parsons, the motive to deviate is a psychological trait or need that *the deviant* carries with him at all times. This need is itself deviant: *it cannot be satisfied by conformity.* Social controls enter merely as reality factors that determine the form and manner in which this need will be satisfied. If one path to deviant behavior is blocked, the deviant will continue searching until he finds a path that is open. Perhaps because this need arises from interpersonal conflict, and is thus socially derived, the image it presents of the deviant as fundamentally immoral, as doing evil because it is evil, has been largely ignored by those objecting to the control theorist's tendency to fall back on natural propensities as a source of the energy that results in the activities society defines as wrong. See Talcott Parsons, *The Social System* (New York: The Free Press, 1951), Chapter 7.

[47] Briar and Piliavin, "Situational Inducements," p. 36.

plete unless it provides an impetus by which the potential for delinquency may be realized.[48]

The impetus Matza provides is a "feeling of desperation," brought on by the "mood of fatalism," "the experience of seeing one's self as effect" rather than cause. In a situation in which manliness is stressed, being pushed around leads to the mood of fatalism, which in turn produces a sense of desperation. In order to relieve his desperation, in order to cast off the mood of fatalism, the boy "makes things happen"—he commits delinquent acts.[49]

There are several additional accounts of "why they do it" that are to my mind persuasive and at the same time generally compatible with control theory.[50] But while all of these accounts may be compatible with control theory, they are by no means deducible from it. Furthermore, they rarely impute built-in, unusual motivation to the delinquent: he is attempting to satisfy the same desires, he is reacting to the same pressures as other boys (as is clear, for example, in the previous quotation from Briar and Piliavin). In other words, if included, these accounts of motivation would serve the same function in the theory that "animal impulses" traditionally served: they might add to its persuasiveness and plausibility, but they would add little else, since they do not differentiate delinquents from nondelinquents.

In the end, then, control theory remains what it has always been: a theory in which deviation is not problematic. The question "Why do they do it?" is simply not the question the theory is designed to answer. The question is, "Why don't we do it?" There is much evidence that we would if we dared.

[48] *Delinquency and Drift*, p. 182.

[49] Matza warns us that we cannot take the fatalistic mood out of context and hope to find important differences between delinquents and other boys: "That the subcultural delinquent is not significantly different from other boys is precisely the point" (*ibid.*, p. 89).

[50] For example: Carl Werthman, "The Function of Social Definitions in the Development of Delinquent Careers," *Juvenile Delinquency and Youth Crime*, Report of the President's Commission on Law Enforcement and Administration of Justice (Washington: USGPO, 1967), pp. 155–170; Jackson Toby, "Affluence and Adolescent Crime," *ibid.*, pp. 132–144; James F. Short, Jr., and Fred L. Strodtbeck, *Group Process and Gang Delinquency* (Chicago: University of Chicago Press, 1965), pp. 248–264.

Chapter III
The Sample and the Data

Western Contra Costa County is part of the San Francisco–Oakland metropolitan area, bounded on the south by Berkeley and on the west and north by San Francisco and San Pablo bays. In the hills to the east live professionals and executives who commute to Berkeley, Oakland, San Francisco, and the major city in the western part of the county, Richmond. The flatland between the hills and the bay is populated predominantly by manual workers and, since the beginning of World War II, by a Negro population that has grown from less than 1 to more than 12 percent.[1]

The Sample

The sample on which the present study is based was drawn as part of the Richmond Youth Project from the 17,500 students entering the eleven public junior and senior high schools of this area in the fall of 1964.[2] This population was stratified by race, sex, school, and grade, producing 130 subgroups, such as seventh-grade non-Negro boys at Granada Junior High School and tenth-grade Negro girls at Richmond High School. In most cases, 85 percent of the Negro boys, 60 percent of the Negro girls, 30 percent of the non-Negro (largely Caucasian but with some Oriental and Mexican–American) boys, and 12 percent of the non-Negro girls were selected randomly for inclusion in the sample.[3] In a few

---

[1] Alan B. Wilson, "Western Contra Costa County Population, 1965: Demographic Characteristics," mimeographed, Survey Research Center, Berkeley, 1966.

[2] Sampling procedures are described in greater detail in Alan B. Wilson, Travis Hirschi, and Glen Elder, "Technical Report No. 1: Secondary School Survey," mimeographed, Survey Research Center, Berkeley, 1965, pp. 3–21. The account presented here depends heavily on this source.

[3] Throughout this chapter, I refer to "non-Negro" students and to girls. In the analysis which follows, "non-Negro" becomes "white," and the girls disappear. Subsequent reference to "white" boys is accurate, because the few Oriental and Mexican–American boys were removed from the non-Negro category. Since girls have been neglected for too long by students of delin-

schools, where these sampling fractions would not produce 25 Negro boys or 25 Negro girls, all Negro boys and girls in the school were included in the sample. This procedure produced a stratified probability sample of 5,545 students: 1,479 Negro boys, 2,126 non-Negro boys, 1,076 Negro girls, and 864 non-Negro girls. Of the 5,545 students in the original sample, complete data were eventually obtained on 4,077, or 73.5 percent. The sources of attrition in the original sample are shown in Table 1.

Table 1 / Disposition of the Original Sample

Source of Attrition	Number	Percent
Permission denied by parent	359	6.5
No response from parent	303	5.5
Transfers and dropouts	345	6.2
Absentees	396	7.1
Errors in response	65	1.2
Completed questionnaires	4,077	73.5
Total original sample	5,545	100.0

Of the several reasons for nonresponse to the questionnaire shown in Table 1, failure to obtain permission from parents bulks largest in the statistics. The school administration required that permission be obtained from a parent or guardian of each child in the sample prior to administration of the questionnaire. After names and addresses were obtained from school records, a letter requesting such permission was sent to all parents. If no response was received within ten days, a follow-up letter was sent explaining the project in greater detail and again requesting permission to include the child in the sample. Finally, field workers called on most non-respondents to seek their permission. In the end, 359 students (6.5 percent of the original sample) were excluded from the survey because their parents refused permission, and an additional 303 students (5.5 percent) were excluded because their parents could not be contacted or failed to respond to the permission request. Before administration of the questionnaire began, then, 12 percent of the original sample had been lost due to failure to obtain permission from a parent. (Actually, many permissions were un-

quency, the exclusion of them is difficult to justify. I hope to return to them soon.

doubtedly denied at the request of the student. Several parents reported directly to us that although they were willing for their child to take part in the survey, the child himself refused to participate.)

By the spring of 1965, when the questionnaire was administered, 345 of the students selected in the fall of 1964 were no longer in the Richmond schools. These dropouts and those who transferred to other school systems are not properly part of the population sampled, since the population at issue is the in-school population during the spring of the school year. While the time gap between the selection of the sampling frame and the administration of the questionnaire makes the response rate look worse than it actually was, it should be noted that the sampling frame did not include students transferring into the school system during the same period.

Three hundred ninety-six students were absent during all administrations of the questionnaire, or did not complete enough of the questionnaire to allow data on them to be retained. (Unless the student completed at least two of the three sections of the questionnaire, he was classified as an absentee, and none of the answer sheets he completed was used in the analysis.)

Finally, screening of the answer sheets on which responses were recorded by the students resulted in the elimination of 65 additional cases as probably invalid.

Weighting Procedures

Five sampling fractions were used in the original sample. Therefore, in order to make population estimates, five weights must be used. While each non-Negro girl in the sample "represents" about 8 non-Negro girls in the population, each Negro boy represents only 1.2 Negro boys in the population. If the non-Negro girls and the Negro boys were simply added together in estimating averages for the population, the resulting statistic would be biased toward the average for Negro boys. Since 130 subgroups were actually sampled, and since different response rates were obtained in each, this logic was extended to the reduced final sample, and two weighting procedures, both of which appear in the present analysis, were employed.

The first procedure, required especially by counter-sorter and similar manual techniques of analysis, is based on the simple notion that if the proportion of the population is the same in all subgroups, the sample statistics are direct unbiased estimates of population parameters. To accomplish such identity, the overall proportion responding in each race-sex category was computed. Cases were then randomly discarded from those subgroups whose response rate exceeded that for the race-sex category as a whole and randomly duplicated in those subgroups whose response rate fell below that of their race-sex category. For example, if Negro boys had an overall response rate of 70 percent, and if 75 of 100 Negro boys in the ninth grade at Harry Ells High School completed the questionnaire, then the data on 5 of the 75 ninth-grade boys at Harry Ells were removed by random selection.

The target proportions for this procedure were set somewhat below the actual response rate for each race-sex category so that for the entire sample 193 cases were removed, and the data on 171 cases were chosen randomly for duplication. Most of the tables presented below are based on the self-weighting sample produced by this procedure. (Within a given race-sex category, about 4 percent of the cases shown in the tables appear twice.)

A second weighting procedure, made possible by computer analysis, involves assigning a weight to each case based on the proportion of the subgroup responding to the questionnaire. Thus, for example, if 20 percent of Negro girls in the tenth grade at a particular school completed the questionnaire, each of these girls is multiplied by 5 in making population estimates. Most of the tables presented below involving means, correlations, and regression coefficients are based on this weighting procedure.

In all cases, then, the statistics presented are population estimates rather than simple averages of the final sample data. The assumption upon which these weighting procedures are based is that the students completing the questionnaire within a subgroup are representative of all the students in that subgroup. Nonresponse bias of course affects the validity of these weighting procedures, as it does any weighting procedure, but to treat the sample as a simple random sample of the population would be to allow both nonresponse and disproportionate sampling to bias the results in unknown ways.

The Data

The data used in the present study come from three sources: school records, the questionnaire completed by the students, and police records.

School Records

The school records which served as a sampling frame contain, in addition to the race, sex, grade, and school information used in sampling, numerous academic achievement test scores and grade-point averages in selected subjects. All students in the district are given a battery of achievement tests in the eighth grade. Scores on these tests for students who were in the seventh grade at the time of administration of the questionnaire were added in the following year.

The Questionnaire

The questionnaire was divided into three sections. For each section, an IBM answer sheet containing the student's name, grade, school, and identification number was prepared. Both faces of the answer sheet were numbered, and these numbers were referred to repeatedly in the questionnaire itself (see Appendix C). Inasmuch as the schools had assumed responsibility for the first administration of the questionnaire, the answer sheets, arranged in alphabetical order by grade, were sent to the schools. Sets of instructions for administration were provided each school. The more difficult questions, such as father's occupation, had been placed at the beginning of each section in order that the teacher could use them as examples in giving instructions to the students. Most of the schools administered the questionnaire one section at a time on three consecutive days, although at least one school administered all three sections during consecutive class periods.

Responsibility for follow-up administrations of the questionnaire was assumed by the research staff of the Richmond Youth Project, the schools having returned all of the questionnaires after one attempt at administration. On the first administration, more than 2,100 students failed to complete the questionnaire satisfactorily. These included students absent on the day the questionnaire was administered, students who did not have sufficient time to complete the questionnaire,[4] and students whose answer sheets suggested misunderstanding of instructions or failure to take the questionnaire seriously.

Answer sheets returned by the schools were checked for completeness and for impossible or illegitimate marks. Lists of students to be included in the follow-up were then prepared by processing unsatisfactory answer sheets through an IBM 1230 mark-sensing machine. If the student had been absent during any portion of the first administration, his answer sheet pertaining to that portion was returned to him on the follow-up; if he had simply failed to complete sections of the questionnaire, his original answer sheet and a questionnaire booklet marked at the point he was to begin were provided; those students whose original answer sheets indicated misunderstanding or facetiousness were given clean answer sheets and special attention in follow-up trips to the school.

In most cases, the schools required that all students failing to complete the questionnaire on the first administration attend follow-up sessions during regular class periods. In some cases, however, attendance was voluntary, and the follow-up was administered before or after regular class sessions.

After the follow-up administrations of the questionnaire had been completed (a process requiring about six weeks), the answer sheets were again screened for reversals (the student marking the wrong side of the answer sheet, an error readily detectable from the pattern of responses), other types of errors, and apparent failure to take the questionnaire seriously. Given the varying range of permissible responses to items, the student merely checking the answer sheet without regard to the questionnaire items soon gave himself away, regardless of whether he was providing random or geometrical patterns of response. As mentioned earlier, 65 cases

[4] A pretest on sixth-grade students had suggested that at least 90 percent of seventh graders could complete each section of the questionnaire in a fifty-minute period. However, in many schools a good portion of the fifty-minute period was apparently used in distributing booklets, answer sheets, and pencils and in giving instructions to the students. In one high school, only one student in five had completed the first section of the questionnaire when it was returned to the project staff.

were eventually eliminated as a result of such checking.[5] (Individual answer sheets were also discarded as a result of such checking, although the bulk of the data on such a student was retained.)

Police Data

An alphabetical list of all 3,605 boys in the original sample was prepared, and records at the Richmond and San Pablo police departments and at the Contra Costa County Sheriff's Office were searched for evidence of contact with the police. Information was obtained on the total number of offenses a boy had committed; his age at first offense; the date of his most recent offense; and the type of offenses committed. These data, which provide information on the bias in the sample with respect to delinquency, as well as an alternative measure of the dependent variable, are described in Appendix C.

Nonresponse Bias

Nonresponse is occasionally used as grounds for dismissing the results of questionnaire studies of delinquency: delinquents are so obviously underrepresented among those completing questionnaires that the results need not be taken seriously. Given the extent of nonresponse to the questionnaire, and given that this is a study of delinquency, it seems necessary to say something about the probable extent of nonresponse bias before presenting the data. Nonresponse *is* related to delinquency. In fact, boys included in the final sample are considerably less likely to be delinquent than are boys who failed to complete the questionnaire. Most studies of delinquency based on natural populations undoubtedly encounter similar or more serious problems of nonresponse, but it is a curious fact that the more careful the data collection process, the more obvious the extent to which it falls short of what we would wish it to be.[6]

[5] As analysis of the nonresponders suggests, reading difficulties appear to account for many of the errors as well as for failure to take the questionnaire seriously.

[6] At the other extreme from the survey in which the sampling frame is carefully defined is participant observation, which always appears to be error-free (until, of course, a second observer attempts to retrace the steps of his predecessor).

On the other hand, it has been argued that the "dropout" or nonresponse problem actually enhances the faith one can have in sample results. For example, Albert J. Reiss and Albert Lewis Rhodes note that low-status boys are more likely to drop out of school and are more likely to be delinquent. They go on to comment: "Confidence in the observed differences presented in this paper is therefore justified since the inclusion of the out-of-school groups would increase the magnitude of the observed differences." [7] The limitations of this argument are clear: if delinquency and social status interact with respect to the response rate, neither the direction nor the magnitude of the bias in the sample is known. In the last analysis, then, we are dealing with an empirical question, and we cannot know what would have been without actually examining the cases not included in the sample.

Nevertheless, in the present case, police and school records on the entire original sample allow us to compare *some* of the results for the final sample with what would have been obtained had the response rate been perfect. In Table 2 the relation between race and official delinquency among boys in the original sample is compared with the relation among boys completing the questionnaire. Looking behind the figures in Table 2, we see that the nonresponse rate for non-Negro boys with police records is somewhat higher than the nonresponse rate for Negro boys with police records; the result is that the differences in delinquency between non-Negro and Negro boys in the final sample are slightly larger than in the original sample. For all practical purposes, however, the relation is unaffected by nonresponse. And this is so in spite of the fact that 64 percent of the Negro boys and 46 percent of the non-Negro boys not completing the questionnaire had police records.

As mentioned earlier, many achievement test scores were available for all boys in the original sample. The effects of nonresponse on the relation between test scores and delinquency are illustrated in Table 3. Looking at the response pattern indicated by Table 3, we see that high-achieving delinquents are only slightly more likely to be included in the final sample than low-achieving

[7] Albert J. Reiss, Jr., and Albert Lewis Rhodes, "The Distribution of Juvenile Delinquency in the Social Class Structure," *American Sociological Review,* XXVI (1961), 721.

Table 2 / Official Delinquency by Race—Boys Only
(in percent)

Original Sample		
	Race	
Official Record	Negroes	Others
No police record	43	68
Police record—no offenses in previous two years	12	8
One offense	18	11
Two offenses	9	5
Three or more offenses	18	8
Totals	100	100
	(1,479) [a]	(2,126)

Final Sample		
	Race	
Official Record	Negroes	Others
No police record	47	74
Police record—no offenses in previous two years	12	7
One offense	19	10
Two offenses	8	5
Three or more offenses	14	3
Totals	100	99
	(1,001)	(1,335)

[a] In all tables, numbers in parentheses represent the total number of cases upon which the percentages are based. In this case, the table says that 43 percent of the 1,479 Negro boys in the original sample had no police record.

delinquents, while high-achieving nondelinquents are much more likely to be included in the final sample than low-achieving nondelinquents. Given the proper set of circumstances, this pattern of nonresponse would tend to exaggerate rather than to obscure differences in delinquency between the high and low achievers. However, in the present case, the number of high-achieving delinquents is too small for this response pattern materially to affect the results, and the relation between Differential Aptitude Test verbal ability and official delinquency is virtually identical in the original and final samples.

Comparison of the relation between grade-point average (in English) and official delinquency among boys in the original and

Table 3 / Official Delinquency by Differential Aptitude
Test Verbal Scores—Non-Negro Boys Only
(in percent)

Original Sample				
	DAT Scores			
Official Record	0–9	10–19	20–29	30 and above
No police record	52	69	78	86
Police record—no offenses in previous two years	11	9	8	5
One offense	16	11	9	7
Two offenses	7	6	2	1
Three or more offenses	14	6	3	2
Totals	100 (378)	101 (615)	100 (370)	101 (170)
Final Sample				
	DAT Scores			
Official Record	0–9	10–19	20–29	30 and above
No police record	55	73	81	89
Police record—no offenses in previous two years	11	7	7	5
One offense	17	10	8	5
Two offenses	7	6	2	0
Three or more offenses	9	4	2	0
Totals	99 (190)	100 (377)	100 (286)	99 (132)

final samples reveals the effect of nonresponse bias anticipated by
Reiss and Rhodes (Table 4). In the original sample, 48 percent of
the boys with the lowest grades in English have no police record,
compared to 90 percent of the boys with the highest grades in
English, a difference of 42 percentage points. In the final sample,
56 percent of the boys with the lowest grades in English have no
police record, compared to 91 percent of the boys with the highest
grades, a difference of 35 percentage points. In other words,
the percentage point difference between boys with the lowest and
boys with the highest grades in English is smaller in the final than
in the original sample. At the serious end of the delinquency scale,
the percentage point difference between those with the highest

Table 4 / Official Delinquency by English Weighted
Average Mark—Non-Negro Boys Only
(in percent)

	Original Sample				
	English Weighted Average Mark				
Official Record	Low 1	2	3	4	High 5
No police record	48	58	75	78	90
Police record—no offenses in previous two years	13	13	7	7	4
One offense	18	14	10	11	5
Two offenses	7	7	4	3	1
Three or more offenses	15	8	4	1	. . .a
Totals	101	100	100	100	100
	(254)	(377)	(308)	(309)	(275)

	Final Sample				
	English Weighted Average Mark				
Official Record	Low 1	2	3	4	High 5
No police record	56	63	79	79	91
Police record—no offenses in previous two years	12	12	6	7	3
One offense	14	14	10	8	5
Two offenses	8	7	3	5	1
Three or more offenses	10	3	2	1	. . .a
Totals	100	99	100	100	100
	(117)	(234)	(196)	(208)	(215)

a Less than one-half of 1 percent.

and those with the lowest grades shrinks from 15 to 10. The net
effect of nonresponse bias in this case is thus slightly to attenuate
the relation. The relation observed in the final sample is weaker
than what would have been observed had there been complete
response to the questionnaire.

The response pattern producing this attenuation is shown in
Table 5; as one can see, it is the response pattern assumed by those
skeptical of the questionnaire method of studying delinquency.
Delinquents are consistently less likely than nondelinquents to
have completed the questionnaire. Furthermore, there is a relation
between the independent variable and the response rate, such that

Table 5 / Percent Completing the Questionnaire by Average
Grade in English and Police Record—Non-Negro Boys Only

	English Weighted Average Mark				
Official Record	Low 1	2	3	4	High 5
No police record	54 (121) ᵃ	67 (220)	66 (232)	69 (240)	79 (247)
Police record	38 (133)	55 (157)	55 (76)	62 (69)	71 (28)

ᵃ Once again, numbers in parentheses represent the total number of cases
upon which the percentages are based. In this case, the table shows that 54
percent of the 121 boys who had no police record and the lowest average
mark in English completed the questionnaire. When only one percentage
figure is given, the complementary percentage can be directly inferred. Thus,
the table also shows that 46 percent of the 121 boys who had no police
record and the lowest average mark in English failed to complete the questionnaire.

those in the "delinquency-prone" groups are less likely to respond,
regardless of their delinquency. Nevertheless, the relation between
this variable and delinquency is virtually identical in both the
original and the final samples. And the same is true of all relations
on which the data allow such comparisons. We, of course, have no
way of knowing how far this lack of effect extends. But dismissal
of the results on the ground that the sample is known to be biased
is not justified. And the consistency of the present results with
those revealed by previous studies, some of which do not have the
same kind of nonresponse problems (and many of which have
more serious problems but have no way of knowing how much or
in what way they affect the results), is, I think, sufficient to affirm
their credibility.

Chapter IV

What Is Delinquency?

Delinquency cannot be usefully defined apart from an attempt to explain delinquency so defined. Neither can delinquency be explained without, at the same time, at least implicitly defining delinquency. The task of this chapter is to extract a definition of delinquency consistent with the theory, to suggest measures of delinquency consistent with the definition, and to relate both the theoretical and the operational definitions to previous speculation and research.

Definitions of Delinquency

In this study, *delinquency is defined by acts, the detection of which is thought to result in punishment of the person committing them by agents of the larger society.* Although this definition is consistent with standard definitions of "deviant behavior" [1] or "delinquent acts," [2] it is not widely used in either delinquency theory or research. Several reasons have been advanced for avoiding this kind of definition of delinquency: (1) it is not interesting, or, at least, it is less interesting than alternative definitions; (2) delinquent acts, by themselves, are inadequate to establish that a person is or is not a delinquent; and (3) delinquent acts are too diverse to be studied as a unit.

---

[1] The most widely quoted definition of deviant behavior is probably Cohen's: "We define deviant behavior as behavior which violates institutionalized expectations—that is, expectations which are shared and recognized as legitimate within a social system." Albert K. Cohen, "The Study of Social Disorganization and Deviant Behavior," *Sociology Today*, ed. Robert K. Merton et al. (New York: Basic Books, 1959), p. 462.

[2] "The delinquent act . . . is behavior that violates basic norms of the society, and, when officially known, it evokes a judgment by agents of criminal justice that such norms have been violated." Richard A. Cloward and Lloyd E. Ohlin, *Delinquency and Opportunity* (New York: The Free Press, 1960), p. 3.

Role Definitions of Delinquency

The most popular definition of delinquency among theorists is the "role" definition:

> We are not so much interested in the person who commits a deviant act once as in the person who sustains a pattern of deviance over a long period of time, who makes of deviance a way of life, who organizes his identity around a pattern of deviant behavior. It is not the casual experimenters with homosexuality . . . that we want to find out about, but the man who follows a pattern of homosexual activity throughout his adult life.
>
> . . . Many kinds of deviant activity spring from motives which are socially learned. Before engaging in the activity on a more or less regular basis, the person has no notion of the pleasures to be derived from it; he learns these in the course of interaction with more experienced deviants. . . . What may well have been a *random impulse* to try something new becomes a settled taste for something already known and experienced.[3]

Defining delinquency as a role makes the explanation of the delinquent act logically equivalent to explanations of why college professors teach: "In this book . . . we are concerned with those forms of delinquent activity which result from the performance of social roles *specifically provided and supported by delinquent subcultures.*" [4] Thus, in spite of Albert K. Cohen's oft-quoted injunction, "In order to build a sociology of deviant behavior, we must always keep as our point of reference deviant *behavior*, not kinds of people," [5] most sociologists, including Cohen, ask: "Why do some people become deviants?" [6]

An unfortunate side effect of the view that the proper focus

[3] Howard S. Becker, *Outsiders* (New York: The Free Press, 1963), p. 30. Emphasis added.
[4] Cloward and Ohlin, *Delinquency and Opportunity*, p. 9. Emphasis in original.
[5] Cohen, in *Sociology Today*, ed. Merton et al., p. 463. Emphasis added.
[6] Cohen's recent paper, "The Sociology of the Deviant Act: Anomie Theory and Beyond," is appropriately abbreviated on the page headings as "The Sociology of the Deviant," since the deviant act is implicitly defined as conversion from a conforming to a deviant mode of life (*American Sociological Review*, XXX [1965], 5–14).

of study should be the criminal rather than the crime is the view that crimes not committed by criminals are essentially unexplainable (Becker's "random impulse"), or that they do not require explanation since there is no variation in criminal activity among noncriminals, a thought that is expressed in this quotation from Jackson Toby:

> I think it is well to bear in mind that the group which Professor Nye calls "most delinquent" would be considered non-delinquents by many criminologists. Whereas nearly everybody commits delinquent *acts* at some time or other, only a very small proportion of the population assumes a delinquent *role*—with all that this implies in the way of a deviant self-concept. . . . Sociologists are, I believe, more concerned with the few who assume a delinquent role than with degrees of delinquent behavior on the part of the many who adhere to a generally law-abiding style of life.[7]

Users of role definitions of delinquency thus treat the delinquent act as nonproblematic, as something whose explanation is given in the explanation of a prior event. The point of reference is *not* delinquent behavior, because delinquent behavior is nothing more than an epiphenomenal outgrowth of the assumption of a delinquent role.

Configurational or Syndrome Definitions of Delinquency

Although linked to a different intellectual tradition, "syndrome" definitions of delinquency have consequences for research and theory much like those of role definitions. In this view, delinquency is defined by a peculiar *configuration* of delinquent acts. It is not the first act, or the third, that defines a boy as "delinquent," but it is some, often ineffable combination of acts that distinguishes the "true" delinquent from the "pseudo"-delinquent and the "true" nondelinquent. At first glance, these definitions may appear unexceptionable:

> For the purposes of the present study . . . delinquency refers to *repeated acts* of a kind which when committed by persons

[7] Jackson Toby, review of *Family Relationships and Delinquent Behavior* by F. Ivan Nye, *American Sociological Review*, XXV (1960), 282–283.

beyond the statutory court age of sixteen are punishable as crimes. . . .[8]

[Delinquency is] behavior by nonadults which violates specific legal norms or the norms of a particular societal institution with sufficient frequency and/or seriousness so as to provide a firm basis for legal action against the behaving individual or group.[9]

The problem is that making the meaning of a particular delinquent act contingent on prior or subsequent acts shifts the focus from what is being done to who is doing it. Thus Sheldon and Eleanor Glueck argue, for example, that gang membership cannot be a cause of "delinquency," because in their sample most of the boys had "become delinquents" prior to joining gangs. Delinquent acts certainly occur after gang membership, but in syndrome definitions, as in the case of role definitions, these acts become "the behavior of a delinquent" and are thus nonproblematic and/or uninteresting.[10]

If, as in the role and syndrome definitions, a person at some point "becomes a delinquent" and at some other point may "leave delinquency," then questions applicable to other roles appear perfectly reasonable when applied to delinquency: "At what age do children become delinquents?" "How long do they remain delinquents?" "What is the typical length of a delinquent career?" "How do the early starters differ from the late starters?" "What are the causes of reform?" [11] In terms of the definition used here, most such questions are meaningless (for example, "What is the typical length of a delinquent career?" becomes "How much time usually elapses between stealing a candy bar and urinating against a wall?") or, at best, unnecessary (for example, "What are the

[8] Sheldon and Eleanor Glueck, *Unraveling Juvenile Delinquency* (Cambridge, Mass.: Harvard University Press, 1950), p. 13. Emphasis added.
[9] William C. Kvaraceus and Walter B. Miller, *Delinquent Behavior: Culture and the Individual* (Washington: National Education Association, 1959), p. 54.
[10] For an extended discussion of the Gluecks' definition and its research implications, see Travis Hirschi and Hanan C. Selvin, *Delinquency Research: An Appraisal of Analytic Methods* (New York: The Free Press, 1967), pp. 60–63. That the Kvaraceus and Miller definition leads to similar conclusions is shown by the following: "As a preventive, 'keeping youth busy' . . . can, at best, only temporarily postpone behavior that is symptomatic of more deep-seated or culturally oriented factors" (*Delinquent Behavior*, p. 39).
[11] For a review of research and theory on such questions, see Barbara Wootton, *Social Science and Social Pathology* (New York: Macmillan, 1959), Chapter V.

causes of reform?" is the same as "What are the causes of non-delinquency?"—which is the same as "What are the causes of delinquency?").

Typological Definitions of Delinquency

Both the role and the syndrome definitions of delinquency are compatible with and, indeed, seem to foster the view that it is illegitimate to consider delinquency as a homogeneous or unidimensional phenomenon. The sheer number of sociologists who have spoken out in favor of this "typological" approach to delinquency attests to its persuasiveness.[12] Just as it is illegitimate to treat all diseases as one, so it is illegitimate to treat all delinquent acts as "delinquency."

Robert M. MacIver states the argument forcefully: "It is vain to seek the causes of crime as such, of crime anywhere and everywhere. Crime is a legal category. The only thing that is alike in all crimes is that they are alike violations of the law." [13] However, if we take his argument at face value, MacIver's conclusion ("It is vain . . .") simply does not follow from his premise. If it did, one could, on a priori grounds, call into question any attempt to explain a natural phenomenon. The only things that all members of any class have in common *by definition* are the things entering the definition. But beyond this definitional homogeneity there is homogeneity *by hypothesis*. MacIver appears to be asserting without logical or empirical evidence that all theories of "crime" are and will be false—that no true *hypothesis* of homogeneity is possi-

---

[12] The list is long and varied. Robert M. MacIver, *Social Causation* (Boston: Ginn, 1940), p. 33; Albert K. Cohen, *Delinquent Boys* (New York: The Free Press, 1955), pp. 172–173; Wootton, *Social Science*, pp. 306–307; Cloward and Ohlin, *Delinquency and Opportunity*, p. 33; Marshall B. Clinard and Andrew L. Wade, "Juvenile Vandalism," *Readings in Juvenile Delinquency*, ed. Ruth S. Cavan (Philadelphia: Lippincott, 1964), pp. 220–226; Robert K. Merton, *Social Theory and Social Structure* (New York: The Free Press, 1957), p. 177; Irwin Deutscher, "New Perspectives for Research In Juvenile Delinquency," *Human Behavior and Social Processes*, ed. Arnold M. Rose (Boston: Houghton Mifflin, 1964), pp. 474–476; John Finley Scott, "Two Dimensions of Delinquent Behavior," *American Sociological Review*, XXIV (1959), 240; Robert A. Dentler and Lawrence J. Monroe, "Social Correlates of Early Adolescent Theft," *American Sociological Review*, XXVI (1961), 733–743. For an extended discussion of the literature and logic of the typological approach from a treatment perspective, see Don C. Gibbons, *Changing the Lawbreaker* (Englewood Cliffs, N.J.: Prentice-Hall, 1965).
[13] *Social Causation*, p. 33.

ble. However, this overlooks a key phrase in MacIver's statement: "Crime is a *legal* category." In the theory MacIver envisions, "crime" would not or could not be defined by the law. If, by definition, their illegality is the only thing crimes have in common, then disregard for their illegality makes them hopelessly heterogeneous, and no theory of crime, so "defined," is possible.

Arguments like MacIver's rest on the acknowledged fact that, as *behavior*, smoking marihuana has little in common with pushing cars over the edge of an embankment. The most commonly advanced argument for subdefinitions of delinquency, however, rests on the heterogeneity of those committing the acts: "Delinquent acts, as such, occur throughout the social structure: although the rates differ, they are committed by females, middle-class adolescents, and residents in rural areas. It is *unreasonable* to assume that a single theory can account for such diverse behavior." [14] Actually, the diversity of the perpetrators of delinquent acts is irrelevant in judging a theory of delinquency unless such diversity is precluded by the theory. If it is unreasonable to attempt to explain delinquent acts because they are committed by girls, the children of rich men, and the children of farmers, then, by the same token, it makes little sense to try to explain urban lower-class male delinquency, because some urban lower-class male delinquents are tall, some have red hair, and some are of Italian extraction.

In brief, then, the definition of delinquency used here is *not the same* as the definitions used or proposed by most students of delinquency. Role definitions of delinquency exclude from consideration the delinquent acts of "nondelinquents," and they exclude from interest the delinquent acts of delinquents: they propose an analogy between delinquency and other social roles that confuses more than it clarifies; they prematurely and unnecessarily restrict

[14] Cloward and Ohlin, *Delinquency and Opportunity*, p. 70. Emphasis added. For an insightful critique of the view that many "factors" mean many theories, see Albert K. Cohen, "Multiple Factor Approaches," *The Sociology of Crime and Delinquency*, ed. Marvin E. Wolfgang et al. (New York: Wiley, 1962), pp. 77–80. There is little difference between the assumption that the many causes of delinquency require many theories and the assumption that the many possible subdimensions of delinquency require many theories. If the number of independent variables can be reduced by abstraction, then so too can the number of dependent variables. Thus it is not perfectly consistent for the opponents of "multiple factor" theories to advocate "multiple effect" theories.

the study of delinquency to small segments of the population while acknowledging that delinquency is prevalent throughout the social structure and without giving any good reason for believing that the causes of delinquent acts are different from one class to another.

Syndrome definitions of delinquency present similar problems. In addition, since they are typically used in empirical studies, their ultimate ambiguity is particularly unfortunate. The not-very-far-beneath-the-surface assumption that delinquency is a disease of which delinquent acts are a symptom allows users of these definitions to diagnose boys committing few delinquent acts as "delinquent" and other boys committing many delinquent acts "non-delinquent." [15]

Unfortunately, it is not possible to claim a theory of crime that would constitute an irrefutable answer to those who argue that delinquency cannot or should not be treated as a homogeneous phenomenon. However, insofar as such judgments are possible, it is true that general explanations, such as social control theories, go as far toward explaining all crime as the special theories designed to account for specific acts go in explaining these specific acts. Furthermore, on the empirical level, the "more regular correlations" between antecedent variables and specific delinquent acts promised by the typological approach have not yet equaled those that do exist between antecedent variables and delinquency defined more generally.[16]

[15] Syndrome approaches tend to lead to the "delinquent-nondelinquent" dichotomization of subjects because, as in any complex typology, it is difficult to rank cases other than those at the extremes. In research designed to predict delinquency, this results in the appearance of the "pseudo-delinquent," presumably a person who appears on the surface to be a delinquent but whom the researcher knows is not really one. Unfortunately, the evidence used to prove that he is not really a delinquent tends to be the variables used to predict delinquency in the first place. For an example of research in which the view that a boy either is or is not a delinquent was a continual source of trouble and eventually of disaster, see Maude M. Craig and Selma J. Glick, "Ten Years' Experience with the Glueck Social Prediction Table," Crime and Delinquency, IX (1963), 249–261. Criticisms of the New York City Youth Board Study are numerous; see, for example, Alfred J. Kahn, "The Case of the Premature Claims: Public Policy and Delinquency Prediction," Crime and Delinquency, XI (1965), 217–228.

[16] The problem with the typological approach is that it begs the question of causal homogeneity by focusing exclusively on the question of behavioral homogeneity. The method of analytic induction is a more sophisticated approach to the same problem, since it judges each case in terms of a causal

Measures of Delinquency

A theory purporting to explain a variety of delinquent acts does not necessarily assume they are strongly related to each other. Thus petty theft may or may not be related to vandalism: given the opportunity to commit an act of vandalism, the theory suggests, the person currently committing petty thefts is more likely to succumb, as common sense holds. But no relation like that suggested by Reiss is required or supposed: "An adolescent boy or girl who is arrested for stealing almost always has also violated sexual conduct norms, and the reverse is usually the case as well." [17]

Among the many items on the questionnaire dealing with delinquent or deviant behavior were those listed below. These were included to serve as an index of delinquency.

1. Have you ever taken little things (worth less than $2) that did not belong to you?
2. Have you ever taken things of some value (between $2 and $50) that did not belong to you?
3. Have you ever taken things of large value (worth over $50) that did not belong to you?
4. Have you ever taken a car for a ride without the owner's permission?
5. Have you ever banged up something that did not belong to you on purpose?
6. Not counting fights you may have had with a brother or sister, have you ever beaten up on anyone or hurt anyone on purpose?

As a group, these six items do not constitute a previously developed "delinquency scale." Rather, they are taken from two different scales: two of the items (No. 1 and No. 5) are part of F. Ivan Nye and James F. Short's seven-item delinquency scale; [18] the remaining four items are from Robert A. Dentler and Law-

hypothesis but does not attempt a priori to settle the question of causal homogeneity.

[17] Albert J. Reiss, "Sex Offenses of Adolescents," *Readings in Juvenile Delinquency*, ed. Ruth S. Cavan (Philadelphia: Lippincott, 1964), p. 229.

[18] F. Ivan Nye and James F. Short, Jr., "Scaling Delinquent Behavior," *American Sociological Review*, XXII (1957), 328. See also F. Ivan Nye, *Family Relationships and Delinquent Behavior* (New York: Wiley, 1958), pp. 13–14.

rence J. Monroe's five-item "theft scale." [19] Although it is often argued that one serious problem in delinquency research is that no two researchers define delinquency and/or their independent variables in *exactly* the same way, the following arguments are advanced for devising a new delinquency scale (based, to be sure, on two existing scales) and for not using a previously developed scale *in toto*.

One of the Nye/Short items was considered not sufficiently serious for use in a population like that studied ("Have you ever driven a car without a driver's license or permit?"). Four of their items do not measure delinquency as the term is defined here ("Have you ever skipped school without a legitimate excuse?"; "Have you ever defied your parents' authority to their face?"; "Have you ever bought or drank beer, wine, or liquor? [Include drinking at home]"; and "Have you ever had sex relations with a person of the opposite sex?"). In addition, Nye and Short asked the students if they had committed the acts "since beginning grade school." Inasmuch as this forces a relation between delinquency and age and obscures reform, it was considered undesirable.

It would have been possible to include Dentler and Monroe's fifth item and thus to replicate their study. However, one of the major arguments of the present study is that the findings of delinquency research are not as dependent on the operational definition of delinquency as has been widely assumed. It is not expected that these variations in the definition of delinquency will produce results inconsistent with those of Nye and Short or Dentler and Monroe.[20] If the results are consistent, then something has been gained by varying the definition of the dependent variable.

The items included in our delinquency scale have logical

[19] "Social Correlates," p. 734.

[20] Nye's inclusion of items like "defying parents' authority" in a study in which relations with parents are the major independent variables appears at first glance to stack the cards heavily in favor of his hypotheses. However, as far as I can determine, Nye's dichotomization of his Guttman scale made this particular item unimportant in determining whether a student was assigned to the "most" or "least" delinquent categories. See *Family Relationships*, pp. 18–19. One item, "drinking at home," may have produced findings not replicable by the measure used here, such as a relation between religiousness and delinquency. See Travis Hirschi and Rodney Stark, "Hellfire and Delinquency," a paper presented at the annual meetings of the Pacific Sociological Association, San Francisco, 1968.

validity, since they measure petty and grand larceny, auto theft, vandalism (malicious mischief), and battery—all offenses that are commonly thought to result in punishment by agents of the larger society, if detected.

Since arguments for the multidimensionality of delinquency are commonly based on inspection of the relations among offenses, the associations among the six items are presented in Table 6.

Table 6 / Correlations Among Self-Report Items— White Boys Only [a]

	1	2	3	4	5	6
1. Theft ($2)	1.00	.45	.26	.27	.28	.27
2. Theft ($2–50)		1.00	.48	.30	.26	.27
3. Theft ($50+)			1.00	.32	.21	.20
4. Auto theft				1.00	.23	.22
5. Vandalism					1.00	.28
6. Battery						1.00

[a] The numbers upon which the correlations are based range from 1,532 to 1,539.

Response categories for all six items were identical. For example:

Have you ever taken little things (worth less than $2) that did not belong to you?
1. Never.
2. More than a year ago.
3. During the last year.
4. During the last year *and* more than a year ago.[21]

Since these response categories measure more than one dimension (recency, persistence, and, indirectly, frequency), no straightforward interpretation of the correlations in Table 6 is possible. One can say, however, that those answering "during the last year *and* more than a year ago" are in some general sense "more delinquent" than those checking some other response category. Thus, the "more delinquent" a boy is as measured by any one of these

[21] Previous studies of self-reported delinquency have typically asked students "how many times" they have committed a particular delinquent act and then for purposes of analysis dichotomized between those "never" committing the act and those committing it once or more. These response categories were designed to produce this information as well as information as to when the most recent acts occurred.

items, the more delinquent he is likely to be as measured by any other item.[22]

In addition to their relations with each other, each item is related in the same manner and in the expected direction to such things as self-reported *truancy* (.24–.33),[23] self-reported school *suspensions* (.18–.28), self-reported *contacts with the police* (.28–.39), and *official delinquency* as measured by police records (.13–.29). An example of a relation between one of these items and delinquency as measured by official records is given in Table 7.

Table 7 / Official Offenses by Theft of Item of Medium Value—White Boys Only
"Have you ever taken something of medium value ($2–50) that did not belong to you?"
(in percent)

Number of Offenses in Previous Two Years	Never	More than Year Ago	During Last Year	During and More
None	85	73	61	55
One	9	14	19	21
Two or more	6	13	20	25
Totals	100 (1,054)	100 (123)	100 (70)	101 (53)

Only 15 percent of the boys who report they have never stolen anything of medium value have police records, whereas 46 percent of the boys who report stealing something of medium value during the previous year and prior to that have been picked up by the police. The six items intended for use as measures of "delinquency" thus have pragmatic validity—they differentiate between boys known to differ on some independently measured aspect of delinquency.

It has been suggested that such validation of self-report items by the use of official data is tantamount to admitting that

[22] The magnitude of these relations suggests at the outset that the goal of explaining 100 percent of the variance in the measure of delinquency is highly unrealistic.
[23] These figures define the range of correlation coefficients for the six items. The smallest correlation with truancy was .24; the largest was .33.

"community definitions of crime (arrest and detention) represent the basic criterion" of delinquency. It has also been argued that "the investigator does not know the honesty" of self-reports.[24] William McCord and Joan McCord have this to say about the relative virtues of official and self-report measures of delinquency:

> Unfortunately, the validity of this [self-report] approach can be established only by intimate and constant observation of the subject or by reference to court convictions. Yet court convictions are the very standard which these sociologists wish to avoid. . . .
>
> We believe that court convictions offer the best opportunity for unbiased identification of criminals. Whereas records for arrests may be subject to the bias of police, and sentences to correctional institutions to the bias of judges, convictions are a result of the operation of the legal system in its most objective form.[25]

The argument that to validate self-report items against official data is to admit the superiority of the latter is, I think, a misinterpretation of the function of validation. Inconsistencies between the two measures can as easily be used against as in favor of the official measure, as Short and Nye have shown.[26] The argument that "court convictions" are less biased than "police records" is a remarkable statement of faith in the ability of a system to correct bias occurring at an earlier point in the adjudication process. How, for example, do judge and jury correct for those persons guilty of crimes who are picked up and released by the police?

Arguments about the overall honesty of respondents in reporting delinquent acts must take one of the following patterns. (1) Respondents will lie in the direction of making themselves look "good"—that is, they will say that they have not committed delinquent offenses when they in fact have. This is the most popular (and cogent) of the "lying" hypotheses, especially when nonanonymous questionnaires are used. (2) Respondents will lie to make

24 William McCord and Joan McCord, *Origins of Crime* (New York: Columbia University Press, 1959), p. 18.

25 *Ibid.*, p. 11.

26 James F. Short, Jr., and F. Ivan Nye, "Reported Behavior as a Criterion of Deviant Behavior," *Social Problems*, V (1957), 207–213. The "inconsistencies" I have in mind here are with respect to the relations between "outside" variables and delinquency as measured by official and self-report methods. If the broken home is related to official delinquency but not to self-reported delinquency, there is good reason to suspect official statistics as a measure of delinquent behavior, which presumably is the basic criterion for judging the validity of measures of "delinquency."

themselves look "bad"—that is, they will say they have committed delinquent acts when they in fact have not. (3) Some respondents will take one approach, some another, such that actual responses are only randomly related to the "underlying" phenomenon. (4) Some respondents will take one approach, some another, such that the relation between actual responses and the "underlying" phenomenon is systematically biased.

In their strongest forms, hypotheses 1, 2, and 3 are clearly false, as Table 7 shows. Boys do admit, and deny, delinquent offenses; and their reports are related to measures beyond the reach of their tendencies to fabricate the past. In fact, the position that respondents will deny delinquent activities on a nonanonymous questionnaire is the least defensible of the three hypotheses on the basis of the data collected.[27] For example, while 19 percent of all white boys said they had been picked up by the police although they had no ascertainable police record, only 10 percent denied having been picked up by the police in spite of records to the contrary.[28]

The most serious argument against the validity of self-report items is that they are systematically biased. If there are systematic differences between the honest and dishonest, many or most of the relations between self-reported delinquency and outside variables may be artifacts of differential honesty. It is impossible to disprove such a hypothesis in the abstract—one cannot show that no antecedent variable can account for observed relations. However, the problem is tractable when a specific antecedent variable is offered as a possible explanation of observed results:

> Suppose respondents varied considerably in their willingness to cooperate with the researchers. The less cooperative ones might have denied what they considered discreditable: delinquencies, unhappy family relations, infrequent church attendance. The more cooperative respondents, on the other hand, might have been more willing to admit such things, thus generating a spurious relationship between confessions and other responses.[29]

[27] However, John P. Clark and Larry L. Tifft ("Polygraph and Interview Validation of Self-Reported Deviant Behavior," *American Sociological Review*, XXXI [1966], 516–523) found that most of the offenses measured here were underreported on their "initial" questionnaire. Nonetheless, the rank correlation between the initial and final sets of scores was .81 for the Dentler–Monroe items, four of which are used in the present index.

[28] See Table 15 and the discussion of race in the next chapter.

[29] Jackson Toby, review of Nye's *Family Relationships*, p. 283.

Suppose Toby's speculation is correct, suppose that uncooperative respondents are more likely to deny delinquent acts, and that, therefore, the uncooperative group is *over*represented among those who say they have *never* taken anything of medium value (see Table 7). This forces one to argue that *un*cooperative children are *less* likely to have been picked up by the police, since only 15 percent of the white boys who say they have never taken anything of medium value have been picked up, while 45 percent of those who admit taking something of medium value "during the last year *and* more than a year ago" have police records.

It is, of course, very difficult to maintain that "cooperativeness" is positively related to having a police record. For almost every item on the questionnaire, those who fail to respond are more likely to have been picked up by the police; and, as we have seen, those who refused to take the questionnaire at all (for whatever reason) are even more likely to have a police record.[30]

Actually, in terms of the data, a superficially more plausible antecedent variable hypothesis with respect to self-reported acts is that cooperative, "good" children might underreport delinquent acts while uncooperative, "bad" children might overreport them— the hypothesis *opposite* to Toby's. This would also generate spurious relations in the direction predicted by most theories: boys who report liking their teachers would report few delinquent acts; boys who report disliking their teachers would report many, and so on. Almost all of the relations reported in a study of this kind could be so explained, if one is willing to take an additional step and argue that police records are biased in the same direction. In order to advance this hypothesis, however, one has to revert to a modified "role" or "syndrome" view of the world, according to which "delinquency" explains everything *except* the commission of delinquent acts.[31]

---

[30] For further evidence of a negative relation between this kind of cooperativeness and delinquency, see Arthur L. Stinchcombe, *Rebellion in a High School* (Chicago: Quadrangle, 1964), pp. 186–189.

[31] In other words, if this "cooperativeness" or "goodness" produces and explains the relations between outside variables and *self-reported* delinquency, then it should also produce and explain relations between outside variables and *actual* delinquency. If this is the argument, then the self-report technique is not called into question, since presumably any method of measurement of delinquency would produce similarly spurious relations. If, on the other hand, the argument is that there are no relations of any kind between the outside variables and *actual* delinquency, then the intermittent efficacy of this "antecedent variable" is, at best, puzzling.

If it is granted that in two meanings of the term the "validity" of the individual self-report items has been provisionally established, then the problem becomes one of combining them to form an index of delinquent activity, and questions of yet another form of validity are thus raised. If the respondents had been asked to report how many times they had committed each of the acts, it would seem consistent with the theory simply to assign each boy a score based on the total number of offenses he reported. However, since the theory assumes that "reform" is not only possible but probable, any scoring procedure that forces an increase over time in the proportion delinquent must be avoided. A theory that assumes that "delinquency" may vary from time to time and may therefore decline with age certainly should not be tested by use of a measure that cannot decline. In other words, the idea that the dependent variable should be the "number of acts" is only elliptically correct. Strictly speaking, the theory suggests that during the time a given independent variable has the value X, the probability of delinquent acts is increased. Thus the period during which one might legitimately take the total number of delinquent acts as a measure of the dependent variable depends upon the independent variable in question. Suppose, to use an example from classical criminological theory, that intelligence is taken as an independent variable on the grounds that persons of low intelligence are more likely to underestimate the risk of detection and are less likely to see the implications of their acts for the interpersonal relations assumed to bind persons to the moral order. If intelligence were taken as constant over time, then, with respect to intelligence, it would seem proper to count *all* delinquent acts occurring after the grounds that involvement in such a relationship tends to remove "age of responsibility" had been reached. In contrast, suppose one from delinquency-inducing situations and at the same time increases the cost of detection.[32] It would obviously be "unfair" to this variable to count acts occurring long before formation of the heterosexual liaison.[33]

[32] This assumption appears to be empirically false, since those who date are more likely to commit delinquent acts (see Stinchcombe, *Rebellion*, p. 126, and Chapter IX, below).

[33] The problem as to when the variables should be measured is not unique plicitly suggest that the *direction* of the relation between some independent to control theories. In fact, "reaction formation" and analogous theories ex-

Since delinquent activity presumably climbs rapidly to a peak at fourteen or fifteen years of age and then declines, it must be assumed that the values of variables conducive to delinquency also change during this period, and thus a fair test of the theory would require restriction of the period during which delinquent acts could have been committed. Otherwise, the current value of the independent variable may not be what it was when the delinquent acts were committed. It was with this problem in mind that students were asked *when* they committed the acts in question.[34] (Sacrificing the number of times the acts had been committed was not considered serious since previous investigators had found it advisable to dichotomize between *no* and *one or more* delinquent acts, using items tapping less "serious" offenses on the whole than those used in the present study.) An index based on the number of *acts committed during the previous year* was considered most appropriate as an operationalization of delinquency in terms of the theory. Two indexes were constructed in addition to this *recency* index: one, based on procedures followed by most investigators of self-reported delinquency, is the total number of delinquent acts ever committed (*standard* index); the other takes both persistence and recency into account and, indirectly, weighs frequency (*persistence* index).[35]

The relations of these indexes to each other and to selected outside variables are shown in Table 8. Each of the indexes is more strongly related to the outside variables than was any single item, although the gain over the most potent single item in some cases is

variables and delinquency depends on when the independent variables are measured.

[34] Actually there was another good reason for restricting the time period— to reduce the relation between age and delinquency and thus obviate the necessity of controlling age in the analysis. This effort was largely successful, although evidence remains that fourteen and fifteen are the peak years for delinquent activity. (The relation between age and delinquency in the present sample is shown in Appendix A.)

[35] More explicitly, the alternative indices were constructed by scoring each of the six items as follows:

Response	Recency	Standard	Persistence
Never	0	0	0
More than a year ago	0	1	1
During the last year	1	1	2
During last year and more than a year ago	1	1	3

not large. Contrary to my expectations,[36] the recency index does not do quite as well as the other indexes in predicting outside variables, even when these variables (for example, truancy) are also restricted to a one-year period. However, the differences are not large, and I consider the gain in conceptual clarity that comes from using an index which depends upon acts committed in the recent past more than sufficient justification for its use, even if it does entail some loss in "predictive" ability.

Table 8 / Correlations Among Alternate Self-Report Indexes and Selected Outside Variables—White Boys Only [a]

	Recency	Persistence	Standard
Recency	1.00	.90	.76
Persistence		1.00	.92
Standard			1.00
Truancy [b]	.39	.42	.42
Suspension [c]	.33	.35	.35
Police contact [d]	.42	.47	.50
Official record [e]	.27	.29	.30

[a] The number of cases upon which these correlations are based is not less than 1,300.
[b] "During the last year, did you ever stay away from school just because you had other things you wanted to do?"
[c] "Have you ever been suspended from school?"
[d] "Have you ever been picked up by the police?"
[e] Scored as total number of delinquent acts recorded by the police.

The relation between an individual item and police records was used earlier as evidence in favor of the validity of self-reports, and it was suggested at that time that arguments about validity based on an empirical relation are a two-way street: if police records support self-reports as measures of the commission of delinquent acts, then self-reports offer evidence that police records are at least partially valid as a measure of the same thing. We are justified in suggesting that police records are less valid as a measure of delinquency as defined here on other grounds. As defined, every delinquent act committed by a person is witnessed by him; he

[36] The recency index is the most badly skewed of the three, and thus on statistical grounds this expectation was naïve. By the same token, the expectation could possibly be saved by the use of an asymmetric measure of association or "corrections" for the number of categories and the like.

cannot commit delinquent acts without knowing it (otherwise, there is nothing to explain). Obviously, the police do not have such omnipresence. Furthermore, the police define some "acts" as delinquent that cannot be considered delinquent by a social control theory (the number is not large). For example, possession of a BB gun purchased by his parents may give a boy a police record, but such an act presumably reflects nothing about the boy's moral or rational stake in conformity. In short, the records of the police are, on a priori grounds, a weaker measure of the *commission* of delinquent acts than presumably honest self-reports. But the relation between self-reported delinquent acts and police records has significance for validity beyond confirming that persons reporting certain acts are more likely to have committed them: the agreement between "commission" and "detection" affirms that the acts are *delinquent* as the term is defined.[37]

In the analysis which follows, I shall in some cases present both the recency index based on self-reported offenses and the number of offenses recorded by the police in the two years prior to and in the year following administration of the questionnaire. I originally intended to compare all of the results obtained from the questionnaire with those that would have been obtained had only official records been available. I assumed that the results would in general be consistent.[38] However, the results turned out to be so independent of the measure of delinquency used that I lost interest in pursuing this exercise further.

[37] In making this point, I reaffirm that the definition of the delinquent act used here is virtually identical to that proposed by Cloward and Ohlin, although, as noted earlier, there is little relation between this definition and that used by Cloward and Ohlin (see *Delinquency and Opportunity*, pp. 2–13).

[38] This assumption was not a result of inspection of the data (see Hirschi and Selvin, *Delinquency Research*, pp. 192–193). For that matter, much analysis suggests that the results would not have been materially altered had some alternate self-report measure of delinquency been used (for example, "Have you ever been picked up by the police?"). Irving Piliavin has conducted extensive analysis of the present data using the self-report measure of offenses, the measure of official delinquency, and a self-report measure of contact with the police. To my knowledge, none of his findings has been contingent on the measure used. While all this is true, the police data generally produce weaker relations with the independent variables than do the self-report measures. For this reason, as well as for the reason that occasional inconsistencies require substantial analysis, the police data are presented mainly when the question of validity of results is particularly crucial or when a discrepancy is suggested by theoretical considerations.

Chapter V

The Social Distribution of Delinquency

Sex, race, social class, neighborhood, mother's employment, the broken home, size of family, and so forth, are the stuff of which most empirical studies, textbooks, and theories of delinquency are constructed. These traditional variables share one thing in common: it is hard to know *why* they are related to delinquency if they are in fact so related. The problem is not that it is difficult to account for observed relations between these variables and delinquency; on the contrary, it is too easy. A strong relation between race and delinquency, for example, can be interpreted by almost any theorist without introducing ad hoc assumptions. Strain, social control, and cultural deviance theories are equally capable of accounting for such a relation. If, as might happen, no such relation appears in a particular study, they are all equally unconcerned. How is it that such variables can always verify but never falsify theory? The answer is that these variables are usually treated as causes of intervening variables, rather than as direct causes of delinquency. Or, to put it differently, they are usually treated as indicators of causal variables: Negroes occupy a highly disadvantageous position in the opportunity structure; the Negro's stake in conformity to conventional expectations is decidedly small; Negro "culture" is lower-class in character; Negro family life produces faulty ego and superego development. A zero relation between race and delinquency would negate the assumed relation between race and these intervening variables, but it would not necessarily call into question the assumed relation between the intervening variables and delinquency.

Interest in many of these variables (for example, the broken home or mother's employment) undoubtedly originally stems from a social control perspective, and hypotheses about their relations with delinquency can thus easily be derived from a control theory. Nevertheless, even if these hypotheses are confirmed, little has been added in the way of confirmation of control theory or refutation of competing theories, since the "intervening" variables are the bones of contention.[1] Therefore, an analysis adequate to the problem would attempt to determine which of the hypothesized intervening variables actually "accounts for" the observed relation (if any) between one of these variables and delinquency.

Although I shall attempt such an analysis with some of these variables, on the whole I consider an alternate procedure preferable—namely, to start as close as possible to the dependent variables and work back to the presumably more numerous causes of the proximate variables. Therefore, in this chapter I shall use two of these traditional variables (social class and race) to describe the distribution of delinquency in the population, to suggest some of the weaknesses and limitations of the data, to indicate the extent to which it is necessary to control these variables in subsequent analysis, and to discuss problems not directly related to the choice between social control and alternative theories. Many remaining traditional variables are discussed in Appendix A.

Social Class

While the prisons bulge with the socioeconomic dregs of society, careful quantitative research shows again and again that the relation between socioeconomic status and the commission of delinquent acts is small, or nonexistent. More than common sense is offended by a finding of no difference, as some of the first investigators to find it suggest in classic understatement: ". . . the findings have implications for those etiological studies which rely upon the assumed class differential in delinquent behavior as a basis for a delinquency theory."[2] One of these investigators suggests fur-

[1] Ruth Kornhauser, "Theoretical Issues in the Sociological Study of Juvenile Delinquency," mimeographed, Center for the Study of Law and Society, Berkeley, 1963, p. 1. David J. Bordua has written: ". . . the ironic thing about theory and research in the subcultural vein is that, as the general thrust of the theories has grown more 'sociological,' the empirical controversies have, in many ways, grown more 'psychological'" ("Sociological Perspectives," *Social Deviancy among Youth: The Sixty-Fifth Yearbook of the National Society for the Study of Education*, ed. William W. Wattenberg [Chicago: University of Chicago Press, 1966], p. 98).

[2] F. Ivan Nye, James F. Short, Jr., and Virgil J. Olson, "Socioeconomic Status and Delinquent Behavior," *American Journal of Sociology*, LXIII (1958), 388.

ther, far-reaching implications of these findings when he states the case for using father's occupation as a measure of socioeconomic status: "Occupation so permeates the lives of those engaged in it that *it is related* not only to income but values, attitudes, and goals as well as setting, to a certain extent, the social relations among societal members." [3]

If socioeconomic status is unrelated to delinquency, then consistency requires that "socioeconomic status" be removed from the dictionary of delinquency theory and research. A sociological language with this term removed is not easily used, as some of those reporting a zero relation between class and delinquency have found.[4] Concern for the discrepancy between self-report and official measures of delinquency thus reflects justifiable concern for broader questions of sociological and criminological theory. Accepting the self-report findings at face value calls into question assumptions basic to such areas as stratification and the family;[5] accepting these findings would also appear simply and directly to falsify delinquency theories based on an assumed relation between social class and delinquency. (However, as we have seen, delinquency theories can survive a zero relation between socioeconomic status and delinquency, even when such an assumed relation was the basis upon which they were originally constructed.)

Are the "criminal classes" really no more criminal than other social classes? Have the theorists, the police, the layman simply been wrong? The list of studies reporting no significant differences is impressive.[6] Furthermore, there are reasons for expecting a dis-

[3] F. Ivan Nye, *Family Relationships and Delinquent Behavior* (New York: Wiley, 1958), p. 25. Emphasis added.

[4] *Ibid.*, especially pp. 111–114.

[5] See, for example, the ideal-type description of the lower class in Joseph A. Kahl, *The American Class Structure* (New York: Holt, Rinehart and Winston, 1964), pp. 210–215. For a brief description of how high-status parents are better able to socialize their children, see D. G. McKinley, *Social Class and Family Life* (New York: The Free Press, 1964), p. 57. These are, of course, but two of the countless references that could be used to show how deeply the assumption of greater criminality among the lower classes is imbedded in American sociology.

[6] Nye, Short, and Olson, "Socioeconomic Status"; Arthur L. Stinchcombe, *Rebellion in a High School* (Chicago: Quadrangle Books, 1964), pp. 81–87; Ronald L. Akers, "Socio-Economic Status and Delinquent Behavior: A Retest," *Journal of Research in Crime and Delinquency*, I (1964), 38–46; Robert A. Dentler and Lawrence J. Monroe, "Social Correlates of Early Adolescent Theft," *American Sociological Review*, XXVI (1961), 733–743. See also, Robert H. Hardt and George E. Bodine, *Development of Self-Report Instruments in Delinquency Research* (Syracuse University, Youth Development Center, 1965), p. 13.

crepancy between the correlates of self-reported and official measures of delinquency. Defenders of what might be called an official
reaction hypothesis have long argued that the police and the courts
create the statistical relations which generate and then confirm
most sociological and common-sense theories of crime. And it *is*
true that the lower-class boy is more likely to be picked up by the
police, more likely to be sent to juvenile court, more likely to be
convicted, and more likely to be institutionalized if convicted,
when he has committed the same crime as a middle-class boy.[7]

Good studies reporting a small relation in the expected direction are Albert
J. Reiss, Jr., and Albert Lewis Rhodes, "Juvenile Delinquency and the Social
Class Structure," *American Sociological Review,* XXVI (1961), 720–732;
Jackson Toby and Marcia L. Toby, "Low School Status as a Predisposing
Factor in Subcultural Delinquency," mimeographed, Rutgers University, New
Brunswick, N.J., about 1962.
[7] Evidence in favor of the official reaction hypothesis was widely reported
prior to the finding that there is little difference between social classes in self-
reported delinquency rates (for a reasonably complete list of such studies, see
Hardt and Bodine, *Development of Self-Report Instruments,* p. vi).
Actually, at any given stage of the adjudication process, the differences may
not be large. In analyzing police dispositions of over 17,000 juveniles picked
up in Oakland, California, during the 1950s, I could find only small differences in disposition between Negroes and whites, between children from
broken and unbroken homes, and between children from high-rate (generally
low socioeconomic status) and low-rate areas, when offense was held constant.
For example, among those picked up on a first offense for burglary, the following percentages were arrested (the most serious disposition):

Parents Together				Parents Not Together			
Low Rate		High Rate		Low Rate		High Rate	
White	Negro	White	Negro	White	Negro	White	Negro
31	29	32	40	42	45	31	45
(329)	(96)	(130)	(191)	(185)	(65)	(86)	(228)

In 21 of 29 comparisons, including those in this table, the Negro arrest
rate is higher than the white rate, with the other variables having less effect
on the severity of disposition. The magnitude of these differences does not
seem to fit with anecdotal accounts of police bias, however. The fact is that the
bias of the policeman is probably less important in generating differences than
is the bias in police procedures, such as surveillance and interrogation. Irving
Piliavin and Scott Briar suggest that, after the nature of the offense and prior
record, the *demeanor* of the offender is the most important determinant of
severity of disposition (see their "Police Encounters with Juveniles," *American Journal of Sociology,* LXX [1964], 206–214). This variable too would
presumably have much of its effect before the question of disposition in the
formal sense arises. That is, boys whose demeanor is "inappropriate" are
simply more likely to appear on police records. (The data upon which the
table is based were made available to me by Piliavin and Briar.)

The findings in the present sample are consistent with previous research: we are dealing with what is, at most, a *very small* relation that could easily be upset by random disturbances of sampling or definition. Father's occupation, for example, offers little in the way of confirmation of conventional theory. The sons of professionals and executives are least likely to have committed many delinquent acts (Table 9), but the sons of white-collar workers are most likely to have committed one or more, and the sons of unskilled laborers are among the least delinquent groups in the sample.

Table 9 / Self-Reported Delinquency by Father's Occupation—
White Boys Only
(in percent)

	Father's Occupation [a]				
Self-Reported Acts	Low 1	2	3	4	High 5
None	62	53	56	49	61
One	16	26	25	28	25
Two or more	23	21	19	23	14
Totals	101	100	100	100	100
	(151)	(156)	(390)	(142)	(282) [b]

[a] 1 = Unskilled labor; 2 = Semi-skilled labor; 3 = Skilled labor, foreman, merchant; 4 = White collar; 5 = Professional and executive.
[b] The total number of students will vary from table to table for several reasons. (1) The response rate was different for almost every item in the questionnaire, and students for whom data were not available on all items in a table are excluded from that table. (2) The table programs employed differed in their definition of "complete data." In one program, tables were based only on those cases for whom data were available on all items in the "run," regardless of the number of items in a particular table. (3) In tables in which self-reported and official delinquency were to be compared, I excluded boys 18 or older because in many cases their records had been removed from police files.

There is much evidence for the validity of the measure of father's occupation as an indicator of socioeconomic status. It is related in the expected direction to such other measures of socioeconomic status as father's education, welfare status, and home ownership. Furthermore, the comparative distributions of father's occupation among Negroes and whites, and among the eleven schools in the study, reflect "known" differences.[8]

[8] For example, of white boys analyzed, 47 percent of those in Portola Junior High in El Cerrito (a high SES school) report that their fathers are profes-

Table 10 / Self-Reported Delinquency by Father's Education—
White Boys Only
(in percent)

Self-Reported Acts	Father's Education				
	Less than High School Graduation	High School Graduate	Trade or Business	Some College	College Graduate
None	55	57	54	61	58
One	26	26	29	18	25
Two or more	19	17	17	21	17
Totals	100	100	100	100	100
	(286)	(398)	(70)	(170)	(271)

Father's education does no better, suggesting at best a trend in the direction of a negative relation between socioeconomic status and the commission of delinquent acts (Table 10). Along the same lines, an index of cultural objects in the home (maps, newspapers, news magazines, books, musical instruments) was found to be unrelated to the commission of delinquent acts.

For that matter, there appears to be little or no relation between the socioeconomic status of an area and its rate of self-reported delinquency. The percentages reporting one or more delinquent acts by school range from 36 percent in Portola, the junior high school highest in socioeconomic status, to 49 percent in El Cerrito, the senior high school highest in socioeconomic status.

Several reasons for doubting the findings of previous self-report studies with respect to the relation between social class and delinquency have been suggested: (1) The self-report measure of delinquency is invalid for this purpose. (2) The samples used in these studies deal only with a restricted class range. (3) The measures of socioeconomic status are invalid. (4) The effects of socioeconomic status are suppressed by the effects of some third variable. (5) Contrary to their assertions, some of the "no-difference" self-report studies do show a relation between socioeconomic status and delinquency.

Evidence supporting the claims to validity of the self-report measure of delinquency has been presented in the previous chap-

sionals or executives, while only 9 percent of those in Downer Junior High in Richmond (a low SES school) classify their fathers in this category.

ter. It is, however, true that the question of validity is never settled once and for all. Martin Gold has observed: "It is striking that all of the studies which find no relationship have employed anonymous, self-administered questionnaires . . . and all of the studies which do find a relationship have employed confidential personal interviews." [9] Gold's explanation of this difference is that high-status adolescents are more likely to report "non-chargeable trivia" on the anonymous questionnaire where the seriousness of the offense cannot be determined. Two items in the self-report index used in this study would allow the student to report the trivial offenses to which Gold alludes: he could steal and break a friend's pencil, thus committing two delinquent offenses. Even so, the relation between socioeconomic status and the self-report index is essentially replicated with each item entering the index, and most of these items do not measure or allow the reporting of trivial offenses.

Although I share the doubters' uneasiness about the finding of no appreciable difference in delinquency by social class, I do not think the validity of the measure of delinquency is the most persuasive line of attack. As has been true with many self-report studies, there will be too much evidence presented subsequently to allow one to doubt seriously the validity of the measure of delinquency.

There is more to be said, however, for the arguments that the samples used in previous self-report studies deal only with a restricted class range and that their measures of socioeconomic status are invalid for the purpose of testing theories of delinquency. The *class* model implicit in most theories of delinquency is a peculiarly top-heavy, two-class model made up of the overwhelming majority of respectable people on the one hand and the lumpenproletariat on the other. The *stratification* model used by delinquency researchers is another thing. Since these studies have typically been based on in-school populations in small towns or cities, the group the delinquency theorists have had in mind may not be well represented, if it is represented at all.

[9] Martin Gold, "A Note on Voss's Article," and Harwin L. Voss, "A Reply to Gold," *Social Problems* XV (1967), 114–120. See also Martin Gold, *Status Forces in Delinquent Boys* (Ann Arbor: Institute for Social Research, 1963), pp. 4–7. Incidentally, it will be recalled that the questionnaire used in the present study, while self-administered, was not anonymous.

For that matter, although stratification theory tends to suggest systematic and continuous variation in values and attitudes by class position, it is only the lowest class that is generally assumed to be extraordinarily "lawless." (In fact, the hallmark of the lower-middle class is often held to be its compulsive concern for "respectability.") If this particular class model is applied to the present sample, the result is a relation between "socioeconomic status" and delinquent activity, whether the latter is measured by self-report or official records (Table 11). Differences like those in Table 11 have been reported many times in research based on official records.[10] They show that boys whose fathers have been unemployed and/or whose families are on welfare are more likely than children from fully employed, self-sufficient families to commit delinquent acts.

Table 11 / Self-Reported Delinquency by Welfare Status and Father's Unemployment [a]—White Boys Only (in percent)

Self-Reported Acts	Some Unemployment		No Unemployment	
	Have Been on Welfare	Never on Welfare	Have Been on Welfare	Never on Welfare
None	38	47	54	60
One	26	36	24	23
Two or more	36	17	22	17
Totals	100	100	100	100
	(47)	(121)	(63)	(905)

[a] In the previous three years.

Now, if those having the attributes normally associated with lower-class status are more likely to be delinquent, then the finding of no differences among socioeconomic classes *as measured by father's occupation or education* is not as serious a blow to delinquency theory as is usually implied. There is further evidence on the same point. In the study in which Nye found no differ-

[10] Dealing with a highly restricted range with respect to socioeconomic status, the Gluecks found "a far greater difference in the work habits of the fathers of the delinquents and non-delinquents . . . than in the kind of occupation in which they were engaged" (Sheldon and Eleanor Glueck, *Unraveling Juvenile Delinquency* [Cambridge, Mass.: Harvard University Press, 1950], p. 106).

ences among socioeconomic strata, he found fairly strong relations between delinquency and many variables that are usually assumed to be consequences and/or correlates of class position: for example, pride in parents, acceptance-rejection of parents, parental appearance, and parental disposition. In fact, one could find evidence in Nye's study for almost all of the reasons Briar and Piliavin give for their contention that social class is (or should be) related to delinquency.[11] In other words, Nye's findings are congruent with Briar and Piliavin's hypotheses *even though* his findings do not support their initial assumption that "class" is related to delinquent behavior.

There is, or may be, one further complication, which bears on the conjecture that the relation between socioeconomic status and delinquency assumed by theory is suppressed by the effects of some third variable. Not only may it be true that the intervening variable is, as expected, related to delinquency; it may also be true that the measure of social class is, as expected, related to the intervening variable. Thus, for example, in Stinchcombe's data social class is reasonably strongly related to curriculum choice, and curriculum choice is reasonably strongly related to delinquency. Yet Stinchcombe's data show no relation between social class and delinquency.[12] We shall find the same configurations in the present data. It is not surprising, then, that we continue to feel that social class *should* be related to delinquency and that we should search for an explanation of the finding of no difference. Further exploration of this problem will be deferred until potentially important third variables have been identified.

Gold repercentaged Nye's table purporting to show no significant relation between socioeconomic status and delinquency and concluded that Nye's findings "do not support the contention that data other than official delinquency figures would reveal no social status differences." [13] Have the presentational procedures used here somehow masked an actual relation between socioeconomic status and delinquency? One possibility occasionally noted is that there may be little or no difference between social classes in the proportion committing any or few delinquent acts whereas at the

[11] Scott Briar and Irving Piliavin, "Delinquency, Situational Inducements, and Commitment to Conformity," *Social Problems*, XIII (1965), 42–43.

[12] Stinchcombe, *Rebellion*, pp. 82–83.

[13] Gold, *Status Forces*, pp. 4–13.

same time there are marked differences in the proportion committing many, serious offenses. Although we have collapsed the distribution of delinquent acts such that there could be variation in
the proportion of really serious offenders within and therefore
between the social class categories, this procedure has not
destroyed an important negative relation between social class and
delinquency (tables 12 and 13).

*Table 12 / Average Number of Self-Reported and Official
Delinquent Acts by Father's Occupation—White Boys Only* [a]

Father's Occupation	Self-Reported Acts	Official Offenses	Number of Boys
Lower	.81	.32	124
Upper-lower	.68	.28	112
Lower-middle	.83	.27	300
Middle	.88	.24	128
Upper-middle	.61	.22	241
Total sample	.76	.26	905

[a] Unless otherwise noted, all tables which follow are restricted to white
boys.

Tables 12 and 13 show the average number of delinquent acts
committed by the boys in each occupational and educational category; they thus allow boys committing many delinquent acts to
have the influence they deserve on the statistics (it will be recalled
that there are six offenses in the self-report index). Again we can
say that the highest status groups in the sample, especially the sons
of professionals and executives, have committed the fewest delinquent acts.[14] But beyond this, the differences are generally small
and erratic. The differences in tables 12 and 13 with respect to
official offenses are, in contrast, completely consistent, offering additional evidence for the validity of the measures of socioeconomic
status.

[14] Much analysis not reported here confirms the general conclusion that the
sons of professionals and executives are least likely to commit delinquent acts
but that outside this group (which itself differs only slightly from the other
groups) there are few differences attributable to social class. It is plausible to
suggest that the higher dropout rate among the lower-status groups could de-
stroy a relation between social class and delinquency. However, the relation is
no stronger among junior than among senior high school students in the present sample, undermining at least partially the dropout argument.

Table 13 / Average Number of Self-Reported and Official
Delinquent Acts by Father's Education

Father's Education	Self-Reported Acts	Official Offenses	Number of Boys
Less than high school graduation	.83	.35	217
High school graduate	.77	.29	285
Trade or business school	.66	.28	50
Some college	.70	.20	128
College graduate	.73	.17	225
Total sample	.76	.26	905

In sum, then, there is in the present sample no important relation between social class as traditionally measured and delinquency. We do find a small group at the bottom of the class
hierarchy whose children are more likely to be delinquent, and, at
the other extreme, we find that the sons of professionals and executives are consistently less likely to be delinquent. The percentage
point differences and/or the number of cases in extreme categories
are, however, small, so small, in fact, that we need not control
social class in subsequent analysis. I shall occasionally examine
relations within socioeconomic status categories if the hypothesis
in question is class specific, and I shall occasionally examine relations between social class and independent variables, but it should
be kept in mind throughout the analysis that alternative explanations involving social class cannot, in the present data, be true.

Race

Forty-two percent of the Negro and 18 percent of the white
boys in the analyzed sample had police records in the two years
prior to administration of the questionnaire.[15] When other measures of "delinquency" are used, the difference between Negroes
and whites is sharply reduced (Table 14). For example, 42 percent of the Negro [16] and 35 percent of the white boys report
having been picked up by the police; 49 percent of the Negro and

[15] In the "original" sample, 57 percent of the Negro and 32 percent of the
white boys had police records. The effect of nonresponse on the relation between race and official delinquency is shown on p. 43.
[16] The 42 percent reporting having been picked up by the police are not
the same 42 percent with police records. See Table 15.

Table 14 / Number of Official Offenses, Number of Times
Picked Up by Police, and Number of Self-Reported
Delinquent Acts, by Race
(in percent)

Number of Acts (or Reported Contacts with Police)	(A) Official Offenses		(B) Self-Reported Police Pickup		(C) Self-Reported Delinquent Acts	
	White	Negro	White	Negro	White	Negro
None	81	57	65	57	56	51
One	10	19	18	20	25	25
Two or more	8	23	17	22	19	24
Totals	99	99	100	99	100	100
	(1335)	(888)	(1302)	(833)	(1303)	(828)

44 percent of the white boys report having committed one or more
delinquent acts during the preceding year. By one measure, then,
the difference between Negroes and whites is 24 percentage points,
by another, it is only 5 percentage points. Resolution of this discrepancy requires some anticipation of subsequent analysis.

In the sample as a whole, Negro boys *should* have at least a
slightly higher rate of self-reported delinquency than white boys:
they are less likely to be well supervised; they are less likely to have
favorable attitudes toward the law and the police; and they are less
likely to be concerned about the consequences of violation of the
law.[17] These differences are not large, and they certainly do not
make a relation between race and self-reported delinquency logically necessary; nevertheless, they do suggest that treatment of the
difference in self-reported delinquency as a "virtually zero" difference tending to refute conclusions based on official data is unwarranted.

On the other hand, the official table (14-A) undoubtedly
overestimates the difference in official delinquent activity. When
answers to the question "Have you ever been picked up by the
police?" are compared with the measure of official delinquency, as
in Table 15, a majority of the white boys responding "Yes" do not
in fact have police records, while over three-fourths of the Negro

[17] For example, 69 percent of the Negro boys and 82 percent of the white
boys in the sample agree with the statement, "Being sent to juvenile court
would bother me a lot." This item, in turn, is reasonably strongly related to
the commission of delinquent acts.

Table 15 / Official Record by Self-Report of Police Contacts,
by Race
(in percent)

| Official Record | "Have you ever been picked up by the police?" | | | |
| | White | | Negro | |
	Yes	No	Yes	No
Yes	45	16 a	76	36 a
No	55	85	24	64
Totals	100	101	100	100
	(448)	(854)	(354)	(479)

a A majority of the boys who reported no police record contrary to what
I found were either picked up by the police after administration of the questionnaire or had been picked up only once several years prior to its administration. In other words, very few students denied serious and recent police
records.

boys giving this response do have police records. (This discrepancy
is anticipated by the difference between tables 14-A and 14-B.)
When the relation between self-reported police contacts and official record is examined separately for each of the schools in the
sample, large differences appear in the "accuracy of recall" of contacts with the police. In three schools, for example, between 65
percent and 80 percent of those white boys reporting having been
picked up by the police do not have police records; in three other
schools, such "inaccuracy" ranges from 36 percent to 40 percent,
figures that are higher but comparable to that of Negro boys in
Table 15. The three schools with "poor recall" about police contacts have very low official delinquency rates among whites, and
very few Negroes. They thus act to exaggerate the differences between Negroes and whites in the population as a whole. Removal
of the students in the virtually "all-white" schools from the sample
results in Table 16, in which the difference in those ever picked up
by the police is reduced to 16 percentage points.

This difference is still large. It does not result from interde-
partmental differences in defining and recording cases by the police; [18] it cannot result from "errors" in data collection such as

[18] The difference holds within each of the schools studied and thus holds
when both white and Negro boys are exposed to the practices of the same
police department(s).

Table 16 / Official Delinquent Acts by Race—"Flat" Schools
Only
(in percent)

Number of Offenses	Negro	White
None	58	74
One	19	14
Two or more	23	12
Totals	100	100
	(713)	(542)

those that may explain the unusually low rate of official delinquency among white boys in two of the schools.[19] Although the
official delinquency rate among Negro boys is partially accounted
for by differences in actual delinquent activity (the self-report
difference between Negro and white boys persists when the controls used in the case of official delinquency are applied), the
discrepancy in the strength of the relation between these two measures of delinquency and race remains to be explained.

In the case of Negroes, the official reaction hypothesis as an
explanation of differential official rates is particularly persuasive. In
this case it does not require imputation to the police of extraordi-
nary powers of discernment, since racial differences are obvious to

[19] The official delinquency rates are low in two of the eleven schools at
least partly because police records of the small city in which they are located
were not searched (an oversight that came to my attention only as a result
of data analysis). However, serious offenses by juveniles in all cities of the
county are recorded in the County Sheriff's Office, and some of the students
in these two schools had been picked up by the police in the two neighboring cities; records at all three of these locations were searched. I say that the
omission of these data partly accounts for the low rates because another virtually all-white school has a delinquency rate comparable to that of the two
schools mentioned, even though its students should have been picked up at
all three locations at which records were searched. For that matter, the Negro delinquency rate in one of these "incomplete data" schools is only slightly
lower than the Negro rate at the complete data schools. Should the official
data be used in the analysis in the face of such highly probable bias? It should
be recalled that the relation between race and school attended is very strong,
much stronger than that to be expected between most independent variables
and school. If a relation between one of my independent variables and school
is plausible (for example, father's occupation, I.Q.), I do not present the relation between this independent variable and official delinquency without first
controlling for school. If school is unrelated to the independent variable, then
the bias in data collection presumably cannot account for observed results.

anyone; the police do patrol more heavily in Negro areas; [20] the police do think that Negroes are unusually likely to commit criminal acts; [21] the police are in general no more enlightened in their attitudes toward Negroes than are others of comparable education and background; and, finally, Negroes are more likely to report "non-delinquent" offenses involving interaction with and requiring definition by officials other than the police. [22]

On the other hand, the official reaction hypothesis aside, there is no reason to believe that the causes of crime among Negroes are different from those among whites. [23] Therefore, any variable related both to race and to official delinquency provides a plausible counter-hypothesis explaining the relation between race and official delinquency. For instance, Negroes in the sample are more likely to have unfavorable attitudes toward the police, attitudes which could act to assure the recording of offenses that might otherwise be forgotten. Also, Negroes are much less likely than whites in the sample to do well on verbal achievement tests, and other analysis suggests that children of both races whose academic achievement is high are much less likely to have been picked up by the police, regardless of the level of their delinquent activity.

In fact, when verbal achievement scores are held relatively constant, the relation between race and official delinquency is con-

[20] William R. Smith, Fred Templeton, and Alan B. Wilson, "The Richmond Police Department: March–May, 1965," mimeographed, Survey Research Center, University of California, Berkeley, 1965, pp. 19–21.

[21] The tendency of the policeman to overestimate markedly the percentage of Negroes among all those arrested by his own department has been noted many times. See William M. Kephart, *Racial Factors and Urban Law Enforcement* (Philadelphia: University of Pennsylvania Press, 1957), pp. 88–91.

[22] They are, for example, more likely to report having been sent out of a classroom and having been suspended from school. In these cases, the differences between Negro and white boys are much greater than in the case of offenses not requiring action on the part of others—for example, cheating on tests, stealing.

[23] Because of the greater unreliability of Negro data, partly stemming from their generally low verbal skills, the bulk of the analysis and the data presented in the remainder of this work is restricted to whites. Before this decision was reached, many tables had been run allowing Negro-white comparisons. In general, the results were consistent—most independent variables had the same relation to official and self-reported delinquency among Negroes as among whites. As suggested, the major difference was that the relations among Negroes were consistently smaller, an attenuation apparently due to greater unreliability of response.

siderably reduced, as Table 17 shows. Given the very strong relation between achievement test scores and official delinquency evident in Table 17, and given the very different distributions of achievement test scores between Negroes and whites, it appears that residual variation in test scores within the categories of Table 17 could account for the Negro-white differences in delinquency that remain. However, more sophisticated analysis [24] of these same data shows that Table 17 approaches the limit with respect to the degree to which Negro-white differences in official delinquency can be reduced in the present sample.[25]

Table 17 / Number of Official Delinquent Acts by Race and Differential Aptitude Test Verbal Scores—"Flat" Schools Only (in percent)

Number of Official Offenses	DAT Scores							
	0–9		10–19		20–29		30 and above	
	Negro	White	Negro	White	Negro	White	Negro	White
None	52	58	65	74	78	81	100	94
One	20	23	19	11	8	15	0	6
Two or more	27	20	15	15	15	5	0	0
Totals	99	101	99	100	101	101	100	100
	(470)	(128)	(194)	(231)	(40)	(130)	(9)	(53)

The present data suggest, then, that differences in academic achievement go a long way toward explaining Negro-white differences in delinquent activity. This is a far from satisfying conclusion. In terms of subsequent analysis, it is important to note that nothing we have seen contradicts the assumption that the causes of delinquency are the same among Negroes as among whites. It follows from this assumption that we need not study Negro boys to determine the causes of their delinquency. If we can further interpret the relation between academic achievement and delin-

[24] In which, for example, the effects of achievement test scores are removed by statistical adjustment rather by creation of *relatively* homogeneous subgroups.
[25] Alan B. Wilson, "Educational Consequences of Segregation in a California Community," mimeographed, Survey Research Center, Berkeley, 1966, p. 62. Wilson's analysis shows that the Negro-white difference persists when the effects of verbal achievement, mother's supervision, number of siblings, family status, and attitudes toward grades are removed.

quency among white boys, we will have further interpreted the original relation between race and delinquency.

The present data also support the conclusion that Negro-white differences are exaggerated by differential police activity. This may not mean that the police are biased against Negroes in the traditional meaning of that term; [26] but it most assuredly means that there is a Negro-white differential that cannot be removed by statistical analysis.

Conclusion

David J. Bordua has noted that sociological theories of delinquency emphasize class position to the virtual exclusion of other characteristics of populations having high rates of delinquency, such as race, geographical origins, and the like.[27] The data presented here suggest that such emphasis is misguided. Social class differences with respect to self-reported delinquency are very small. I have attempted to demonstrate that the traditional methodological criticisms of the self-report technique cannot, in the present instance, account for this finding. There are, of course, difficulties in such a demonstration. There is still room for doubt. Let us, then, grant skepticism all it desires: Assuming the self-report technique were perfectly valid, what kind of relation should we expect to find between social class and the commission of delinquent acts? A correlation of .8? A correlation of .2? I suggest that the maximum relation the skeptic can reasonably claim is defined by the relation between social class and *official* delinquency, which is not very strong (see tables 12 and 13).[28]

Yet the relative impotence of social class as traditionally defined and measured as a determinant of the commission of delin-

[26] See p. 68, n. 7.
[27] David J. Bordua, "Some Comments on Theories of Group Delinquency," *Sociological Inquiry*, XXXII (1962), 245–260.
[28] The methodological critic must suggest that if the errors he detects were eliminated or the procedures he advocates adopted, something drastic would happen to the findings of research. In this connection the following comment on a long-standing dispute between methodologist and researcher is most instructive: "Sociological criticism . . . of the Gluecks often is well taken but seems to have led to an agreement to ignore their findings. The results of *Unraveling Juvenile Delinquency* agree fairly well with those of comparable control group studies" (Bordua, "Some Comments on Theories," p. 259).

quent acts should not be construed as showing that social class is unimportant in other aspects of delinquency. It is of the essence of social class that it can create differences in reward where none exists in talent, that it can impose differences in punishment where none exists in obedience to rules. The evidence that the lower-class boy is more likely than the middle-class boy to end up in juvenile court and in the reformatory is no more open to doubt than is the evidence that he is less likely to end up in college. Social class would be an important factor in education even if there were no differences in academic ability among the social classes.

By the same token, the present findings cannot be taken as showing that differences in the social status *of juveniles* are unimportant in the causation of delinquency. In the following chapters it is apparent that the child not likely to be going anywhere (but down) is more likely to commit delinquent acts. The class of the father may be unimportant, but the "class" of the child most decidedly is not.

Chapter VI

Attachment to Parents

Control theory assumes that the bond of affection for conventional persons is a major deterrent to crime. The stronger this bond, the more likely the person is to take it into account when and if he contemplates a criminal act. The ability to take something into account, however, suggests the corollary ability to do something about it, and crimes are of course committed in the face of strong attachments to conventional others. Yet the attached person, by his greater efforts to avoid detection and by his unwillingness to take the risks the unattached freely takes, proves the potency of his attachment even as he commits the crime. In fact, when detection is certain, the attached person may hit upon unusual means for preventing those whose opinion he values from gaining knowledge of his act: "I intend to kill my wife after I pick her up from work. I don't want her to have to face the embarrassment that my actions will surely cause her." [1]

A persistent image in delinquency theory is that of a child *already* without a family—at least without a family whose unhappiness is of concern to him. Like most such images, this one contains much that is true. Since most delinquent acts are committed outside the home, since few delinquencies are committed at parental urging, and since most detected acts cause parents embarrassment and/or inconvenience, it is not surprising that an image of the delinquent as not only physically but emotionally free of his parents has developed.

But a social vacuum is abhorrent to theories based on the assumption that the delinquent act is "positively" motivated.[2] If behavior is normatively oriented, if man requires social support for his actions, then there must be others who are willing to praise and reward that which parents condemn. As a consequence, in most

---

[1] Charles Joseph Whitman, quoted by *Newsweek*, August 15, 1966.

[2] Muzafer Sherif and Carolyn W. Sherif, *Reference Groups: Explorations into Conformity and Deviation of Adolescents* (New York: Harper and Row, 1964), especially pp. 271–273.

sociological theories of delinquency the gang rushes in to fill the void created by estrangement from parents. The incontestable fact that most delinquent acts are committed with companions is taken as evidence supporting this view. Walter C. Reckless goes so far as to say: "There is almost every reason to admit that companionship is one of the most important, universal causes of crime and delinquency among males." [3] But the link between "companionship" and delinquency is still a matter of dispute, and the Gluecks, unimpressed by a mountain of sociological theory and research, and by their own data which shows a strong relation between delinquency and the delinquency of companions, could still argue that boys become delinquents *before* they choose their companions.[4]

And, indeed, studies of neglected children, of the psychopathic personality, appear to support the Gluecks' view. They suggest that the capacity to form attachments to others may be generally impaired so that the child who feels nothing for his parents is less likely to feel anything for anyone else. They suggest that the freedom that severance of the bonds to family creates is *not* immediately lost by being swallowed up in a new group, that there are those outside the "web of group affiliations" who have in some sense lost the capacity to belong. Delinquents may be with other boys when they commit their delinquent deeds, but this does not necessarily mean that these acts are a response to pressures emanating from a moral community.

For that matter, no good evidence has been produced to show that attachment to peers is actually conducive to delinquency. Unless delinquent behavior is valued among adolescents, there is no reason to believe that attachments to other adolescents should produce results different from those obtaining from attachments to conventional *adults*. Predictions about the effects of peer attachments thus hinge on the assumed conventionality or nonconventionality of peers. If the peer "culture" requires delinquent behavior, then presumably attachment would foster conformity— that is, delinquency. However, if the peer culture is identical to

[3] Walter C. Reckless, *The Crime Problem*, 3rd ed. (New York: Appleton-Century-Crofts, 1961) p. 311.
[4] Sheldon and Eleanor Glueck *Unraveling Juvenile Delinquency* (Cambridge, Mass.: Harvard University Press, 1950), p. 164.

the conventional culture, then attachment to persons within this culture should foster conformity to conventional standards.

No such ambiguity adheres in predictions about the effect of attachments to teachers and the school. Teachers, by inclination and law, espouse conventional standards. Here, again, however, the question of the extent of carry-over from attitudes toward parents to attitudes toward teachers is of interest, as is the question of the relative importance of attachments to persons variously located in conventional society.

In this and following chapters, I examine attachments to parents, teachers, and peers. Although I shall devote much of the analysis to factors affecting attachment (and some to the effects of attachment on other elements of the bond to conventional society), the burden of the argument rests on the relations between the various attachments and delinquency. I shall begin by assuming that all "others" are conventional and only later investigate the effects of attachment to persons not conforming to the conventional model.

Attachment to Conventional Parents

Although denied in some theories and ignored in others, the fact that delinquents are less likely than nondelinquents to be closely tied to their parents is one of the best documented findings of delinquency research.[5] As is true with most well-established relations in the field of delinquency, there are many ways of accounting for this relation.

In the light of the cultural deviance perspective, the child unattached to his parents is simply more likely to be exposed to "criminogenic influences." He is, in other words, more likely to be free to take up with a gang. His lack of attachment to his parents is, in itself, of no moral significance.[6]

Strain theory appears to have particular difficulty with the relation between attachment to parents and delinquency, and it is

[5] Ibid., especially Chapter 11; F. Ivan Nye, Family Relationships and Delinquent Behavior (New York: Wiley, 1958), Chapter 8.

[6] Edwin H. Sutherland and Donald R. Cressey, Principles of Criminology, 7th ed. (Philadelphia: Lippincott, 1966), especially pp. 225–228.

therefore largely ignored by strain theorists.[7] (If, for example, there are systematic differences in the adequacy of socialization between social classes, then no differences in pressures to deviate are required to explain the differential rates of deviation.)

It is in control theory, then, that attachment to parents becomes a central variable, and many of the variations in explanations of this relation may be found within the control theory tradition. Perhaps the major focus of attention has been on the link between attachment and the adequacy of socialization, the internalization of norms. As is well known, the emotional bond between the parent and the child presumably provides the bridge across which pass parental ideals and expectations.[8] If the child is alienated from the parent, he will not learn or will have no feeling for moral rules, he will not develop an adequate conscience or superego.[9] Among those with a more psychoanalytic orientation, actual separation from the parent, especially the mother, is held to be more serious than lack of attachment to a physically present mother.[10] In fact, the maternal deprivation hypothesis has received endorsement reminiscent of that granted feeble-mindedness hypotheses in the early years of the twentieth century: ". . . on the basis of this varied evidence it appears that there is a very strong case indeed for believing that prolonged separation of a child from his mother (or mother-substitute) during the first five years of life stands foremost among the causes of delinquent character development and persistent misbehaviour." [11]

[7] Robert K. Merton suggests that persons in the social class with the highest rate of crime tend to be inadequately socialized. However, Cloward and Ohlin are more consistent in this regard and explicitly deny variations in the adequacy of socialization as a cause of delinquency. For Merton's position, see Social Theory and Social Structure (New York: The Free Press, 1957), p. 141. One of the clearest statements in the literature with respect to the varying assumptions of the strain, cultural deviance, and control theories on this point may be found in Richard A. Cloward and Lloyd E. Ohlin, Delinquency and Opportunity (New York: The Free Press, 1960), p. 106.

[8] David G. McKinley, Social Class and Family Life (New York: The Free Press, 1964), p. 57. McKinley argues that the higher the status of the parent, the stronger the emotional bond between the parent and the child.

[9] Nye, Family Relationships, p. 71; William McCord and Joan McCord, Origins of Crime (New York: Columbia University Press, 1959), pp. 198–199.

[10] Kate Friedlander, The Psycho-Analytical Approach to Juvenile Delinquency (New York: International Universities Press, 1947), p. 70.

[11] John Bowlby, Forty-Four Juvenile Thieves (London: Bailliero, Tindall and Cox, 1946), p. 41, quoted by Barbara Wootton in Social Science and Social Pathology (New York: Macmillan, 1959), p. 137. Wootton's treat-

Like the feeble-mindedness hypothesis, this form of the maternal deprivation hypothesis can take little comfort from quantitative research based on reasonably large samples of noninstitutional populations. McCord and McCord [12] and Nye [13] both report no difference in delinquent behavior between those whose homes were broken before five years of age and those whose homes were broken later. And in the present data those living with both parents prior to age five are just as likely to have committed delinquent acts as children separated from one or both parents during this period.[14]

Explanation of the effects of attachment to the parents on delinquent behavior by reference to the internalization of norms (or, as is common in social control theories, by reference to "internal" or "personal" control) [15] creates difficulties in explaining variations in delinquent activity over time. If the conscience is a relative constant built into the child at an early age, how do we explain the increase in delinquent activity in early adolescence and the decline in late adolescence? It is also easy to slip into mere tautology when the locus of control is placed inside the person. Reiss, for example, defines personal control as "the ability of the individual to refrain from meeting needs in ways which conflict with the norms and rules of the community." After relating psychiatric classifications to rates of recidivism, Reiss concludes that his *observations* show "that delinquent recidivists are less often persons with mature ego ideals or non-delinquent social roles and appropriate and flexible rational controls which permit the individual to guide action in accord with non-delinquent group expectations." [16] Given commonly accepted meanings of the terms

ment of the maternal separation studies is clearly "devastating"—but it is difficult to imagine any kind of social research that would satisfy the criteria of evaluation she uses. If the results are consistent and reasonably conclusive, Wootton does not hesitate to conclude that "homely truths" are lurking behind a "pretentious scientific facade."

[12] McCord and McCord, *Origins of Crime*, p. 83.

[13] Nye, *Family Relationships*, p. 47.

[14] In a book first published in 1953, Bowlby states that there is "no room for doubt" about the proposition that "prolonged maternal deprivation" causes severe psychiatric disturbance (John Bowlby, *Child Care and the Growth of Love* [Baltimore: Penguin Books, 1963], p. 50).

[15] Nye, *Family Relationships*, pp. 5–6; Albert J. Reiss, Jr., "Delinquency as the Failure of Personal and Social Controls," *American Sociological Review*, XVI (1951), 196–207.

[16] *Ibid.*, pp. 196 and 204.

in this statement, it could never be shown to be false. In fact, explanation of the recidivism of those delinquents with mature ego ideals and nondelinquent social roles is virtually ruled out. The only way their recidivism can be explained is to admit error in the psychiatric classifications. In other words, the explanation is beyond the reach of empirical observation.

These difficulties are avoided if we ignore internalization and assume that the moral element in attachment to parents resides directly in the attachment itself. If the bond to the parent is weakened, the probability of delinquent behavior increases; if this bond is strengthened, the probability of delinquent behavior declines. Attachment may easily be seen as *variable* over persons and over time for the same person.

There are many elements of the bond to the parent, all of which may not be equally important in the control of delinquent behavior. Let us therefore look more closely at the process through which attachment to the parent presumably works against the commission of delinquent acts.

The child attached to his parents may be less likely to get into situations in which delinquent acts are possible, simply because he spends more of his time in their presence. However, since most delinquent acts require little time, and since most adolescents are frequently exposed to situations potentially definable as opportunities for delinquency, the amount of time spent with parents would probably be only a minor factor in delinquency prevention. So-called "direct control" is not, except as a limiting case, of much substantive or theoretical importance.[17] The important consideration is whether the parent is psychologically present when temptation to commit a crime appears. If, in the situation of temptation, no thought is given to parental reaction, the child is to this extent free to commit the act.

Which children are most likely to ask themselves, "What will my parents think?" Those who think their parents know where they are and what they are doing. Two items on the questionnaire bear directly on such virtual supervision: "Does your mother (father) know where you are when you are away from home?"

17 Items measuring the amount of time spent talking with parents, working around the house, and the like, are related to the commission of delinquent acts in the expected direction, but these relations are uniformly weak.

And, "Does your mother (father) know whom you are with when you are away from home?" The response categories were: "Usually," "Sometimes," and "Never." The two mother items, which correlated .59, were combined, equally weighted, so that the mothers of boys obtaining a score of 4 "usually" know where they are and whom they are with. The relation between this index of supervision and self-reported delinquency is shown in Table 18.

Table 18 / Self-Reported Delinquency by Mother's Virtual Supervision
(in percent)

Self-Reported Acts	Mother's Supervision				
	Low 0	1	2	3	High 4
None	0	28	45	59	63
One	45	31	26	21	26
Two or more	55	41	29	20	12
Totals	100	100	100	100	101
	(11)	(29)	(236)	(252)	(698)

The skewness of the distribution evident in the bottom row of Table 18, together with hindsight, suggests that the boys should have been allowed to report that their mothers "almost always" know where they are and whom they are with, since the majority of boys in the sample are, according to this measure, well and equally supervised. Even so, the range of virtual supervision present in the table is sufficient to produce marked variation in delinquent activity: children who perceive their parents as unaware of their whereabouts are highly likely to have committed delinquent acts. Although only 11 boys say their mothers never know where they are and whom they are with, all 11 have committed delinquent acts in the year prior to administration of the questionnaire. The majority of the sample who in this sense usually have their mothers with them are much less likely to have committed delinquent acts than those who, at least sometimes, feel they have moved beyond the range of parental knowledge or interest.

We assume that the supervision illustrated in Table 18 is indirect, that the child is less likely to commit delinquent acts not because his parents actually restrict his activities, but because he shares his activities with them; not because his parents actually know where he is, but because he perceives them as aware of his location. Following this line of reasoning, we can say that the more the child is accustomed to sharing his mental life with his parents, the more he is accustomed to seeking or getting their opinion about his activities, the more likely he is to perceive them as part of his social and psychological field, and the less likely he would be to neglect their opinion when considering an act contrary to law— which is, after all, a potential source of embarrassment and/or inconvenience to them.

Several items on the questionnaire are appropriate as measures of the intimacy of communication between parent and child. The boys were asked: "Do you share your thoughts and feelings with your mother (father)?" And, "How often have you talked over your future plans with your mother (father)?" Independent analysis reveals that these items are sufficiently correlated to justify combining them on empirical as well as conceptual grounds. They were combined, equally weighted, such that boys with highest scores often share their thoughts and talk over their plans with their parents, while the boys with the lowest scores never have such communication with their parents. This index, which I shall call an index of intimacy of communication (A), is correlated .25 with mother's virtual supervision, and .26 with father's virtual supervision.[18]

A second index of intimacy of communication (B), distinguished from the first by the fact that the flow of communication is from the parent to the child rather than from the child to the parent, was constructed from the following items: "When you don't know why your mother (father) makes a rule, will she explain the reason?" "When you come across things you don't understand, does your mother (father) help you with them?" And, "Does your mother (father) ever explain why she feels the way she does?"

As would be expected, the two indexes of intimacy of communication are strongly correlated (for mothers, the correlation is .42; for fathers, .52). The second index is even more strongly correlated with virtual supervision than the first (for mothers, r

---

[18] Each index is constructed separately for each parent. The correlations are thus between, for example, intimacy of communication with mother and mother's virtual supervision.

= .35; for fathers, $r = .40$). Both indexes appear in subsequent analysis.

As Table 19 illustrates, the intimacy of communication between child and parent is strongly related to the commission of delinquent acts. Only 5 percent of the boys who often discuss their future plans and often share their thoughts and feelings with their fathers have committed two or more delinquent acts in the year prior to administration of the questionnaire, while 43 percent of those never communicating with their fathers about these matters have committed as many delinquent acts. As reported earlier, how-

Table 19 / Self-Reported Delinquency by Intimacy of Communication (A) with Father [a]
(in percent)

Self-Reported Acts	Little Intimate Communication			Much Intimate Communication	
	0	1	2	3	4
None	39	55	55	63	73
One	18	25	28	23	22
Two or more	43	20	17	15	5
Totals	100	100	100	101	100
	(97)	(182)	(436)	(287)	(121)

[a] The comparable index of intimacy of communication with the mother is more badly skewed (boys are more likely to report intimate communication with the mother) and is slightly less strongly related to delinquency.

ever, those who spend much time talking with their parents are only slightly less likely than those who spend little time talking with their parents to have committed delinquent acts. All of which suggests that it is not simply the fact of communication with the parents but the focus of this communication that is crucial in affecting the likelihood that the child will recall his parents when and if a situation of potential delinquency arises.

If we assume that the child considers the reaction of his parents, he must then ask himself a further question: "Do I care what my parents will think?" Most studies of the effects of parent-child relations concentrate on this second question. Thus affectional identification, love, or respect is taken as the crucial element of the bond to the parent. Even if the child does in effect consider the opinion of his parents, he may conclude that parental reaction is not sufficiently important to deter him from the act (given, of course, a certain risk of detection). This conclusion is presumably more likely the less the child cares for his parents.

Since most items measuring aspects of parent-child relations reflect to some extent the favorability of the child's attitudes toward his parents, this dimension is both easy and difficult to measure. (The ubiquity of the favorability-unfavorability dimension may well be the reason that many analyses seem to suggest that everything the parent does "matters" with respect to delinquency.) Perhaps the best single item in the present data is: "Would you like to be the kind of person your mother (father) is?"

Table 20 / Self-Reported Delinquency by Affectional Identification with the Father [a]
(in percent)

Self-Reported Acts	"Would you like to be the kind of person your father is?"				
	In Every Way	In Most Ways	In Some Ways	In Just a Few Ways	Not at All
None	64	65	58	48	41
One	21	24	25	30	22
Two or more	16	11	17	22	38
Totals	101	100	100	100	101
	(121)	(404)	(387)	(172)	(138)

[a] The relation between identification with the mother and delinquency is somewhat stronger than the relation shown in the table. I do not combine the items for the two parents because such a combination has little, if any, additional effect. As discussed below, part of the reason for the lack of additive effect is that the boys in the sample tend very strongly to have similar attitudes toward both parents.

As affectional identification with the parents increases, the likelihood of delinquency declines (Table 20). On the basis of measures available,[19] it appears reasonable to suggest that the ex-

[19] Indexes of emotional attachment to the father and to the mother produce relations only slightly stronger than that shown in Table 20. The items available for measuring attachment to the parents on the original questionnaire are a source of some uneasiness, since they are uniformly indirect. For example, the most direct items on the questionnaire are: "Does your father seem to understand you." "Have you ever felt unwanted by your father." And, "Would your father stick by you if you got into really bad trouble."

tent and nature of communication between the parent and the child are as important as feelings of affection for the parent. We have had some indications already, however, that distinctions between the dimensions of attachment to the parent may be artificial. Let us therefore examine the joint effects of intimacy of communication and identification with the father (Table 21).

Table 21 / Percent Committing Two or More Delinquent Acts by Index of Intimacy of Communication with Father and Identification with Father

	Intimacy of Communication				
	Low				High
"Like to be like father?"	0	1	2	3	4
In every way	—[a]	—	10	19	10
	(3)	(8)	(31)	(42)	(21)
In most ways	—	16	13	9	3
	(10)	(31)	(153)	(117)	(61)
In some ways	36	19	15	18	3
	(25)	(59)	(141)	(102)	(31)
In just a few ways	—	20	23	—	—
	(15)	(44)	(70)	(19)	(4)
Not at all	59	24	28	—	—
	(41)	(33)	(32)	(4)	(2)

[a] Too few cases for stable percentages.

As would be expected, those who identify with their fathers tend to discuss their personal problems with them, and vice versa, with few students reporting no desire to emulate the father on the one hand and extensive intimate communication with him on the other. Even so, each of these dimensions appears to have an independent effect on the likelihood that the child will commit delinquent acts. With few exceptions, as the intimacy of communication increases, the less likely the child is to have committed delinquent acts, regardless of his identification with his father. The only boys for whom the relations do not hold quite as expected are

(An index composed of these items, equally weighted, is used in subsequent analysis. It is called an index of attachment.) Nevertheless, in a separate study of a subsample of the students used here, Irving Piliavin asked a series of direct questions about the child's emotional attachment to his parents (for example, "Are you interested in what your father thinks of you?"). The relations between Piliavin's items and delinquency appear to be no stronger than those reported here.

those reporting a very high level of identification with the father. Given prevailing cultural prescriptions about the kinds of attitudes one should express toward one's parents, we would expect a lower level of validity at this end of an attachment scale.

Without misevaluating the significance of the feeling of affection of the child for the parent, we can say that the psychological presence of the parent depends very much on the extent to which the child interacts with the parent on a personal basis. The idea that those committing criminal acts as often do not think of the consequences of their acts for those whose opinion they value as they do not care about the consequences of their acts is supported by these data.

Consistent with much previous research, then, the present data indicate that the closer the child's relations with his parents, the more he is attached to and identifies with them, the lower his chances of delinquency. It is argued here that the moral significance of this attachment resides directly in the attachment itself. The more strongly a child is attached to his parents, the more strongly he is bound to their expectations, and therefore the more strongly he is bound to conformity with the legal norms of the larger system.

Attachment to Unconventional Parents

The major alternative to this explanation is found in theories of cultural deviance. According to one variant of cultural deviance theory, the values of many parents (largely in the lower class), while not explicitly criminal, are at least conducive to criminality.[20] According to a second variant of this perspective, there are areas of society in which crime is openly encouraged: "Stealing in the neighborhood was a common practice among the children and approved of by the parents." [21]

If either view is accurate, alienation from parents should not work to produce delinquency in all segments of the sample. If some parents in the sample hold criminal values, lack of attach-

[20] Walter B. Miller, "Lower Class Culture as a Generating Milieu of Gang Delinquency," *Journal of Social Issues*, XXIV (1958), 5–19.
[21] Cloward and Ohlin, *Delinquency and Opportunity*, p. 153, quoting C. R. Shaw, *The Jack-Roller* (Chicago: University of Chicago Press, 1930), p. 54.

ment to them may have effects opposite to the effects of lack of attachment to conventional parents, and the effects of attachment on delinquency for the sample as a whole may be attenuated.[22] Are some children in this sample likely to be delinquent *because* they are attached to their parents?

There are several ways to approach this question.[23] We have previously identified one group of parents whose sons have relatively high rates of delinquency. This group, those who have been unemployed and/or on welfare, should also be the group in the sample most likely to be members of the "lower-class culture." Does attachment to parents in this group have less effect on—or is it actually conducive to—delinquency? Table 22 provides an ambiguous answer to the question.

Table 22 suggests that boys strongly attached to a lower-class father are as likely to be delinquent as boys weakly attached to a lower-class father, with boys moderately attached to a lower-class father somewhat less likely to commit delinquent acts. It thus appears to support both the lower-class culture thesis and the view that lack of attachment to a lower-class father is conducive to delinquency. Attachment to a father who in effect encourages delinquency is conducive to delinquency; on the other hand, alienation from such a father need not be expressed in adherence to conventional forms of conduct. In fact, the child unattached to a nonconventional father is, like the child unattached to a conventional father, free to commit delinquent acts without too much concern for the consequences.

This interpretation of Table 22 entails acceptance of the view

[22] Nye (*Family Relationships*, p. 72) recognizes this problem but does not pursue it further. See also Martin Gold, *Status Forces in Delinquent Boys* (Ann Arbor: Institute for Social Research, 1963), pp. 40–41.
[23] Not the least important of which is examination of previous research on delinquency. Although they do not directly address this question, the McCords' data on type of discipline, criminality of father, and conviction for crimes may be taken to suggest that attachment to a criminal father reduces one's chances of crime (McCord and McCord, *Origins of Crime*, especially p. 94). The families of the Gluecks' delinquents were lower class and highly likely to have members with criminal records (67 percent of the fathers and 45 percent of the mothers), yet the Gluecks' data show strong negative relations between attachment to parents and delinquency (Glueck and Glueck, *Unraveling*, pp. 93–134). On the other hand, Hamblin, Abrahamson, and Burgess conclude that attachment to parents *fosters* delinquency among most slum youth (Robert L. Hamblin, Mark J. Abrahamson, and Robert L. Burgess, "Diagnosing Delinquency," *Trans-Action*, I [1964], 10–15).

Table 22 / Percent Committing Two or More Delinquent
Acts [a] by Intimacy of Communication with Father and
Father's Employment History/Welfare Status

Intimacy of Communication	No History of Welfare or Unemployment		History of Welfare and/or Unemployment	
High	10	(325)	25	(60)
Medium	17	(331)	17	(76)
Low	29	(193)	27	(64)

[a] The trends observable in the table hold true regardless of the point at which delinquency is dichotomized.

that there is a substantial number of fathers in the sample who either approve of or are neutral to delinquency. Without denying the existence of fathers who encourage delinquency, we may still assume they are too rare to account for the results in the right-hand column of the table. By questioning one of the theories with which we interpret the data, we call the data themselves into question. Let us assume that only one cell in Table 22 is out of line. If it is the upper right-hand cell, the cultural deviance theory is disconfirmed; if it is the middle right-hand or the lower right-hand cell, the cultural deviance theory is confirmed. Since such a minor fluctuation in the data would lead to drastically different conclusions, the matter is worth pursuing further.

Let us take the lower-class culture thesis at its word. The number of persons sharing in or influenced by this culture is very large, from 40 to 60 percent of the population. Parents within this culture are not likely to be too disturbed by the delinquencies of their children because the rules being violated are those of a class to which they do not belong. In fact, since delinquency "derives from a positive effort to achieve what is valued within [the lower-class] tradition, and to conform to its explicit and implicit norms," [24] attachment to members of the lower-class culture should foster delinquency, and lack of attachment might even foster conformity to middle-class norms, that is, nondelinquency.

Our first attempt to test this hypothesis was inconclusive, presumably because of the small number of cases in the lower-class group. Given the estimates of the size of the lower class provided by advocates of the lower-class culture thesis, however, many fami-

[24] Miller, "Lower Class Culture," p. 19.

lies in the sample in addition to the unemployed and those on welfare should be firmly lower class. We therefore returned to father's occupation as a measure of class status and reintroduced Negro boys to assure that we were dealing with a group sufficiently low in class status to provide a reasonable test of the hypothesis (Table 23).

Table 23 / Percent Committing Two or More Delinquent Acts by Intimacy of Communication with Father, Race, and Father's Occupation—Boys Living with Real Father

Father's Occupation	Intimacy of Communication	Race			
		Negro		White	
Unskilled labor	High	12	(43)	10	(48)
	Medium	20	(66)	14	(68)
	Low	28	(57)	25	(41)
Semi- and skilled labor	High	15	(63)	11	(164)
	Medium	15	(39)	19	(179)
	Low	21	(35)	31	(100)
White collar	High	—a	(15)	19	(58)
	Medium	—	(16)	16	(77)
	Low	—	(9)	39	(28)
Professional	High	—	(16)	8	(109)
	Medium	—	(7)	13	(94)
	Low	—	(6)	22	(58)

a Too few cases for stable percentages.

The message in Table 23 is clear: regardless of the class or racial status of the parent, the closer the boy's ties to him, the less likely he is to commit delinquent acts. We may infer, then, that those lower-class boys committing delinquent acts are not finding support for their actions from their parents or from their "class culture." If alienation from lower-class parents is conducive to delinquency, as the table clearly shows it is, then Sykes and Matza's argument against the view that delinquency springs from deviant class values is supported: "There is a strong likelihood that the family of the delinquent will agree with respectable society that delinquency is wrong, even though the family may be engaged in a variety of illegal activities." [25]

[25] Gresham M. Sykes and David Matza, "Techniques of Neutralization: A Theory of Delinquency," *American Sociological Review*, XXII (1957), 665.

Attachment and Exposure to Criminal Influences

A second approach to the cultural deviance perspective on the effects of attachment involves a choice between intervening variables. In control theory, lack of attachment to the parents is directly conducive to delinquency because the unattached child does not have to consider the consequences of his actions for his relations with his parents. In cultural deviance theory, in contrast, lack of attachment to the parents merely increases the probability that the child will be exposed to criminal influences, that he will learn the attitudes, values, and skills conducive to delinquency. Being free of parental control is not enough to produce delinquency; a learning process must intervene: "If the family is in a community in which there is no pattern of theft, the children do not steal, no matter how much neglected or how unhappy they may be at home." [26]

It would perhaps be difficult to find a community in which there was no pattern of theft, and therefore difficult directly to falsify this proposition. However, this proposition assumes that certain experiences must intervene if attachment to the family is to influence delinquent conduct. If we can measure some of these experiences, we can determine whether they affect the influence of attachment to parents on the likelihood the child will *steal*.[27]

If it is true that lack of attachment to parents has no direct effect on delinquency, then among those whose exposure to "criminal influences" is identical, the effects of attachment to parents should be considerably reduced, if not eliminated. In Chapter VIII the influence of peers on delinquent conduct is examined in some detail. Suffice it to show here that, as cultural deviance theory predicts (and as control theory also predicts), the delinquency of one's friends is strongly related to one's own record of delinquent conduct.

Table 24 indicates that three-fourths of those boys with four or more close friends who have been picked up by the police have

26 Sutherland and Cressey, *Principles of Criminology*, p. 227.
27 Four of the six items in the self-report index involve theft.

themselves committed delinquent acts in the previous year, while only slightly more than one-fourth of those with no delinquent friends have committed delinquent acts during the same period. Percentaged in the other direction, the table would show that of those boys committing two or more delinquent offenses 82 percent have had at least one close friend picked up by the police, while only 34 percent of those committing no delinquent acts have delinquent friends.[28]

Table 24 / Self-Reported Delinquency by Friends' Contacts with the Police
(in percent)

| Self-Reported Acts | "Have any of your close friends ever been picked up by the police?" | | | | | |
	No	One	Two	Three	Four or More	Don't Know
None	73	51	41	32	25	61
One	20	27	37	24	30	24
Two or more	7	21	21	44	45	15
Totals	100	99	99	100	100	100
	(520)	(164)	(99)	(62)	(208)	(227)

The magnitude of this relation adds plausibility to the thesis that exposure to criminal influences must intervene if lack of attachment to the parent is to result in delinquency. However, a direct test of this hypothesis requires that we examine the effects of attachment to parents and "criminal influences" simultaneously, as in Table 25.

With respect to the issue at hand, Table 25 supports control theory. Regardless of the delinquency of his friends, the child attached to his father is less likely to commit delinquent acts. Among those with no delinquent friends and among those with several delinquent friends, the weaker the attachment to the father, the greater the likelihood of delinquency.[29]

[28] In calculating these percentages, I have excluded the boys who had no knowledge of their friends' contacts with the police.

[29] Gary Jensen has examined the relation between attachment to parents and delinquency with much more extensive controls for "criminal influences" and "definitions favorable to violation of law" than those used here—with the same result: attachment to parents has an independent effect on the commission of delinquent acts.

Table 25 / Percent Committing Two or More Delinquent
Acts by Intimacy of Communication with Father and
Delinquency of Friends

Intimacy of Communication	Number of Friends Picked Up by Police		
	None	One–Two	Three or More
High	4 (190)	16 (85)	30 (63)
Medium	9 (184)	22 (88)	39 (77)
Low	11 (87)	23 (53)	53 (83)

We should not allow selective emphasis to take us too far
from the data, however, since in all other respects Table 25 offers
impressive evidence in favor of a cultural deviance interpretation.
Children unattached to their parents are much more likely to have
delinquent friends (this fact is of course expectable also from a
social control perspective), and delinquency of companions is
strongly related to delinquency regardless of the level of attachment to the father. It is the latter fact that poses problems for
control theory. It will therefore be discussed in some detail in
Chapter VIII.

Father or Mother?

The empirical evidence that the father is more important
than the mother in the causation of delinquency is matched on
the whole by evidence that he is less important.[30] The theoretical
literature also offers us a choice.[31] As a general orientation to such
problems, control theory offers little in the way of preconceptions
or solutions: although akin to psychoanalytic theory in many respects, it has not tended to develop beyond common sense (or,
perhaps better, it has not gotten away from common sense) in
describing the mechanisms through which relations with parents
affect the morality of the child. As a consequence, research from
within the control tradition on the relative importance of the

[30] McCord and McCord, Origins of Crime, p. 116; Nye, Family Relation-
ships, p. 156; Robert G. Andry, "Parental Affection and Delinquency," The
Sociology of Crime and Delinquency, ed. Marvin E. Wolfgang et al. (New
York: Wiley, 1962), pp. 342–352.
[31] Gold, Status Forces, pp. 39–41; Talcott Parsons, "Age and Sex in the
Social Structure of the United States," in Essays in Sociological Theory (New
York: The Free Press, 1954), pp. 89–103.

father and the mother in the causation of delinquency has been radically empirical. The general strategy is to compare the effects on delinquency of attitudes toward the father with the effects of attitudes toward the mother, to compare the effects of the father's "role model" with the effects of the mother's "role model," and so on. The result is often a long list of complicated, ostensibly empirical conclusions. For example: "Maternal and paternal passivity differ in their relationships to criminality. Maternal passivity is similar in effect to maternal neglect. Paternal passivity resembles paternal warmth in its relation to crime." [32]

Since almost all items used in the present study were repeated for both parents, it would be easy to address again the question of the relative importance of parents using procedures widely used in the past. However, the ultimate complication and ambiguity of the conclusions of these studies suggest the need for a modified approach.

Nye concludes that "the father's behavior is more often significantly related to delinquent behavior than is the behavior of mothers," but he suggests that this is a consequence of greater variation in paternal behavior and thus does not reflect greater intrinsic importance of the paternal role.[33] Given the interrelations among Nye's independent variables, it is possible that he simply measured items relevant to the father more often than he measured items relevant to the mother. For that matter, one strong mother item would swamp numerous father items and make attitudes toward the mother easily more important than attitudes toward the father. The hypothesis Nye offers to explain the greater apparent importance of fathers, that the greater homogeneity of mothers' role definitions accounts for the relative absence of significant relations between their behavior and delinquency, is not supported by his own data, since on most items the variation for mothers is as great as that for fathers.[34]

One way to avoid counting the number of significant relations, many of which may duplicate each other, is to compare the

[32] McCord and McCord, Origins of Crime, p. 116.
[33] Nye, Family Relationships, p. 156.
[34] Gold (Status Forces, pp. 129–137) also argues that relations with the father are more important than those with the mother in the control of delinquency. I think it fair to say that Gold's data offer, at best, very weak evidence in favor of this position.

overall effects of a variety of mother items with the overall effects of the same father items. If we select the items important for both the father and the mother, this comparison should be meaningful, at least within the context of the data at hand. We have previously seen that supervision by the mother and the intimacy of communication with and attachment to the father are importantly related to delinquency. An index of disciplinary techniques used by the parents should also be included, since discipline has "obvious" connections to delinquency, and analysis not reported has shown that it is weakly but tenaciously related to delinquency.[35] When these items are simultaneously related to delinquency separately for the father and mother, the results are those shown in tables 26 and 27.[36]

For present purposes, the important statistic in tables 26 and 27 is the coefficient of multiple correlation, R. For the mother items, it is .35, for the father items, .33. For all practical and theoretical purposes, the conclusion that attitudes toward and relations with the mother and the father are equally important in the causation of delinquency appears justified. It is of course true that we can reach no final answer to this question, since it is possible that some item not included may differentiate markedly between the parents. However, since the items included are those upon which theory has traditionally focused, and since experience shows that the point of diminishing returns is reached very rapidly in this

[35] Items included in the index are: "Do your parents ever punish you by slapping or hitting you?" "By not letting you do things you want to do?" "By calling you bad names?" And, "By nagging or scolding you?"
As is now expected, the use of any disciplinary technique is positively related to delinquent behavior. Since the application of "negative sanctions," from slapping by the mother to imprisonment by the state, generates an empirical relation which suggests that the effort at control has the effect opposite of that intended, some recent writers have reached the conclusion that the "real" purpose of punishment is to generate that which it is ostensibly designed to prevent. See, for example, Kai T. Erikson, "Notes on the Sociology of Deviance," *The Other Side*, ed. Howard S. Becker (New York: The Free Press, 1964), pp. 9–21.
[36] The analytic technique producing tables 26 and 27, which I use occasionally throughout the study, is discussed in Appendix B. The partial regression coefficients show the linear effect of an independent variable on delinquency when the effects of the other variables included in the table have been removed. Thus, for example, in table 26, a change in age of one year produces an average increase of .05 in the number of delinquent acts, regardless of intimacy of communication with mother, attachment to mother, and so on.

Table 26 / Self-Reported Delinquency and Selected Mother Items—Boys Living with Real Father and Real Mother

| Variable | Zero-Order Correlations | Partial Regression Coefficients | |
		Raw	Normalized
Intimacy of communication (A)	−.17	−.06	−.06
Intimacy of communication (B)	−.22	−.04	−.05
Attachment	−.22	−.08	−.11
Supervision	−.27	−.24	−.20
Disciplinary techniques used	+.11	+.05	+.07
Age	+.09	+.05	+.08
Number of siblings	+.11	+.06	+.09

(R = .35) Number of cases = 955

kind of analysis,[37] the conclusion of no difference would seem adequate.

A more important question, especially with respect to control theory, is whether attachment to *a* parent is as efficacious as attachment to both parents in preventing delinquent conduct. It may be, for example, that the boy strongly attached to his mother is unlikely to be delinquent regardless of his feelings toward his father; it may be that strong attachment to both parents adds little in the way of control. If true, this would help explain the fact that the one-parent family is virtually as efficient a delinquency-controlling institution as the two-parent family, contrary to expectations deriving from "direct control" hypotheses. The solution to this problem would appear to be straightforward: we examine the combined effects of attachments to the father and the mother to determine whether there is an increment over the effects of attachment to a single parent.

[37] ". . . in general, the increase in the multiple correlation which results from adding variables beyond the first five or six is very small" (Quinn McNemar, *Psychological Statistics* [New York: Wiley, 1949], p. 163). In the present case, we have already reached the point of rapidly diminishing returns, since the second index of intimacy of communication contributes very little. Of course, as McNemar adds, if we were to add variables that were much more highly correlated with delinquency and/or variables having small relations with those already used, this statement would not apply. There are no parental items in the present data more highly correlated with delinquency than those used, and we would not expect to find important parental items having small relations with those already included in the analysis.

The multiple correlation of all of the items in tables 26 and 27 with delinquency is .36. Since we began with a multiple correlation between the mother items and delinquency of .35, the conclusion that knowing attitudes toward both parents adds *nothing* to our ability to predict delinquency is inescapable. (The multiple correlation cannot decline when additional variables are added. Thus some increment is eventually a logical necessity.) This conclusion, despite its statistical correctness, appears to be in direct conflict with common sense. Suppose, for example, a boy loves his

Table 27 / Self-Reported Delinquency and Selected Father Items—Boys Living with Real Father and Real Mother

Variable	Zero-Order Correlations	Partial Regression Coefficients	
		Raw	Normalized
Intimacy of communication (A)	−.20	−.09	−.09
Intimacy of communication (B)	−.23	−.02	−.02
Attachment	−.24	−.08	−.11
Supervision	−.24	−.17	−.16
Disciplinary techniques used	+.12	+.04	+.07
Age	+.09	+.05	+.08
Number of siblings	+.12	+.06	+.08

(R = .33) Number of Cases = 940

mother and hates his father; suppose his relations with one parent are warm and intimate while his relations with the other are cold and distant. Surely it seems reasonable to think that it would help to know these facts—they would, after all, lead to opposite predictions. Although this argument sounds plausible, it contains errors of assumption and fact.

The argument is, after all, based on a confusion of statements of existence with statements of frequency. There are, no doubt, adolescents who love one parent and hate the other, but, however true this may be, it tells us virtually nothing about the frequency of such discrepancies. In fact, adolescents whose attitudes toward and relations with one parent differ markedly from those with the other parent are very rare (Table 28). The correlations in Table 28 show why, on statistical grounds, knowledge of attitudes toward both parents adds little to our ability to predict delinquency. In most cases, to know attitudes toward one parent is to know attitudes toward the other, at least with respect to those attitudes relevant to delinquency.[38]

These correlations, and the corollary finding that the multiple correlation based on both parents is for all intents and purposes equal to the multiple correlation based on a single parent, suggest that research systematically comparing the effects of attitudes toward the mother with those of attitudes toward the father without ever asking how these attitudes are related to each other may be

Table 28 / Correlations Between Father and Mother Items [a]

Index	Correlation
Intimacy of communication (A)	.75
Intimacy of communication (B)	.77
Attachment	.74
Disciplinary techniques used	.68
Supervision	.80

[a] The correlations in this table are based on 909 white boys living with their real fathers and mothers.

seriously misleading.[39] It is not surprising that such analysis can produce differences between the father and the mother that "make sense" with respect to delinquency. We could do the same by comparing tables 26 and 27: these tables show that supervision by the mother is "more important" than supervision by the father; that intimacy of communication with the father is more important than intimacy of communication with the mother; and so on. Although in these cases the differences may not be statistically significant, eventually such differences would of necessity appear.

Since we assume that in considering a delinquent act the child takes into account the reactions of his parents, we naturally assume that he takes into account the reaction of each parent. But

[38] I have attempted by several methods to determine whether attitudes toward the father and the mother interact in their effects on delinquency. The results have been consistently negative. (On the basis of previous research, it is plausible to guess that the weaker the attachment to one parent, the more important is attachment to the other. The differences I have found point in this direction, but they are too small to merit attention.)

[39] Although Nye does not report the relations between the mother and father items he examines, the marginal distributions in his study frequently suggest that the relations could be as strong as those reported here (see Family Relationships, especially pp. 74–76).

the latter requires a calculus of pleasure beyond the grasp of man. Compare the potential delinquent's situation with that of the professor assigning grades in a course. The grade assigned (the delinquent act) will normally be correlated with each of the measures of performance gathered during the term. However, as the diminishing returns problem in multiple correlation suggests, given enough measures of performance (all more or less highly correlated with each other), it is conceivable that some will add nothing to the explained variance in final grades. It would then be correct to say that these particular measures of performance did not "count." Given the fixed and limited values of his final grades, and given the limitations on his capacities to consider simultaneously the various bits of information available to him, there was simply more information available to the professor than he could use. If the professor, in the quiet of his study, with time to consider and weigh alternatives, and with several options open to him, cannot assure us that he will "count" the first midterm, why should we expect the adolescent, who has vague fears in place of concrete scores, who has to decide in a matter of moments which course of action to take, who may experience pressures against his better judgment, and the like, to "count" his father?

We should not expect this. And, in the control theory, we do not have to expect it. Relations with and attitudes toward the parents are in some sense equivalent to the professor's answer to the question, "How good a student is he, really?" Answers to this question will presumably be correlated with final grades; but if we were to break the question into component questions, we would undoubtedly quickly find components that contribute nothing additional to the final result.

The alternative is to argue that relations with parents are somehow built into the child, that crime satisfies special psychological or social needs stemming from relations with the parents. If the child has needs stemming from his relations with each parent, and if these needs must somehow be satisfied, then the personality of each parent will show in the actions of the child, as in these findings reported by the McCords: "Passive mothers produced high proportions of sexual criminals and traffic offenders, yet their sons did not commit crimes of violence; . . . overprotective mothers had high proportions of 'violent criminals' and traffic offenders among their sons but a very low proportion of sexual criminals." [40] Although we cannot prove that the McCords' statistically significant findings will never again appear in the literature of crime and delinquency, we can ask: Why, if A (sex crimes) is psychologically compatible with B (traffic offenses), and B is psychologically compatible with C (crimes of violence), should we not expect in the next study to find A, B, and C or A and C turning up together for both types of parents? And, we can also ask: Why, if specific crimes satisfy specific psychological needs, are persons committing any given crime much more likely than "noncriminals" to commit every other type of offense? [41]

Conclusion

It is thought that one reason lower-class children have high rates of delinquency is that they have little respect for and do not establish intimate ties with their parents.[42] Related to this is the view that even if the lower-class parent does command the respect and affection of his children, such ties are not as conducive to conformity as is true for the middle-class parent simply because the "model" is himself less likely to exhibit conventional behavior.

Data bearing on the argument that lower-class children have less respect for and establish less intimate ties with their parents have been incidentally presented in this chapter. Tables 22 and 23 show a very small relation in the predicted direction: for example, in Table 22, 38 percent of the sons of those having no history of welfare or unemployment are high on intimacy of communication compared to 30 percent of the sons of those who have been on welfare or have been unemployed. These differences are about the same as those revealed by previous research.[43]

If the view that the lower-class parent is less likely to command the respect and affection of his children finds very weak

40 McCord and McCord, *Origins of Crime*, p. 151.

41 For evidence of the versatility of delinquents, see Albert K. Cohen, *Delinquent Boys* (New York: The Free Press, 1955), pp. 29–30. There is, to be sure, much evidence of versatility in the present data; see Table 6, page 56.

42 Gold, *Status Forces*, pp. 124, 136; McKinley, *Social Class and Family Life*, p. 57.

43 Gold, *Status Forces*, pp. 136–137.

support in these data, the view that even if he does command their respect and affection such ties will not be conducive to conformity receives no support at all. The child attached to a low-status parent is no more likely to be delinquent than the child attached to a high-status parent.

It seems clear, then, that the lower-class parent, even if he is himself committing criminal acts, does not publicize this fact to his children. Since he is as likely to express allegiance to the substantive norms of conventional society as is the middle-class parent,[44] he operates to foster obedience to a system of norms to which he himself may not conform.

If the child does not care or think about the reaction of his parents, their control over him is seriously reduced. While we have emphasized that the child may not care about the reaction of his parents, the data appear to emphasize that he may not think about their reaction. In the ideal control situation, parents are the center of a communication network that is staffed by adult authorities, relatives, neighbors, other children, and the child himself. A traditional explanation of the ineffectiveness of disorganized areas in controlling deviant behavior emphasizes their anonymity, the failure of adult authorities, relatives (who are back in the old country or back on the farm), and neighbors to communicate relevant information to the parents. This factor is undoubtedly important in determining the overall rate of delinquency in an area. Within the context of the present data, however, the decisive links in this communication network are those between parent and child. If the child does not communicate with his parents, if he does not tell them of his activities, then he does not have to concern himself with their imagined reactions to his behavior. If, by the same token, they do not tell him how they feel about his behavior, this too frees him from an important source of potential concern. He can act in the present without worrying about reenacting the scene at some later date before a possibly disapproving audience; today's play, in other words, will at no time in the future be reviewed.[45]

44 "A growing body of research has documented the higher degree of intolerance for deviant behavior among those of low education and socioeconomic position" (Stanton Wheeler, "Sex Offenses: A Sociological Critique," *Sexual Deviance*, ed. John Gagnon and William Simon [New York: Harper and Row, 1967], p. 90).

45 For a study of communication between delinquents and adults outside the family that suggests similar conclusions, see James F. Short, Jr., Harvey

In the next chapter I look at the effects on delinquency of performance in and attitudes toward the school. For now, it is worth mentioning that the child doing poorly in school is less likely to report close communication with his parents. We could explain this relation by noting that some families are less intellectual or, at least, less verbal than others. While there may be something to this argument, it is also a fact that we are all more willing to pass on to others our successes as opposed to our failures. Success in the wider world may thus serve to raise the level of intimate, personal communication within the family; failure may serve to retard it. Thus the power of the family as a controlling agency may at least partially depend on the school performance of the child.

Marshall, and Ramon J. Rivera, "Significant Adults and Adolescent Adjustment: An Exploratory Study," *Journal of Research in Crime and Delinquency*, IV (1967).

Chapter VII
Attachment to the School

Between the conventional family and the conventional world of work and marriage lies the school, an eminently conventional institution. Insofar as this institution is able to command his attachment, involvement, and commitment, the adolescent is presumably able to move from childhood to adulthood with a minimum of delinquent acts.

Since the school is a manifestly middle-class institution and delinquency has long been considered a predominantly lower-class phenomenon, the major lever for prying open the secrets of the school in the production of delinquency has been to assess its impact on the lower-class child. This approach has taken two major forms.

On the one hand, the lower-class boy's day-to-day experience in the school is shown to be unpleasant, degrading, and demoralizing. Although she might wish to do otherwise, the middle-class teacher tends to punish the fidgety, unambitious, and dirty lower-class boy. Furthermore, children from classes above him dominate extracurricular affairs, refuse to date him, and refuse to admit him into their cliques. To the degree that all this matters to him, the lower-class boy is held to face a problem of adjustment: "To the degree to which he values middle-class status, either because he values the good opinion of middle-class persons or because he has to some degree internalized middle-class standards himself, he faces a problem of adjustment and is in the market for a 'solution.' " [1]

On the other hand, the lower-class boy's everyday experience in the school is deemphasized, and his relation to *education* as it bears on social mobility becomes the major focus of attention. Although this second view appears to assume many of the same experiences within the school, the lower-class boy's inability to

[1] Albert K. Cohen, *Delinquent Boys* (New York: The Free Press, 1955), p. 119.

pursue an education (either because of lack of money or appropriate values) is seen as the major reason for his "turning to delinquency." [2]

The relations reported earlier in this study—and elsewhere—do not justify great reliance on "social class" as a starting point for an explanation of delinquency. Nevertheless, some of the assumed correlates of social class, notably academic competence and school performance, are more than adequate as a basis for discussion of the effects of school experience on delinquency.

Ability and Performance

Academic competence [3] is of such obvious importance in academic performance and commitment to the school and to the educational system that its assumed lack of relation to delinquency must be considered one of the wonders of modern social science. Literally hundreds of studies have been devoted to the relation between academic competence and crime. Historical trends (and inconsistencies) in attitudes and findings concerning this relation are exemplified in the following quotations.

> If poverty is the mother of crime, lack of sense is its father. (nineteenth century)

> Feeble-minded persons become criminals because they cannot foresee and appreciate the consequences of their acts.[4] (circa 1915)

> . . . as the techniques for more accurate measurement of intelligence have been refined, the foundations of the once widely

[2] Richard A. Cloward and Lloyd E. Ohlin, *Delinquency and Opportunity* (New York: The Free Press, 1959), especially chapters 4 and 5.

[3] For several reasons I use "academic competence" rather than "intelligence" throughout the present discussion. First, the test scores I use, although undoubtedly highly correlated with tests designed to measure intelligence, are not, strictly speaking, intelligence tests. Second, all the argument requires is the assumption that there are differences in academic ability and that these differences can have an effect on one's life. The sources of differences in academic ability are not at issue. Third, a basic trait of brightness or stupidity is not required by the discussion. Many delinquent acts are undoubtedly stupid if the risks and rewards are calculated by conventional standards of value, but this does not require us to assume that the acts are stupid when judged by the actors' standards of value.

[4] *The Sutherland Papers*, ed. Albert K. Cohen et al. (Bloomington: Indiana University Press, 1956), p. 239. Sutherland is summarizing a theory to which he does not subscribe.

held belief in the existence of a negative correlation between intelligence and criminality have crumbled away. . . .[5] (1959)

In short, coming from families of inferior socio-economic status and *having limited intellectual capacity* leads to an unfavorable attitude toward school, and an unfavorable attitude toward school predisposes a boy to associate with delinquents.[6] (1962)

Indicative of the extent to which "intelligence" has moved from the status of an all-important cause of delinquency (in the first three decades of the century) to the status of a variable that was once thought to be important is the fact that Jackson and Marcia L. Toby react with surprise to their finding that low intellectual status is related to the acquisition of delinquent friends.[7]

The present theory does not depend upon a relation between academic competence and delinquency. It would therefore be possible simply to ignore studies that include some measure of academic competence. However, we are presumably dealing with a rational world in which conjectural and empirical relations between variables have implications for other relations. Thus it would be puzzling, at best, if delinquency were related to dropping out of school, school retardation, interest in school, "poor reputation" at school, and so on, without being related to academic competence. By the same token, it would be puzzling if attachment and commitment to a system were not related to possession of those characteristics the system rewards and, indeed, spends much of its effort attempting to foster.

Academic competence may be used to make another point about the theoretical location of some of the variables examined in this study. Academic competence is not assumed to be a cause of delinquency in the sense that the less competent person is more likely to underestimate the risk of detection and less able to see the implications of his acts for the interpersonal and object relations that would otherwise bind him to the conventional order. Instead, in a system in which competence is rewarded and incom-

---

[5] Barbara Wootton, *Social Science and Social Pathology* (New York: Macmillan, 1959), p. 302. Wootton adds: "And what has happened to intelligence has happened to one supposed peculiarity of offenders after another."

[6] Jackson and Marcia L. Toby, "Low School Status as a Predisposing Factor in Subcultural Delinquency," mimeographed, Rutgers University, New Brunswick, N.J., about 1962, p. 27. Emphasis added.

[7] *Ibid.*, pp. 16 and 21.

petence is therefore punished, the cost of detection is assumed to be reduced for the incompetent because his ties to the conventional order have *previously* been weakened. In other words, the academically incompetent person may be very well able to foresee the consequences of his acts; the problem is that, for him, the consequences are less serious. Academic competence is thus assumed to operate through attachment, commitment, involvement, and belief to produce delinquent acts.

The effects of such variables as academic competence may vary from one group to another: for example, academic competence may have little effect on attachment to parents. These outside variables may also vary in importance over time: for example, as education becomes more universal in a system, academic competence should become more potent as a factor affecting attachment to that system. Stated more generally, the factors affecting the strength of the bond to a conventional system are assumed to be numerous and variable; they do not receive systematic attention here because the task of showing that the bond to the conventional order is strongly related to the commission of delinquent acts is considered logically prior.

The relation in the present sample between a central measure of academic competence and delinquency is shown in Table 29. All of the numerous test scores available on school records produce results similar to those in Table 29: the higher the boy's score, the less likely he is to have committed delinquent acts and the less likely he is to have been picked up by the police.[8] Most textbooks to the contrary, I do not think this result can be treated as an additional example of the inconsistency of delinquency research. In fact, several recent investigations show relations like that in Table 29.[9]

Remarks on the ability of the competent to avoid detection

[8] Given the possibility of bias in the police data related to school attended, I felt it necessary to reexamine the relation between academic competence and official delinquency holding school constant. The relation is present within all schools in the sample.

[9] Toby and Toby, "Low School Status," p. 17 (the Tobys' measure of intellectual level is based on the student's ability-group placement and the perceptions of fellow students); Albert J. Reiss, Jr., and Albert L. Rhodes, "The Distribution of Juvenile Delinquency in the Social Class Structure," *American Sociological Review*, XXVI (1961), 723; James F. Short, Jr., and Fred L. Strodtbeck, *Group Process and Gang Delinquency* (Chicago: University of Chicago Press, 1965), pp. 237–238.

Table 29 / Self-Reported and Official Delinquent Acts
by Differential Aptitude Test Verbal Scores
(in percent)

Self-Reported Acts	(A) DAT Scores				
	0–9	10–19	20–29	30–39	40 and above
None	55	53	58	66	81
One	24	25	28	21	10
Two or more	21	22	14	13	10
Totals	100 (224)	100 (452)	100 (319)	100 (140)	101 (21)

Official Acts	(B) DAT Scores				
	0–9	10–19	20–29	30–39	40 and above
None	68	80	89	93	100
One	17	10	8	7	0
Two or more	15	10	3	0	0
Totals	100 (232)	100 (464)	100 (324)	100 (142)	100 (21)

appear frequently in the delinquency literature (even among those who *deny* a relation between academic competence and official delinquency).[10] The data in Table 29 do not wholly undermine such skepticism, since academic competence is considerably more strongly related to official than to self-reported delinquency. However, if, as is implied, differences in ability to avoid detection account for the difference between the competent and the incompetent, there should be no difference between them on self-reported delinquency. (In fact, if there is really no difference in their propensity to commit delinquent acts, the academically competent should have a higher rate of actual delinquency, given their presumed ability to avoid the clutches of the law.) Since there is a relation between academic competence and self-reported delin-

10 George B. Vold, *Theoretical Criminology* (New York: Oxford University Press, 1958), pp. 88–89; Milton L. Barron, *The Juvenile in Delinquent Society* (New York: Alfred A. Knopf, 1954), pp. 113–116.

quency, no explanation based solely on the ability of the competent to avoid detection is adequate. How, then, is the relation to
be explained?

Possession of the skills measured by paper and pencil tests
makes school a place of potential achievement and satisfaction in a
way that it can never be for those not possessing such skills. The
ability simply to solve intellectual puzzles is itself rewarding and,
so long as the goals of education are accepted, inability to solve
them is punishing. The academically competent boy is more likely
to do well in school and more likely as a result to like school. The
boy who likes school is less likely to be delinquent. Thus, by
hypothesis, academic competence is linked to delinquency by way
of success in and attachment to the school. The best measure of
success in school is undoubtedly grade-point average. Although
overall grade-point averages were not available when the analysis
was conducted, grades in required subjects such as English and
mathematics were available for most students in the sample. The
correlation between Differential Aptitude Test verbal scores and
average marks in English is .39, as would be expected not only
from the hypothesis advanced here. However, the nontrivial prediction that average marks are more closely related to delinquency
than test scores is also confirmed, as Table 30 shows.[11]

The better a student does in school, the less likely he is to
have committed delinquent acts and the less likely he is to have
been picked up by the police. There is no reason to think that
commission of the acts involved in these measures of delinquency
could affect marks in English or mathematics. However, the tendency of teachers to reward good behavior somewhat independently of actual performance is occasionally cited as a possible
explanation of observed relations between school performance and
delinquency. Wootton, for example, says: "Much of this evidence
[that delinquents have poor school records], however, is based
upon the assessments of schoolmasters, which can hardly be regarded as objective, or as reasonably certain to be free of bias.

[11] For self-reported delinquency, the correlations with Differential Aptitude Test verbal scores and average grades in English are .08 and .18, respectively, and, for official delinquency, .19 and .22. The greater strength of
the relation between grades and self-reported delinquency may not be apparent in the table. (Incidentally, with the present sample, correlations of
.08 would not occur as a result of sampling from a population in which the
true relation is zero more than once in a hundred samples.)

Delinquent children are likely to be unpopular with their teachers. . . ." [12]

To test Wootton's explanation, I reexamined the relation between grades and delinquency among those whose classroom behavior had been sufficiently circumspect during the previous year to avoid being sent out of the classroom. (Which, by the way, was no mean feat, inasmuch as 53 percent of the white boys reported not having been sent out during the previous year.) The relation

Table 30 / Self-Reported and Official Delinquent Acts
by English Average Mark [a]
(in percent)

Self-Reported Acts	English Average Mark			Official Acts	English Average Mark		
	0–49	50–79	80–99		0–49	50–79	80–99
None	52	53	64	None	73	81	91
One	23	30	23	One	14	11	5
Two or more	26	17	12	Two or more	12	7	4
Totals	101	100	100	Totals	99	99	100
	(242)	(337)	(357)		(258)	(351)	(361)

[a] The relation between average grades in mathematics and delinquency is virtually identical. The distribution of grades is tri-modal. Each of the categories in the table embraces one of these modes. The off-mode students are consistently more likely to be delinquent, suggesting an effect attributable to change in academic performance or age. In any event, the collapsing procedure does not misrepresent the strength of the relation.

between grades and delinquent acts, both self-reported and official, persists essentially unchanged within this group.

Before examining the additional links in the causal chain hypothesized here, let us look at the implications of these data for other theories of delinquency. As sociological theories have moved from an image of the delinquent as an organism reacting mindlessly to forces in his environment (an assumption not far beneath the surface in many of the quantitative studies of the last fifty years) to an image of the delinquent as a symbol-using, self-reflective human being, there has been a natural tendency to overreact to the earlier model. In some theories the delinquent is now not only just as capable as anyone else, he is in fact, if anything, a

[12] Barbara Wootton, Social Science, p. 134.

little more capable: "Delinquents tend to be persons who have been led to expect opportunities because of their potential ability to meet the formal, institutionally established criteria of evaluation. . . . The available data support the contention that the basic endowments of delinquents, such as intelligence . . . , are the equal of *or greater than* those of their nondelinquent peers." [13]

Theories like Richard A. Cloward and Lloyd E. Ohlin's that focus on a sense of unjust deprivation presuppose a reasonably capable delinquent. But they presuppose more than this. The delinquent is aware of his intellectual talents; he is aware of them because others have recognized them. It is because of this awareness and the heightened expectations it produces that the potential delinquent finds his "lack of opportunity" particularly galling. If he were not competent, if other people did not recognize his competence,[14] then his lack of opportunity, which, to be sure, would be much more profound,[15] would not upset him in the same way.

The theory advanced here also suggests that self-perceived ability is important in the causation of delinquency. The boy who sees himself as capable of doing well in school is likely to find school tolerable and relevant to his future, regardless of his ability as measured in some more objective way. It is of course assumed that objective ability heavily influences subjective self-assessments and that this in turn partially accounts for the relation between objective ability and delinquency. In any event, the hypothesis advanced from the present perspective would be *opposite* to that advanced by Cloward and Ohlin. The more competent a boy thinks he is, the less likely he is to commit delinquent acts. This hypothesis is supported by Table 31.

Table 31 shows that 13 percent of those who consider themselves "among the best" in school ability have committed two or more delinquent acts, while 35 percent of those who consider themselves "below average" in school ability have committed two or more delinquent acts. As the table also shows, the distribution

[13] Cloward and Ohlin, *Delinquency and Opportunity*, p. 117. Emphasis added.
[14] *Ibid.*, pp. 113–121.
[15] Theories based on injustice in the American system must be careful not to make their potential delinquent too competent, since it is well established that personal competence can to some extent neutralize structural barriers to opportunity.

Table 31 / Self-Reported and Official Delinquent Acts
by Self-Ratings on School Ability [a]
(in percent)

Self-Reported Acts	Self-Rating			
	Among Best	Above Average	Average	Below Average
None	67	56	57	36
One	20	27	23	29
Two or more	13	16	20	35
Totals	100	99	100	100
	(135)	(379)	(619)	(94)

Official Acts	Self-Rating			
	Among Best	Above Average	Average	Below Average
None	89	86	79	66
One	8	7	12	17
Two or more	3	6	9	18
Totals	100	99	100	101
	(136)	(380)	(626)	(96)

[a] "What grades are you capable of getting?" produces similar results. An index based on the two items did not add sufficiently to the variance explained to justify its use.

of self-ratings of ability is peculiarly distorted if distributions of objective measures are taken as the standard. Less than 8 percent of the white boys in the sample rate themselves as below average in school ability. This suggests that the "accuracy" of self-perceptions of ability may be a function of actual ability, such that the less gifted are less likely to be aware of the nature of their gifts [16] and are thus saved from some of the consequences of their "structural position" in the system. (The absence of a subjective lower class in America presumably reflects the operation of similar distorting influences.)

Of course, opportunity theory introduces complications not covered by the analysis to this point. The person most likely to be delinquent is not only objectively competent, he is also aware of

[16] On one level they may be perfectly aware of their relative position—the "distortion" is thus ideological or semantic. The step from "actual" to "reported" perceptions might be as follows: "Yes, I'd say most guys are smarter than I am. I'd say I'm about average." The question is then which of these two self-conceptions is most determinative of subsequent behavior.

Table 32 / Percent Committing One or More Delinquent
Acts by Differential Aptitude Test Verbal Scores and
Self-Perceived Scholastic Adequacy, by Race
(in percent)

	White Boys						
	Self-Reported Delinquent Acts				Official Delinquent Acts		
	Self-Perceived Scholastic Adequacy				Self-Perceived Scholastic Adequacy		
Test Score	Above Average	Average	Below Average	Test Score	Above Average	Average	Below Average
0–9	41	46	55	0–9	29	33	38
	(34)	(136)	(29)		(34)	(138)	(29)
10–19	45	42	71	10–19	16	20	30
	(123)	(260)	(42)		(123)	(264)	(43)
20–29	44	37	—a	20–29	11	11	—
	(158)	(137)	(11)		(159)	(138)	(11)
30 and above	30	46	—	30 and above	4	12	—
	(134)	(24)	(0)		(134)	(24)	(0)

	Negro Boys						
	Self-Reported Delinquent Acts				Official Delinquent Acts		
	Self-Perceived Scholastic Adequacy				Self-Perceived Scholastic Adequacy		
Test Score	Above Average	Average	Below Average	Test Score	Above Average	Average	Below Average
0–9	49	48	58	0–9	39	42	67
	(103)	(248)	(50)		(104)	(255)	(55)
10–19	39	46	—	10–19	31	33	—
	(56)	(126)	(2)		(58)	(129)	(2)
20–29	42	—	—	20–29	16	—	—
	(31)	(19)	(0)		(31)	(19)	(0)
30 and above	—	—	—	30 and above	—	—	—
	(6)	(2)	(0)		(6)	(2)	(0)

a Too few cases for stable percentages.

his competence *and* barred by injustice in the system from the opportunity due him.

It is not far-fetched to assume that opportunities for Negroes, as a group, are at best equivalent to those of the lower-class boys treated by Cloward and Ohlin. There is, in fact, a further parallel between Negroes in the sample and the lower-class boys Cloward and Ohlin assume to be particularly prone to delinquency: Negroes tend to aspire to the material aspects of middle-class culture rather than to its life style.[17] Thus, according to unjust deprivation theories, the competent Negro boy who is at the same time aware of his ability should be most likely to be delinquent. Table 32 contains the data relevant to this point.

None of the 6 Negro boys in Table 32 with test scores of 30 or above who also see themselves as above average has ever been picked up by the police. Outside this small elite group, the trends on both actual and self-perceived ability are opposite to those suggested by the Cloward–Ohlin hypothesis. The more academically competent a boy is and/or the more competent he sees himself to be, the less likely he is to be delinquent, regardless of his position in the opportunity structure.[18]

Attachment to the School

To this point I have shown that students with little academic competence and students who perform poorly are more likely to commit delinquent acts, and I have argued that the link between ability and performance on the one hand and delinquency on the other is the bond to the school. (Although for present purposes I focus on attachment, ability and performance undoubtedly also affect and reflect involvement in school-related activities and commitment to education.) If the hypothesis is correct, then ability and performance must be related to attitudes toward school. Every

[17] This question is discussed further in Chapter IX.
[18] It is somewhat misleading to speak of competence and opportunity as varying independently. Generally speaking, the less competent a boy is, the smaller his opportunities. These data are thus not incompatible with a general "opportunity" theory; they are, however, incompatible with theories that use competence to generate *strain*. A key element in Cloward and Ohlin's theory is the ascription of blame for failure. The boy who sees himself as competent is more likely to blame the system for his failure and is therefore more likely to become delinquent. This problem is also treated in Chapter IX.

student was asked the direct question, "In general, do you like or dislike school?" The correlation between Differential Aptitude Test verbal scores and this item is .11; the correlation between English average marks and liking school is .23. With respect both to delinquency and to liking school, the statistical data to this point are thus consistent with the proposed causal chain. The variables further removed by hypothesis from the dependent variable(s) do in fact have weaker relations with them than the hypothesized proximate variables.

Table 33 / Self-Reported and Official Delinquent Acts by Attitudes Toward School
(in percent)

Self-Reported Acts	"Do you like school?"			Official Acts	"Do you like school?"		
	Like	Neither Like nor Dislike	Dislike		Like	Neither Like nor Dislike	Dislike
None	68	49	33	None	87	79	65
One	23	27	18	One	8	12	16
Two or more	9	25	49	Two or more	5	10	19
Totals	100	101	100	Totals	100	101	100
	(580)	(648)	(72)		(582)	(657)	(74)

The next step in the chain, then, is the relation between liking school and delinquency, shown in Table 33. Table 33 represents a correlation of .28, again consistent with the hypothesized causal chain. Tabular analysis is occasionally said to exaggerate the strength of relationships. The idea, it seems, is that a relation may appear to be substantial in a table when it represents a correlation coefficient that would be classified only as "weak" or "moderately weak." Reality, this argument suggests, belies appearances. Actually, the argument that the correlation coefficient minimizes relations is equally persuasive. Given the conceptual distance between the two measures and the strength of relations traditionally unearthed in delinquency research, the relation between liking school and delinquency shown in Table 33 is very strong, despite the magnitude of the correlation coefficient. Over 79 percent of the boys committing two or more delinquent acts are found among the 55 percent who are indifferent to or dislike school. It is not surprising that attitudes toward school have played a central part in sociological theories of delinquency. In theory, the question becomes: *Why* are boys who do not like school so much more likely to be delinquent?

Sociological theories of delinquency are so complicated with respect to this question that straightforward tests of their hypotheses are difficult. The "criminogenic" effect of attitudes toward school is sometimes held to depend upon *why* the student does not like school.[19] In other studies, "attitudes toward school" has drifted to the point that it is no longer a cause of delinquency but is instead part of the descriptive characterization of the delinquent: delinquents do not like school.[20] In general, however, it may be said that dislike for school is usually seen as a source of *motivation* to delinquency. Delinquency is a means of relieving frustration generated by unpleasant school experience.[21]

Table 33, which shows that 49 percent of the boys who *dislike* school have committed two or more delinquent acts in the previous year, compared to only 9 percent of those who like school, is consistent in this respect with a frustration hypothesis. Looked at in another way, however, Table 33 suggests that indifference to school is more frequently the hallmark of the delinquent than is active alienation. Of the 247 boys in this table who have committed two or more delinquent acts, 161 or 65 percent say they neither like nor dislike school. Comparable figures obtain when official acts are taken as the measure of delinquency. Students who dislike school are clearly more likely than indifferent students to have committed delinquent acts, but this table does not support the view that acute discontent or intense frustration are in any sense necessary conditions for delinquency.

Although there is little difference between the variables used here to explain lack of attachment to the school and those used by strain theorists to explain the generation of problems of adjustment, less emotion is built into the present model than is required by strain theory. The image of the delinquent deriving from strain theory is that of a boy who finds school too much to tolerate, yet

[19] See Cloward and Ohlin, *Delinquency and Opportunity*, pp. 96–97.
[20] Sheldon and Eleanor Glueck, *Unraveling Juvenile Delinquency* (Cambridge, Mass.: Harvard University Press, 1950), Chapter 12, especially pp. 143–144.
[21] Cohen, *Delinquent Boys*, pp. 112–119.

who continues to care for success either within the school or within the larger society. In control theory, delinquency is not seen as compensation for previous frustration and failure; it is not seen as an alternate route to some remote goal (boys do not steal bubble gum because they wish to be rich and famous). Boys who do badly in school reduce their interest in school (they may of course actually come to hate it) and are thus free to this extent to commit delinquent acts. They do not continue to desire success; they are not *forced* by their desires into delinquency.

Table 34 / Self-Reported and Official Delinquent Acts by Concern for Teachers' Opinions (in percent)

Self-Reported Acts	"Do you care what teachers think of you?"			Official Acts	"Do you care what teachers think of you?"		
	A Lot	Some	Not Much		A Lot	Some	Not Much
None	66	53	36	None	83	83	72
One	22	27	27	One	10	8	17
Two or more	12	20	36	Two or more	7	9	11
Totals	100	100	99	Totals	100	100	100
	(588)	(503)	(209)		(591)	(508)	(213)

The question, "Do you care what teachers think of you?," is thus germane to control theory not only because it is a central measure of attachment to a conventional figure, but also because it bears on the motivational assumptions explicit in competing theories. As Table 34 shows, the less a boy cares about what teachers think of him, the more likely he is to have committed delinquent acts. This relation too is very strong, and it is perfectly congruent with control theory. Yet it poses such problems for a strain theory that one would think it had never before been observed or surmised.[22]

If one measures any source of alleged pressure in a strain theory, whether it be some form of "success aspirations," "concern

[22] It has of course been surmised. John I. Kitsuse and David C. Dietrick ("Delinquent Boys: A Critique," *American Sociological Review*, XXIV [1959], 208–215) draw from Cohen's own statements the conclusion that working-class boys may not care what middle-class people think.

for the opinion of others," or "internalization of middle-class norms," one finds *variation*. All people are not equally concerned about success or the opinion of others. Since these "concepts" often enter strain theories as *constants*, of what significance is the not very surprising finding that they are in fact variables? If strain is an important element of a theory of delinquency, then presumably the greater the strain the greater the chances of delinquency. What one invariably finds, however, is that the higher a person is on the assumed source of strain, the *lower* his chances of delinquency, as in Table 34.[23]

Durkheim's theory of anomic suicide, the acknowledged model for many strain theories of delinquency, illustrates this problem. Durkheim emphasized "overweening ambition" as a cause of suicide, an element of this theory that survives in theories of delinquency. If ambition is a cause of suicide, then ambition should be positively related to suicide. Would a test of Durkheim's theory reveal such a relation? Durkheim himself suggests it would not: "Now he is stopped in his tracks; from now on nothing remains behind or ahead of him to fix his gaze upon. Weariness alone, moreover, is enough to bring disillusionment, for he cannot in the end escape the futility of an endless pursuit." [24] It is hard to imagine a man with high aspirations making ready to kill himself. As Durkheim saw, at some time prior to the act of self-destruction, the suicide's desire for future gain must leave him. His previous desire may accentuate his despair, but it is his despair and not his desire that kills him. As with all theories based upon a paradoxical conversion of virtue into vice, Durkheim's theory of anomic suicide thus suggests both a positive and a negative relation between the same variables, *depending upon the time at which they are measured*. The hypothesis that ambition leads to suicide cannot be falsified by showing that *the absence of ambition* precedes suicide.

Clearly, however, strain theory suggests that, among those whose aspirations are blocked, the higher the aspiration, the more serious the consequences of blockage. In other words, if one desires success and is continually frustrated in his attempts to reach

[23] Any "desire" item is sufficient to show the logical difficulties one encounters in attempting to test a strain theory. Caring what teachers think is equivalent in form to caring for success or valuing middle-class status.

[24] Emile Durkheim, *Suicide* (New York: The Free Press, 1951), p. 256.

this goal, then he is more likely to turn to crime than is the person who does not care for success.

Let us be perfectly clear on this point. Cohen suggests that to the degree that a lower-class boy values the good opinion of middle-class persons, he is more likely to become a delinquent. The item, "Do you care what teachers think of you?," would appear to be an excellent indicator of the degree to which a boy values the good opinion of middle-class persons. But valuing the opinion of middle-class persons is strongly negatively related to delinquency. The more a boy cares about the good opinion of middle-class persons, the less likely he is to become delinquent.

Of course, Cohen does not say that *any* boy who values the opinion of middle-class persons is more likely to become delinquent; he says that *lower-class* boys—boys who are picked on, discriminated against, laughed at—who also value the opinion of middle-class persons are more likely to become delinquent. The theory advanced here clearly suggests the opposite view—that the boy who values the opinion of middle-class persons is less likely to become delinquent regardless of how he is treated or how he sees himself treated in the school.

The item, "Teachers pick on me," would appear to be a good indicator of the second element of Cohen's theory, since it is treatment in the school and not the fact of social class itself that is important in a status frustration theory. Table 35 thus provides a direct test of competing theories. According to Cohen's theory, the boy who *cares* what teachers think of him and who sees himself as picked on by teachers should be most likely to be delinquent. According to control theory, the boy who does not care what teachers think of him and who sees himself as picked on by teachers should be most likely to be delinquent. Twenty-four percent of the boys Cohen's model focuses upon have committed two or more delinquent acts, while 52 percent of the control theorist's boys have committed two or more delinquent acts (columns 1 and 3, Table 35). And, in general, boys who value the good opinion of middle-class persons are less likely to be delinquent regardless of how they see teachers as treating them.

It is at this point that the final *deus ex machina* of strain theory makes its appearance. It can be argued that the boys who say they do not care really do care. The "reaction formation" mechanism may already have converted real concern into apparent lack of concern. Thus the ultimate prediction about a relation between a source of strain and delinquency from a reaction-formation strain theory could be identical to that from a control theory, and the data irrelevant to a choice between them.

Let us keep trying. No device for the transmutation of *subjective* frustration is available to the strain theorist. When it comes

Table 35 / Self-Reported Delinquent Acts by Concern for Teachers' Opinion and Perceptions of Teachers' Treatment (in percent)

	"Teachers pick on me."								
	Agree			Undecided			Disagree		
Self-Reported Acts	"Do you care what teachers think of you?"								
	A Lot	Some	Not Much	A Lot	Some	Not Much	A Lot	Some	Not Much
None	38	36	25	52	38	40	69	59	40
One	39	36	23	23	35	24	21	24	30
Two or more	24	28	52	25	28	36	10	17	30
Totals	100	100	100	100	101	100	100	100	100
	(37)	(45)	(44)	(61)	(72)	(50)	(482)	(386)	(113)

to his central hypothesis that "the intense frustration [of lower-class boys in school] consequently motivates them toward delinquent patterns of behavior in an attempt to recoup their loss of self esteem," [25] he is forced to abide by the data.

Presumably such frustration cannot or should not be measured by combining measures of aspiration with measures of achievement, since, as suggested earlier, the higher the aspiration the less the delinquency, regardless of the achievement, and we therefore know in advance that the outcome is an inconclusive falsification of strain theory.[26] Also, since frustration is ultimately subjective, it should not be inferred from objective discrepancy between aspirations and achievement when and if subjective mea-

[25] Delbert S. Elliott, "Delinquency, School Attendance, and Dropout," *Social Problems*, XIII (1966), 307. Elliott is summarizing the views of Cohen and of Cloward and Ohlin.
[26] The place of ambition in the causation of delinquency is discussed in some detail in Chapter IX.

sures are available. (Such inferences of frustration from objective discrepancies are at the root of most strain theories, and the requirement that the actor as well as the observer be aware of the discrepancy is part of the reason that in these theories delinquents are assumed to have broad perspectives on the social order.)

If school-generated *frustration* is an important motivational source of delinquent activity, then those who feel nervous and tense in school should be more likely to be delinquent than those who do not. Yet they are not appreciably more likely to have committed delinquent acts, as Table 36 shows. According to Table 36, school-generated frustration is virtually unrelated to the commission of delinquent acts. There is a slight tendency for greater delinquency among those who feel nervous and tense in school, but this difference is insufficient grounds upon which to base an explanation of delinquency. On several counts, then, we can say that the delinquency of the boys in this sample does not appear to be based on the drives presumably created by a situation of strain.[27]

The boy who does not like school and who does not care what teachers think of him is to this extent free to commit delinquent acts. Positive feelings toward controlling institutions and persons in authority are the first line of social control. Withdrawal of favorable sentiments toward such institutions and persons at the same time neutralizes their moral force.[28] Such neutralization is, in a control theory, a major link between lack of attachment and delinquency. If a person feels no emotional attachment to a person or institution, the rules of that person or institution tend to be denied legitimacy. Just as the child who does not like his parents is likely to consider their rules "unfair," so the child who does not like school or does not care "what teachers think" is likely to believe that the school has no right to control him.

The items used as measures of attachment to the school, "Do you like school?" and "Do you care what teachers think of you?," are, as would be expected, substantially related to an item designed to tap feelings about the scope of the school's legitimate authority:

---

[27] See Short and Strodtbeck, *Group Process*, p. 233.

[28] "The establishment of sensitivity to the attitudes of approval and esteem, again both external and internal, is one of the most fundamental requirements of adequate socialization of the individual and serves as the central core of his motivation to conformity" (Talcott Parsons, *The Social System* [New York: The Free Press, 1951], p. 264).

"It is none of the school's business if a student wants to smoke
outside the classroom." This item, in turn, is very strongly related
to delinquency (Table 37). Students who actually smoke are very
likely to feel that the school's authority over smoking should be
limited. Nevertheless, such rejection of the school's authority is
conducive to delinquency among those who do not smoke as well
as among those who do (see Table 56).

Table 36 / Self-Reported and Official Delinquent Acts
By School-Generated Emotional Tension
(in percent)

Self-Reported Acts	"I feel nervous and tense in school."				
	SA [a]	A	U	D	SD
None	56	50	58	58	55
One	15	24	24	25	28
Two or more	29	26	18	17	18
Totals	100	100	100	100	101
	(52)	(165)	(195)	(628)	(255)
Official Acts	"I feel nervous and tense in school."				
	SA	A	U	D	SD
None	81	81	81	81	82
One	12	13	7	10	11
Two or more	8	6	12	9	7
Totals	101	100	100	100	100
	(52)	(168)	(197)	(634)	(256)

[a] SA = strongly agree A = agree; U = undecided; D = disagree; SD = strongly disagree.

Beginning, then, with variation in academic competence, we
have traced a path through attachment to the school and support
of the school's authority to delinquency. Let us now look at the
simultaneous effects of the variables thus far discussed (Table
38).

The first thing we note in Table 38 is that this set of school
items, although not chosen specifically for this purpose, accounts
for more of the variance in delinquency than the father-mother
items combined. (The coefficient of multiple correlation is .41,
whereas for the father-mother items it is .36.) Second, as was

expected, academic competence has little direct effect on the commission of delinquent acts when the effects of school performance and attitudes toward school are removed. Third, the effects of academic performance are not eliminated when attachment to the school is taken into account. (Presumably academic performance influences and reflects elements of the bond to the school not yet considered.) Fourth, when the effects of academic competence,

Table 37 / Self-Reported and Official Delinquent Acts by Scope of School's Authority (in percent)

Self-Reported Acts	"None of school's business if student wants to smoke outside the classroom."				
	SA	A	U	D	SD
None	33	54	62	64	67
One	29	26	23	24	22
Two or more	38	20	15	12	11
Totals	100	100	100	100	100
	(261)	(258)	(182)	(196)	(404)

Official Acts	"None of school's business if student wants to smoke outside the classroom."				
	SA	A	U	D	SD
None	69	83	83	83	88
One	16	9	7	12	8
Two or more	15	8	10	5	4
Totals	100	100	100	100	100
	(265)	(262)	(185)	(196)	(405)

grades, and attitudes toward school are taken into account, the relation between self-perceived school ability and self-reported delinquency disappears (in fact, it reverses). Actually, however, given the assumption that objective ability and actual performance affect self-perceived ability, which, in turn, affects attitudes toward teachers and the school, the relation between self-perceived ability and delinquency cannot be considered spurious: analysis not presented shows that those who see themselves as having little scholastic ability are more likely to be delinquent when both verbal test scores and grade-point average are held relatively constant. Self-

Table 38 / Self-Reported Delinquent Acts and Selected School Items

Variable	Marginal Relations		Partial Regression Coefficients	
	Sample Number	Average No. Del. Acts	Raw	Normalized
Likes school				.20[a]
Yes	442	.48	−.18[b]	−.08
Indifferent	476	.91	+.09	+.04
No	43	1.95	+.87	+.16
Cares what teachers think				.09
A lot	424	.56	−.08	−.04
Some	394	.77	+.01	.00
Not much	143	1.34	+.21	+.07
None of school's business if student smokes				.23
Strongly agree	202	1.41	+.48	+.17
Agree	208	.75	−.03	−.01
Undecided	149	.61	−.09	−.03
Disagree	141	.50	−.19	−.06
Strongly disagree	261	.48	−.20	−.08
Rates self on academic ability				.03
Among best	110	.58	+.04	+.01
Above average	311	.64	+.03	+.01
About average	485	.84	−.02	−.01
Below average	55	1.10	−.08	−.02
English average mark			−.005	−.11
Differential Aptitude Test verbal score			−.006	−.05
Total sample (R = .41)	961	.76		

[a] Underlined *beta* coefficients summarize the effects of all categories of the nominal variable. See the literature cited in Appendix B.

[b] These regression coefficients show, for example, that boys who like school have, on the average, committed 1.05 fewer delinquent acts than boys who do not like school, after differences in academic competence, school performance, and other attitudes toward school and toward their own ability are taken into account.

perceptions of ability thus affect delinquency independently of "actual" scholastic ability but not, obviously, independently of attitudes toward teachers and the school. Fifth, and finally, the three attitudinal measures, as expected, retain an effect on delinquency when the effects of the competence and performance variables are removed.

Parents, Teachers, and the School

Some control theorists have suggested that lack of respect for and attachment to parents tends to spread to adult authorities and conventional institutions in general. The Simmelian notion that one is cast adrift by one group only to be swallowed up by another is not, in this view, accurate, at least if attention is restricted to conventional groups.[29] The view that lack of attachment in one setting is not compensated for by stronger attachments in another setting but tends to spread from one setting to another is supported by the present data: students with weak affectional ties to parents also tend to have little concern for the opinion of teachers and tend not to like school.[30]

In Table 39 we examine the joint effects on delinquency of attitudes toward teachers, the school, and the father. As Table 39

Table 39 / Percent Committing One or More Delinquent Acts by Intimacy of Communication with Father, Liking of School, and Concern for the Opinion of Teachers

	"Do you like school?"					
	Yes			No		
Intimacy of Communication with Father (A)	"Do you care what teachers think of you?"					
	A Lot	Some	Not Much	A Lot	Some	Not Much
High	26	33	—[a]	35	43	54
	(181)	(75)	(17)	(90)	(74)	(32)
Medium	33	34	—	41	52	65
	(122)	(81)	(16)	(87)	(155)	(53)
Low	25	42	—	52	58	72
	(54)	(48)	(11)	(66)	(80)	(71)

[a] Too few cases for stable percentages.

[29] Cf. Muzafer Sherif and Carolyn W. Sherif, Reference Groups: Exploration into Conformity and Deviation of Adolescents (New York: Harper and Row, 1964), pp. 240, 247, 272.

[30] For example, of the 330 students classified as "low" on intimacy of communication with the father, 35 percent like school, while 58 percent of the 469 students "high" on intimacy of communication with the father like school.

shows, a favorable attitude toward school protects the child from delinquency regardless of the intimacy of his ties with his father and regardless of his concern for the opinion of teachers. In every comparison possible in the table, the boys who do not like school are more likely than those who like school to have committed delinquent acts. Concern for the opinion of teachers is also related to delinquency regardless of attitudes toward school or intimacy of communication with the father. Intimacy of communication with the father, in contrast, is only weakly related to delinquency when the child likes school, but retains its original effect among students not liking school. Although the interaction in this case is only suggestive, we shall encounter interactions of the same form in subsequent analysis. These interactions suggest that among those with high stakes in conformity, additional attachments and commitments are less important than among those with low stakes in conformity. Since it is possible to derive this specification from control theory, the whole problem will be taken up in more detail in subsequent chapters.

Conclusion

In this chapter I have presented a simple causal chain and examined data relevant to it. The causal chain runs from academic incompetence to poor school performance to disliking of school to rejection of the school's authority to the commission of delinquent acts. All statistical relations relevant to this causal chain have been presented, and all are in fact consistent with it. Given the general consistency of the statistical results with those produced by previous research, I have chosen to emphasize data bearing on their *interpretation*.

Specifically, I have emphasized lack of intellectual skills as a general forerunner of delinquency. James F. Short and Fred L. Strodtbeck suggest that members of delinquent gangs tend to lack other things as well: skill in interpersonal relations, social assurance, knowledge of the job market and of the requirements of modern industry, and even sophistication in their relations with girls. In other words, according to Short and Strodtbeck, members of delinquent gangs tend to be characterized by a general "social disability."[31]

Although the nonintellectual aspects of the delinquent's "disability" have received much attention in the theoretical literature on delinquency,[32] there are difficulties with such an emphasis in the present study. For one thing, there is no obvious way with our theory to get from "social disability" to delinquency: social disability is just not theoretically relevant. We cannot say, as do Short and Strodtbeck, that boys lacking social skills have difficulty satisfying their dependency needs and that "delinquency creates situations in which [these] needs may be met."[33] The fact that variables are ignored says nothing against a theory as long as the ignored variables are empirically unimportant. In the present case, there is little evidence that social disability is important. Although few items for testing hypotheses about its effects are available, it does not appear that boys committing delinquent acts are any more likely to suffer from lack of social assurance than are boys refraining from such acts. There is no relation between delinquency and responses to "It is hard for me to talk to people when I first meet them" or "It is hard to tell other people how I feel."

For that matter, these data appear to be consistent with other data reported in the literature. The Tobys present evidence at least indirectly supportive of my emphasis on intellectual as opposed to other forms of disability: "At first we thought that intellectual status was but one of several types of school status and that any one of them would have the same preventive effect on the development of delinquency. Further investigation showed this hypothesis to have been in error. . . . Neither generalized popularity (interpersonal status) nor athletic prestige served to prevent the acquisition of delinquent friends if intellectual status is controlled."[34]

The Tobys suggest that the academically competent are less likely to be delinquent because they have prospects for the future

[31] Group Process, Chapter 10, pp. 217–247. See also Robert A. Gordon, "Social Level, Social Disability, and Gang Interaction," American Journal of Sociology, LXXIII (1967), 42–62.

[32] See Cohen, Delinquent Boys, pp. 109–119; and Cloward and Ohlin, Delinquency and Opportunity, pp. 97–101.

[33] Group Process, pp. 243–247.

[34] "Low School Status," pp. 16 and 21.

they do not wish to jeopardize. We will explore the impact of plans for the future in a subsequent chapter. For now it is sufficient to note that academic ability and school performance influence many if not most of the variables that turn out to be important predictors of delinquency. If social skill and social status do not perform their traditional functions in the theory advanced here, there are yet hierarchies of ability and ambition that do the job as well.

Chapter VIII

Attachment to Peers

Most delinquent acts are committed with companions;[1] most delinquents have delinquent friends.[2] The meaning of these simple facts is a matter of wide dispute. However, before addressing the controversy over their interpretation, let us ascertain whether the present data are consistent with previous research on the extent to which delinquents associate with delinquents.

As was shown in Table 24, three-fourths of those boys with four or more close friends who have been picked up by the police have committed delinquent acts in the previous year, while only slightly more than one-fourth of those with no delinquent friends have committed delinquent acts during the same period. The table also shows that of those boys committing two or more delinquent offenses, 82 percent had at least one close friend picked up by the police, while only 34 percent of those committing no delinquent acts had friends picked up. By this measure, then, the present data are highly consistent with previous research: boys who commit delinquent acts are much more likely than those who do not to have delinquent friends.

Indirect evidence of the extent to which delinquency and delinquent friends go together is given by the relation between the attitudes of adults toward one's friends and one's own delinquency. As Table 40 illustrates, those whose friends are admired by teachers are unlikely to have committed delinquent acts, while those whose friends are disliked by teachers are very likely to have committed such acts. Although parents are less likely than teachers to disapprove of one's friends (suggesting greater variation in

---

[1] See the summary of Thomas G. Eynon's "Factors Related to Onset of Delinquency," Ph.D. dissertation, The Ohio State University, 1959, in Walter C. Reckless, *The Crime Problem*, 4th ed. (New York: Appleton-Century-Crofts, 1967), pp. 403–406.

[2] Sheldon and Eleanor Glueck, *Unraveling Juvenile Delinquency* (Cambridge, Mass.: Harvard University Press, 1950), pp. 163–164.

Table 40 / Self-Reported Delinquency by Teacher's
Attitudes Toward Friends
(in percent)

Self-Reported Acts	"How much do you think most teachers like the group of friends you go with?"			
	Very Much	Fairly Well	Not Much	Not at All
None	70	60	40	19
One	22	25	24	32
Two or more	8	15	36	49
Totals	100	100	100	100
	(218)	(592)	(133)	(59)

parental standards or knowledge), the same relation obtains between parental approval of friends and delinquency.

The testimony of several indicators is clear: delinquents are
very likely to have delinquent friends; nondelinquents are very
unlikely to have delinquent friends. It is not surprising that, after
comparing such relations in the Gluecks' *Unraveling Juvenile Delinquency* with other relations reported in that study, Reckless
could conclude: "Of all the factors in the entire study, the amount
or degree of relationship between the presence or absence of delinquent companions and the condition of delinquency or nondelinquency was found to occupy first place. . . . [Companionship] is
unquestionably the most telling force in male delinquency and
crime. . . ."[3].

Looking at the same data, the Gluecks had reached a rather
different conclusion. Most delinquents have delinquent friends;
therefore, "Birds of a feather flock together."[4] The Gluecks' birds-
of-a-feather conclusion has been characterized as cavalier; yet it is
an apt formulation of a central assumption of control theories:
"Those boys who have high stakes will tend not to befriend peers

[3] Reckless, *The Crime Problem*, 2nd ed. (1955), p. 77. In subsequent
editions of his book, Reckless drops his summary of the Gluecks' study with
respect to the importance of companions, apparently in recognition of their
arguments about causal order, but he maintains his earlier position on the
importance of the companionship factor. For a methodological examination
of the Gluecks' solution to the problem of causal order with respect to the
relation between delinquency and the delinquency of companions, see Travis
Hirschi and Hanan C. Selvin, *Delinquency Research* (New York: The Free
Press, 1967), pp. 54–58, 60–63.

[4] Glueck and Glueck, *Unraveling*, p. 164.

whose stakes are low since the latter are more likely to 'get into trouble.' Boys with low stakes, on the other hand, will tend to avoid those who are 'chicken' and to seek out those with congruent interests and freedom to act. These processes are not different logically from those involved in the formation of most youth groups." [5]

In one view, then, the companionship factor is a central cause of juvenile delinquency. In another view, companionship with delinquents is an incidental by-product of the real causes of delinquency. There are many variations on these basic, if extreme, positions.

In some forms of differential association theory, the child has no particular propensities to delinquency prior to his association with delinquents. Only after he somehow acquires delinquent friends does he learn the values, attitudes, and skills conducive to delinquency and thus become a delinquent himself.[6] Other statements of differential association theory grant that children differ with respect to their delinquency potential, but appear to argue that this potential is realized mainly or largely through companionship with delinquents.[7]

There are also two basic approaches to this question within control theory. One assumes a causal ordering opposite to that assumed by differential association theorists. Thus the Gluecks argue that their delinquents had committed delinquent acts before the age at which boys usually join gangs. Since gang membership follows delinquency, it cannot be a cause of delinquency, accord-

[5] Scott Briar and Irving Piliavin, "Delinquency, Situational Inducements, and Commitment to Conformity," *Social Problems*, XIII (1965), 40.

[6] There is much justification for references to the theory of differential association as the theory of *accidental* differential association, since at many points such theorists appear to be denying that there are variations in individual personality or life experience other than differential association relevant to crime. See for example, Donald R. Cressey, "The Development of a Theory: Differential Association," *The Sociology of Crime and Delinquency*, ed. Marvin E. Wolfgang et al. (New York: Wiley, 1962), pp. 81–90; and Howard S. Becker, *Outsiders* (New York: The Free Press, 1963), pp. 41–46.

[7] This version of differential association theory arises to explain the correlations implicitly denied in the general statement of the theory. Differential association is the all-encompassing intervening variable; against this standard, nothing else is very important. See Edwin H. Sutherland and Donald R. Cressey, *Principles of Criminology*, 7th ed. (Philadelphia: Lippincott, 1966), especially chapters 6–10. For development of the position that the use of a theoretical intervening variable as a standard against which to judge the importance of empirical variables is misleading, see Hirschi and Selvin, *Delinquency Research*, Chapter 8.

ing to the Gluecks.[8] A second approach from a control theory perspective takes the question of causal ordering as less crucial, suggesting that the relation between gang membership (or the delinquency of companions) and delinquency is spurious. The boy takes up with delinquents *and* commits delinquent acts because he has lost his stake in conformity.

Suppose we were testing the latter version of control theory by examining the relation between delinquency of companions and delinquency with the effects of stakes in conformity removed. If the relation between delinquency of companions and delinquency were to disappear when the effects of stakes in conformity were removed, it could be persuasively argued that the original relation was spurious only if it could be established that delinquency of companions did not cause the variations in stakes in conformity. If association with delinquents produces such variations, we would be controlling an intervening variable, and the statistical configuration adduced to show the spuriousness of the effect of association with delinquents would actually show *how* such association produces delinquency.

The first step in testing this model, then, is to determine the causal ordering of stakes in conformity and delinquency of companions. Actually, much research and speculation suggest a causal ordering opposite to that assumed by control theory. I shall therefore examine several hypotheses about the effects of peers in general and delinquent peers in particular on attitudes relevant to delinquency before taking up the more general problem of choosing between control and cultural deviance models of the relations among stakes in conformity, delinquency of companions, and delinquency.

Attachment to Peers and Stakes in Conformity

Richard R. Korn and Lloyd W. McCorkle suggest that the delinquent is excessively dependent on "acceptance by certain

[8] The Gluecks' position on this question has been stated more fully in publications subsequent to *Unraveling*. See, for example, Sheldon Glueck, "Ten Years of *Unraveling Juvenile Delinquency*, An Examination of Criticisms," *The Journal of Criminal Law, Criminology and Police Science*, II (1960), 296.

others." [9] The "certain others" are delinquent themselves. Now, if the delinquent is unusually dependent on the acceptance of other delinquents, he is, it can be assumed, open to their influence. William C. Kvaraceus and Walter B. Miller, in like manner, find that the delinquent has the personal characteristics necessary to admit social influence from the peer group. In order to get along in lower-class street-corner groups, they say: "One must possess . . . the capacity to interact and to subordinate self to the over-all needs of the group. . . . Similar skills and drives in the case of the middle-class boy are often directed toward the Eagle Scout Badge." [10] Cohen goes one step further, saying that "relations with gang members tend to be intensely solidary and imperious"— that "satisfactory emotional relationships with his peers are likely to be more important" to the lower-class (potentially delinquent) than to the middle-class (nondelinquent) child.[11] More recently, Muzafer and Carolyn Sherif find it "ironic" but true that "those personal characteristics ordinarily prized in social life—friendliness, sociability, loyalty—[are] associated with longer and more serious participation in activities labeled 'antisocial.' " [12]

There is considerable speculation, then, that relations with peers, especially among delinquents, are sufficiently strong to produce marked attitudinal and behavioral changes. What changes can be expected from attachment to peers? On the basis of survey data, James C. Coleman suggests that attachment to peers may weaken ties to parents (and thus contribute to delinquency): "Our adolescents today are cut off, probably more than ever be-

[9] Richard R. Korn and Lloyd W. McCorkle, *Criminology and Penology* (New York: Holt, 1959), p. 352.

[10] William C. Kvaraceus and Walter B. Miller, *Delinquent Behavior: Culture and the Individual* (Washington: National Education Association, 1959), p. 69.

[11] Albert K. Cohen, *Delinquent Boys* (New York: The Free Press, 1955), pp. 31 and 101. Cohen has since changed his mind, agreeing that "the solidarity of the gang is not very impressive." See Albert K. Cohen and James F. Short, Jr., "Juvenile Delinquency," *Contemporary Social Problems*, ed. Robert K. Merton and Robert A. Nisbet, 2nd ed. (New York: Harcourt, Brace and World, 1966), p. 118. Cohen and Short also drop the assertion that a theory of delinquency must explain the phenomenon as a consequence of "positively defined delinquent cultural patterns" that *require* delinquency (1st ed. [1961], p. 106). They maintain allegiance, however, to the general propositions from which this assertion derives. For example, "Behavior Is Oriented to the Maintenance and Enhancement of Favorable Judgments from Our Status Reference Groups" (2nd ed., p. 109).

[12] Muzafer Sherif and Carolyn Sherif, *Reference Groups: Exploration into Conformity and Deviation of Adolescents* (New York: Harper and Row, 1964), p. 66.

fore, from the adult society. They are still oriented toward fulfill-
ing their parents' desires, but they look very much to their peers
for approval as well. Consequently, our society has within its midst
a set of small teen-age societies, which focus teen-age interests and
attitudes on things far removed from adult responsibilities, and
which may develop standards that lead away from those goals
established by the larger society." [13]

Cohen suggests a second consequence of attachment to peers.
Such attachment is incompatible with the pursuit of long-range
goals. The "corner boy," being strongly attached to his peers, neglects personal success. The evidence Cohen cites for this contention was collected using the technique employed by Coleman, the
forced-choice question: "This [survey] question . . . involves
. . . the corner-boy emphasis on primary-group solidarity and loyalty *versus* the college-boy emphasis on personal advancement.
Thirty-four percent of the middle-class boys, fifty-one percent of
the working-class boys chose to 'go along with the rest of the
club.' " [14]

Several testable hypotheses are implicit and explicit in the
statements of those upholding the view that attachment to peers
precedes and produces the attitudes and values that lead eventually to delinquency. Consistent with this view is the hypothesis
that *delinquents are as strongly or more strongly attached to their
peers than nondelinquents.* The examples cited produce two additional hypotheses testable with the present data: *the stronger the
attachment to peers, the weaker the attachment to parents*; and,
*the stronger the attachment to peers, the weaker the commitment
to individualistic success values.*

Taking the view that attachment to others is conducive to
conformity to conventional norms, control theorists advance hypotheses opposite to these. The lack of attachment to others and
the absence of commitment to individualistic success values lead
to association with delinquents (that is, with others similarly lacking in attachment and commitment). Since delinquents are less

[13] James C. Coleman, *The Adolescent Society* (New York: The Free Press,
1961), p. 9. Cohen takes the view that attachment to the gang is both consequence and cause of the breakdown of attachment to parents (*Delinquent
Boys*, pp. 31–32, 153–154).
[14] *Ibid.*, p. 107. In the hypothetical case cited, the boy was forced to
choose between a trip with the boys and books and tools necessary in studying to be an electrician.

strongly attached to conventional adults than nondelinquents, they are less likely to be attached to each other. One of the clearest statements of this view is provided by Lewis Yablonsky: "The youth most susceptible to violent-gang membership emerges from a social milieu that trains him inadequately for assuming constructive social roles. In fact, the defective socialization process to which he is subjected in the disorganized slum fosters a lack of social 'feelings.' At hardly any point is he trained to have human feelings of compassion or responsibility for another." [15]

It seems reasonable to conclude that persons whose social relations are cold and brittle, whose social skills are severely limited,[16] are incapable of influencing each other in the manner suggested by those who see the peer group as the decisive factor in delinquency. As Jack L. Roach and Orville R. Gursslin have said about cultural deviance explanations of lower-class social disorganization: "On theoretical ground it seems implausible to assume that social actors who have cognitive restrictions, a deficient self-system, and a limited role repertory, possess the requisite attributes for the elaboration of intricate cultural and social patterns." [17]

Attachment to Peers and Parents

Let us begin by examining the assertion that boys who like their friends, who are "oriented toward" and attached to them, are less likely to feel the same way about their parents.

The data upon which Coleman bases his conclusion that concern for the opinion of peers may be conducive to delinquency because it implies estrangement from parents and receptivity to unconventional values are open to other interpretations. He concludes, for example, that "the elites in [the sample] are not closer to their parents than are the students as a whole, but are pulled slightly farther from parents, closer to fellow adolescents as a

[15] Lewis Yablonsky, *The Violent Gang* (New York: Macmillan, 1963), p. 196.

[16] For a discussion of the "social disability" of gang boys and a view of their relations to each other similar to Yablonsky's, see James F. Short, Jr., and Fred L. Strodtbeck, *Group Process and Gang Delinquency* (Chicago: University of Chicago Press, 1965), Chapter 10; and Robert A. Gordon, "Social Level, Social Disability, and Gang Interaction," *American Journal of Sociology*, LXXIII (1967), 42–62.

[17] Jack L. Roach and Orville R. Gursslin, "The Lower Class, Status Frustration, and Social Disorganization," *Social Forces*, XLIII (1965), 507.

source of approval and disapproval" [18] on the basis of a finding that elites are less likely to choose "parents' disapproval" as a source of concern from a list that includes "teachers' disapproval" and "friends' disapproval." Coleman neglects the possibility that those who choose peers over parents may very well have closer relations with their parents than those who choose parents over peers (as his data in fact hint). In no case is the inference that "the pulls [between parents and peers] are extremely strong" warranted by the data Coleman presents.

Table 41 / Attachment to Mother by Attachment to Friends (in percent)

"Would you like to be the kind of person your mother is?"	"Would you like to be the kind of person your best friends are?"		
	In Most Ways	In a Few Ways	Not at All
In every or most ways	47	23	18
In some ways	31	41	29
In a few ways	12	23	26
Not at all	10	14	28
Totals	100 (330)	101 (710)	101 (152)

The methodological model that produces "findings" like Coleman's has theoretical counterparts in all areas of sociology. Affection, like time and energy, is assumed to be inherently limited. Thus, if middle-class boys are more likely than lower-class boys to choose material rather than friendship values when they are given a choice ("pick one"), then it seems to follow that middle-class boys place less value on friendship than lower-class boys. Or, as in Coleman's procedure, love of peers must imply lack of love for parents.

But does it? The most meaningful way of answering this question is to relate measures of attachment to parents to measures of attachment to friends. Fortunately, the item used earlier as a central measure of attachment to parents ("Would you like to be the kind of person your mother [father] is?") was also asked with respect to best friends. The relation between these measures of attachment is shown in Table 41. According to these measures, the

[18] *Adolescent Society*, p. 6.

idea that children closely tied to their friends are less likely to be closely tied to their parents is false. On the contrary, children attached to their peers are *more* likely to be attached to their parents. The relation is in the opposite direction from that implied by forcing the child to choose between his peers and his parents.

If the technique Coleman uses is taken as the starting point for answering questions about the relative importance of peers and parents, we compare those *apparently* oriented toward peers with those *apparently* oriented toward parents with respect to attachment to parents. A questionnaire item, "What would be the *worst* thing about getting caught for stealing?," like Coleman's items, forced a choice between the unfavorable reactions of parents and those of friends. The relation between this choice and identification with the mother is shown in Table 42.

Table 42 / Identification with the Mother by Source of Greater Concern in Being Caught for Stealing (in percent)

"Would you like to be the kind of person your mother is?"	"Worst thing about getting caught for stealing"	
	Parents' Reaction	Friends' Reaction
In every or most ways	29	29
In some ways	36	37
In a few ways	20	21
Not at all	15	13
Totals	100	100
	(607)	(282)

In this case, those choosing the reactions of friends as the worst thing about being caught for stealing are as likely to be attached to their mother as those choosing parental reaction as the direst consequence of detected theft. By both counts, then, the conclusion that attachment to peers implies lack of attachment to parents is not justified.

Attachment to Peers and Individualistic Goal Striving

Another way in which close ties to peers are thought to lead at least indirectly to delinquency involves the assumption that such ties are in some way incompatible with an emphasis on personal advancement. In this view (as was true with respect to ties to parents), it is tacitly assumed that success comes to the cold, hard-driving man who is unplagued by sentimental attachments to other persons. The precondition and price of success is loneliness; the unsuccessful are compensated by warm, intimate relations with their families and peers.

An index of achievement motivation, discussed more fully in the following chapter, was used in testing these ideas. It was constructed from the following items: "How important is getting good grades to you personally?" "Whatever I do, I try hard." And, "I try hard in school." Table 43 shows the relation between this index and a measure of attachment to peers.

Table 43 / Achievement Motivation by Attachment to Peers [a]
(in percent)

Index of Achievement Motivation	"Would you like to be the kind of person your best friends are?"		
	In Most Ways	In a Few Ways	Not at All
High	47	30	25
Medium	35	46	35
Low	18	24	40
Totals	100	100	100
	(314)	(673)	(142)

[a] The item "Do you respect your best friends' opinions about the important things in life?" is related in about the same manner as the above item to the index of achievement motivation.

Again, these data are *not* consistent with the picture painted by many delinquency theorists. "Full and intimate participation in a close-knit primary group" [19] may indeed provide substitute satisfaction for working-class boys not likely to achieve social mobility, but it appears that the conventional value system sullies even this source of satisfaction, since the friends of those not conforming to the conventional pattern, like the nonconformer himself, fall short of the ideal posed by this pattern.

Thus far the evidence is clear that attachment to peers does

[19] See Cohen, *Delinquent Boys*, pp. 101–109.

not produce attitudes and values conducive to delinquency. On the contrary, those attached to their peers are less likely to have the attitudes and values traditionally used to account for the presumed relation between attachment to peers and delinquency. If lack of attachment to parents and lack of achievement motivation are conducive to delinquency (as they in fact are), then the hypothesis that attachment to adolescent friends is conducive to delinquency is difficult to justify on theoretical grounds.

Attachment to Peers and Delinquency

If the previous findings undercut the theoretical rationale for believing that the personal relations of delinquents are unusually warm, Table 44 shows there is no empirical justification for this belief. As was true for parents and teachers, those most closely attached to or respectful of their friends are least likely to have committed delinquent acts. The relation does not appear to be as strong as was the case for parents and for teachers (see pp. 92 and 123), but the ideas that delinquents are unusually dependent upon their peers, that loyalty and solidarity are characteristic of delinquent groups, that attachment to adolescent peers fosters nonconventional behavior, and that the delinquent is unusually likely to sacrifice his personal advantage to the "requirements of the group" are simpy not supported by the data.

This conclusion may appear to give a great deal of weight to one empirical relation. Let us therefore examine the data from several points of view. As was suggested in Chapter IV, defining delinquency by the number of acts the child has committed is not deemed appropriate by advocates of delinquent subculture theories. To many of these theorists, the delinquent is a person assuming a delinquent role. Presumably, then, he sees himself and is seen by others as a delinquent. It could be that persons assuming a delinquent role have the characteristics ascribed to them by theorists using a role definition of delinquency and that the measure I have used to this point is irrelevant to a test of such theories.

The questionnaire item, "Do you ever think of yourself as a delinquent?," appears to have face validity as a measure of the assumption of a delinquent role. Insofar as delinquency is a well-defined social role, occupants of this role should be expected to

Table 44 / Self-Reported Delinquent Acts by Identification
with Best Friends
(in percent)

Self-Reported Acts	"Would you like to be the kind of person your best friends are?"		
	In Most Ways	In a Few Ways	Not at All
None	64	54	47
One	21	26	26
Two or more	15	19	27
Totals	100	99	100
	(353)	(748)	(160)

know that they are delinquents and what this entails in the way of
"appropriate" behavior. This item may also lay claim to other
forms of validity, as Table 45 shows.

As would be expected from role or self-concept theory, the
boy who has committed delinquent acts and/or whose attitudes
are "appropriate" to a delinquent is more likely to see himself as a
delinquent. Using this measure of delinquency and an alternative
measure of respect for peers, we obtain results much like those
shown in Table 44: the less the boy respects the opinions of his
friends, the more likely he is to think of himself as a delinquent
(Table 46). Looked at in another way, Table 46 shows that 60
percent of the 55 boys who "often" or "all the time" see themselves as delinquent have little or no respect for the opinions of
their best friends, while only 31 percent of the 716 boys who never

Table 45 / Correlations Between "Do You Ever Think of
Yourself as a Delinquent?" and Selected Variables

Item	Correlation [a]
"Does anyone else ever think of you as a delinquent?"	.60
Self-report index of delinquency	.35
Recent official delinquent acts	.18
"Have you ever stayed away from school just because you had other things you wanted to do?"	.27
"Being sent to juvenile court would bother me a lot."	.27

[a] The number of cases upon which the correlations are based is not less
than 1,478.

see themselves as delinquent have friends whose opinions are not considered worthy of respect.

Although unlikely, it is possible that among boys who see themselves as delinquent and whose friends are also delinquent the trends observable in the tables presented thus far do not hold. That is to say, *gang* delinquents may be highly attached to their friends even though in general as delinquent activity increases attachment to friends declines. Therefore, I shall isolate those boys in the sample most likely to be members of gangs and examine their attitudes toward their friends.

Table 46 / Self-Perceived Delinquency and Attachment to Peers
(in percent)

"Do you ever think of your-self as a delinquent?"	"Do you respect your best friends' opinions about the important things in life?" [a]			
	Completely	Pretty Much	A Little	Not at All
Never	75	58	49	52
Once in a while	22	39	43	33
Often	1	2	5	8
All the time	1	1	1	5
Don't know what the word means	1	1	2	2
Totals	100 (140)	101 (670)	100 (394)	100 (60)

[a] Twelve boys who report having no best friends are omitted from the table.

One direct measure of the delinquency of friends is available on the questionnaire: "Have any of your close friends ever been picked up by the police?" If there are members of delinquent gangs in the present sample, they should be concentrated among those who are themselves delinquent and whose friends have been picked up by the police. In attempting to test the hypothesis that *within* the delinquent gang relations between peers are somehow closer than among delinquents in general, I used two separate measures of ego's delinquency: the self-concept measure discussed earlier and the item "Have you ever been picked up by the police?" (largely on the grounds that the wording is identical to the "close friends" item). In both cases, the following typology results:

Type 1. Member of Delinquent Gang. Both the student and his close friends are delinquent.

Type 2. Evil Companions. The student is nondelinquent; his close friends are delinquent.

Type 3. Bad Apple. The student is delinquent; his close friends are not.

Type 4. Good Boy. Both the student and his close friends are nondelinquent.

In both cases, too, the results are similar (Table 47).

A person's opinions of other persons will often reflect his own characteristics as well as those of the persons he is evaluating. Nevertheless, in this case, the hypothesis that the raters are applying standard criteria to friends who differ in the extent to which they measure up to these criteria could account for all the differences in the columns of Table 47. The delinquent with no delinquent friends is as likely to respect his friends' opinions as is the nondelinquent with no delinquent friends (comparing the "Bad Apples" with the "Good Boys"). And, the fact that the boy with "Evil Companions" is more likely than the "Gang Member" to respect his delinquent friends *could* result from the fact that his friends are actually "less delinquent" than the friends of the "Gang Member." However, since there is no way with the present data to remove the residual variation in the delinquency of friends, we must conclude that the more delinquent the child *and* the more delinquent his friends, the less likely he is to feel that his friends are worthy of respect.

Since it is unreasonable to suggest, as does Table 47, that about 30 percent of the boys in the sample belong to delinquent gangs, let us look only at the 41 boys who "often" or "always" think of themselves as delinquent and who have had close friends picked up by the police.[20] In this group, which should have a very heavy concentration of gang boys, if there are any in the sample, 66 percent report having little or no respect for the opinions of their best friends. The trend in Table 47 continues. There is no

---

[20] Only 6 boys in the sample who report having no close friends picked up by the police "often" or "always" think of themselves as delinquent.

Table 47 / Percent Having Little or No Respect for the
Opinions of Close Friends by Delinquent Gang Typology

	Measure of Student's Delinquency	
Gang Type	Picked Up by Police	Sees Self as Delinquent [a]
Delinquent gang	48 (303)	52 (293)
Evil companions	41 (217)	36 (222)
Bad apple	24 (50)	25 (138)
Good boy	25 (456)	25 (363)

[a] At least "once in a while." Friends are considered delinquent in this table
if any have been picked up by the police.

sudden reversal as we approach the group upon which sociological
theory has traditionally focused.

Yet another approach to the importance of attachment to
peers in the control or causation of delinquency is provided by the
question, "What would be the *worst* thing about being caught for
stealing?" Two of the responses available to the students were:
"Your parents would be angry" and "Your friends would look
down on you." This version of the forced-choice method suggests
that attachment to peers is more important as a *deterrent* of delinquency than is attachment to parents, since those concerned about
their friends' reaction are less likely to commit delinquent acts
than those concerned about the reaction of parents (Table 48).

As is apparent in the total row of Table 48, the students are
more likely to worry about the reactions of their parents than of
their friends by a ratio of more than two to one. Even so, those
worried about peer reactions are less likely to have committed
delinquent acts. An explanation is suggested by separate analysis:
while children oriented toward their friends are as likely to have
favorable attitudes toward parents as children "preferring" parents
over peers, the converse is not true. Children preferring parents to
peers are not as likely to have favorable attitudes toward peers as
children preferring peers to parents. In other words, children worried about the reactions of their peers tend to have two sources of
concern, while those worried first about their parents' reaction
tend to have only one.

Table 48 / Self-Reported Delinquent Acts by Worst Thing
About Getting Caught for Stealing
(in percent)

	"Worst thing about get- ting caught" [a]	
Self-Reported Acts	Parents' Reaction	Friends' Reaction
None	50	60
One	29	26
Two or more	21	14
Totals	100	100
	(643)	(300)

[a] Options not shown in the table are "The police might not treat you right" and "Don't know." Forty-three students checked "police," and 284 checked "Don't know."

As I have suggested earlier, forced-choice items of this type are potentially misleading insofar as they give rise to statements about the relative importance of significant others in the prevention of delinquency. As Table 49 shows, the potential reactions of friends act as a deterrent largely when the friends themselves are law-abiding. The worst that can happen to *some* boys is that they incur the displeasure of friends who have themselves been in trouble with the law. When this is so, the chances that they will commit delinquent acts are high indeed.

Table 49 / Percent Committing One or More Delinquent
Acts Among Those Whose Friends' Reaction Would be
the Worst Thing About Getting Caught for Stealing,
by Number of Friends Picked Up by the Police

Number of Friends Picked Up			
None	One	Two–Three	Four or More
28	32	50	80
(132)	(47)	(26)	(40)

The imagery evoked by contemplation of a criminal act and its possible consequences has been little studied. For present purposes it is enough to show that "the worst that can happen" is contingent upon the respect one has for those whose ill-opinion is most feared. Among those more concerned with their friends' than their parents' opinion, the frequency of delinquent acts rises sharply as respect for this opinion declines: 23 percent of those whose respect for their friends' opinion is "complete" and 56 percent of those who have "little or no" respect for their friends' opinion have committed delinquent acts. Among those concerned first with the opinions of parents, the same trend is observable. And this, of course, is in one sense the basic argument of all that has been said before.

Table 50 / Average Number of Self-Reported Delinquent Acts by Number of Delinquent Friends and Identification with Friends

"Like to be like best friends?"	Number of Close Friends Picked Up by Police		
	None	One–Two	Three or More
In most ways	.33 (215)	.82 (72)	1.56 (54)
In a few ways	.41 (325)	.88 (183)	1.63 (195)
Not at all	.51 (59)	.78 (42)	1.82 (59)

Sutherland, it will be recalled, states that crime is more likely the more intense the association with criminals. "Intensity," he says, "has to do with such things as the prestige of the source of a criminal or anti-criminal pattern and with emotional reactions related to the associations." [21] These data suggest the opposite conclusion. In a study designed to test Sutherland's theory, Short measures the intensity of association with delinquents by asking the question, "Have any of your *best* friends been juvenile delinquents while they were your best friends?" [22] He found a correlation of .58 between this item and the criterion. Although Short's item undoubtedly taps aspects of intensity as it is defined by Sutherland, it leaves the distinct impression that the warmer one's relations with one's delinquent friends, the more likely one is to be delinquent. And this is the impression that the present data seem to contradict.

Let us test directly the hypothesis emerging from control theory and apparently, although thus far indirectly, supported by the

[21] Sutherland and Cressey, *Principles of Criminology*, p. 82.

[22] James F. Short, Jr., "Differential Association and Delinquency," *Social Problem*, IV (1957), 233–239.

data: given that one associates with "criminals," the *less intense* one's associations with them, the *more likely* one is to commit criminal acts. The relevant data are presented in Table 50. The hypothesis is confirmed. The more a boy respects his delinquent associates the less likely he is to commit delinquent acts. This hypothesis is not inconsistent with Short's findings. Table 50 in fact replicates Short's findings and confirms the hypothesis.

Is not this conclusion self-contradictory? Can we really say that the more a boy admires or respects his delinquent friends, the less likely he is to be delinquent himself? There are several ways out of this implausible situation. We could, for example, assume that those who least respect their friends have friends least worthy of respect (assuming the application of conventional standards, an assumption made reasonable by previous data [see especially Table 47]). Given this assumption, the difficulty disappears: the operative variable is delinquency of friends; attachment to friends is irrelevant. But this would be dodging the issue. We assert that, holding delinquency (or worthiness) of friends truly constant at any level, the more one respects or admires one's friends, the less likely one is to commit delinquent acts. We honor those we admire not by imitation, but by adherence to conventional standards (see also Table 23).

Peers, Stakes in Conformity, and Delinquency

Let us return now to the significance of these findings for the question of the causal ordering among stakes in conformity, delinquency of companions, and delinquency. In its pure, if extreme, form, the causal model of these relations stemming from control theory would be that shown in Figure 1.

A second model, and the one to which we have thus far devoted greatest attention, begins with membership in a peer group or delinquent gang and suggests that such membership affects attitudes toward conventional persons and institutions and is of course conducive to delinquency in its own right. This model is represented in Figure 2.

The models represented by figures 1 and 2 differ in two ways.

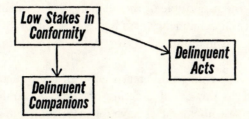

Figure 1. Hypothesized relations among stakes in conformity, delinquency of companions, and delinquent acts (derived from social control theory).

First, in the "adolescent culture" model delinquency of companions has a direct (causal) effect on the commission of delinquent acts, while in the "control" model the relation between delinquent acts and delinquency of companions is spurious. Second, the causal ordering of stakes in conformity and delinquency of companions is reversed from one model to the other: in the control model low

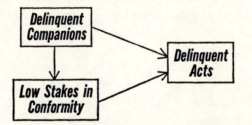

Figure 2. Hypothesized relations among stakes in conformity, delinquency of companions, and delinquent acts (derived from adolescent culture and delinquent subculture theories).

stakes in conformity lead to the acquisition of delinquent friends; in the adolescent culture model delinquent friends reduce one's stake in conformity. We should at this point modify the control model to take into consideration what we have learned from the data. As Hanan C. Selvin and I have suggested with respect to the Gluecks' findings: "Given the magnitude of the relations between delinquency and delinquent companions reported in the Gluecks study, . . . it is unlikely that they could show this relation to be spurious." [23] And the same considerations apply to the present

---

[23] Hirschi and Selvin, Delinquency Research, p. 70.

data. Given the magnitude of the relation between delinquency of companions and delinquency, it is highly unlikely that this relation will disappear when the effects of stakes in conformity are removed.

The only remaining difference between these theories is thus with respect to the causal ordering of stakes in conformity and delinquency of companions. I have for this reason compared assertions stemming from these divergent theoretical traditions about the consequences of peer group membership and about the quality of interpersonal relations within the delinquent gang. The evidence favors the causal ordering assumed by the control theory. The direction of the observed relations is in all cases opposite to that predicted by adolescent and delinquent subculture theories. Attachment to peers does not foster alienation from conventional persons and institutions; it if anything fosters commitment to them. There is no foundation for the belief that the delinquent gang is an intensely solidary group comprising "the most fit and able youngsters in their community." On the contrary, those committing delinquent acts are not likely to think much of each other; distrust and suspicion, not intense solidarity, are the foundations of the delinquent gang.

These data reduce the plausibility of the contention that associations with peers produce the attitudes and values that, in turn, produce delinquency. The directions of the relations between attachment to peers and stakes in conformity are opposite to those that would obtain if such attachments reduced one's stake in conformity. The directions of these relations are those that would obtain if the absence of stakes in conformity led to association with boys similarly lacking in stakes in conformity. If the low-stake boy's attitudes and values are consistent with those of his friends, and the high-stake boy's are relatively free of peer influence, then it is necessary to argue, contrary to well-established principles, that the less the person respects his associates, the more heavily he will be influenced by them.

If it is granted that the revised social control model (Figure 1, adding an arrow from delinquent companions to delinquent acts) fits the data to this point better than the adolescent culture model (Figure 2), we must ask how this model differs from that to be derived from cultural deviance theory. The clearest statements of the relations among these three classes of variables are probably those of Sutherland and Cressey. For example: "Probably delinquency and crime are related to the school in much the same way they are related to family conditions, namely through the effects which school activities have on the students' associations with delinquent and anti-delinquent behavior patterns." [24] In the pure cultural deviance theory, then, birds do not have feathers: they merely take up with those in nearest proximity to them. Attitudes toward the family and the school affect delinquency only insofar as they affect one's exposure to delinquent patterns—that is, to delinquents. Figure 3 shows the model derived from this theory.

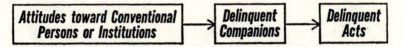

Figure 3. Hypothesized relations among attitudes toward conventional institutions, delinquency of companions, and delinquent acts (derived from Sutherland and Cressey). The empirical variables included under "Conventional Persons or Institutions" are of course the same variables included under "Stakes in Conformity" in the control theory. Since they have no direct relevance to crime in the cultural deviance theory, they should not be labeled "stake" items or "unfavorable" attitudes. They are, under the terms of the theory, morally neutral.

The models represented by figures 1 and 3 differ only in that Figure 1 suggests a direct effect on delinquency of attitudes toward conventional institutions that is denied by Figure 3. In Table 51 I examine the simultaneous effects of stakes in conformity and delinquency of companions on delinquent behavior. The stake items were chosen to represent attachment to parents, attachment to the school, and commitment to conventional achievement. Only one of the stake items, "It is none of the school's business if the student wants to smoke outside the classroom," is not in the terms of the differential association theory morally neutral.

All of the stake items in Table 51 are related to delinquency regardless of the delinquency of one's companions; delinquency of

24 Principles of Criminology, p. 250.

Table 51 / Self-Reported Delinquent Acts and Number of
Delinquent Friends with the Effects of Selected Stakes in
Conformity Removed

| Variable | Marginal Relations | | Partial Regression Coefficients | |
	Sample Number	Average No. Del. Acts (R)	Raw	Normalized
Number of delinquent friends				.27
None	486	.41	−.26	−.11
One	138	.77	−.03	−.01
Two	92	.90	+.09	+.02
Three	53	1.38	+.41	+.08
Four or more	169	1.64	+.57	+.18
Likes school		−.31	−.33	−.16
Agrees none of school's business if student smokes		+.28	+.08	+.10
Close communication with father [a]		−.25	−.14	−.13
High achievement orientation [b]		−.30	−.09	−.12
Age		+.07	−.03	−.04
(R = .50)	938	.79		

[a] Index of intimacy of communication with father is discussed in Chapter
VI, page 93.
[b] Index of achievement orientation is discussed in Chapter IX, page 179.

companions is strongly related to delinquency regardless of stakes
in conformity. The model stemming from control theory is thus
consistent with these data. Boys with low stakes in conformity are
more likely to have delinquent friends (see Table 52), and both
delinquency of companions and stakes in conformity are independently related to the commission of delinquent acts.

The model derived from differential association theory fails to
predict and is incapable of accounting for the relation between
stakes in conformity and delinquency that survives control for
exposure to "criminogenic influences." My interpretation of this
theory is, I think, fair. Sutherland and Cressey, and other members
of this school, repeatedly deny direct causal significance to the
variables here used to represent stakes in conformity. If there is
injustice in the representation of the theories, it enters with the

conclusion that the social control theory leaves something out. In its strong forms, social control theory is as much falsified by these data as is the cultural deviance theory: there is an effect of delinquent gang membership much beyond that suggested by the "birds-of-a-feather" proverb.

It appears, then, that "good" boys with delinquent friends are more likely to commit delinquent acts than are boys with an equivalent stake in conformity but without delinquent friends, and that "bad" boys are less likely to commit delinquent acts if their friends are law-abiding than are equally "bad" boys with delinquent friends. Control theory has no difficulty with the "bad" boys: attachment to conventional peers, like attachment to conventional adults, should reduce delinquency. The difficulty is in trying to explain the impact of delinquent friends on the boy with high stakes in conformity: to account for the commission of delinquent acts in spite of strong stakes in conformity, one must presumably introduce or posit unusual motivation. Since delinquent friends are, according to argument and data presented earlier, unlikely to exert such influence, they have in effect been eliminated as a source of motivation to delinquency capable of accounting for the delinquent acts of high-stake boys.

Before modifying the theory to account for the impact of delinquent friends on high-stake boys, let us determine whether such an explanation is required by the data. We do this by examining the effects of delinquency of friends among those with high and among those with low stakes, as in Table 52.

Table 52 somewhat reduces the friction between the theory and the data. Boys with high stakes in conformity are unlikely to have delinquent friends. (Twenty-two percent of those with the highest stakes in conformity have had friends picked up by the police, while 58 percent of those with the lowest stakes have had friends picked up.) Furthermore, the greater the stake in conformity, the less the impact of delinquent friends. (The number of high-stake boys with many delinquent friends is very small. However, if the four highest-stake categories were collapsed, the conclusion—based on a seemingly adequate number of cases—would remain.)

As is true in any case of interaction, the statement that the impact of delinquent friends depends on stakes in conformity implies a corollary statement: the greater the number of delinquent friends, the greater the impact of stakes in conformity. The low-stake boy with no delinquent friends is more likely to have committed delinquent acts than the high-stake boy with no delinquent friends, but the low-stake boy is *much more likely* than the high-stake boy to have committed delinquent acts when they both have several delinquent friends.

Table 52 / Average Number of Self-Reported Delinquent Acts by Stake in Conformity and Number of Delinquent Friends

Friends Picked Up by Police	Stake in Conformity [a]							
	Low 0	1	2	3	4	5	6	High 7
None	.68	.23	.48	.41	.28	.41	.26	.21
	(114)	(34)	(40)	(70)	(25)	(59)	(65)	(80)
One–two	1.20	1.04	.84	.76	.73	.56	.31	.31
	(55)	(37)	(22)	(42)	(14)	(27)	(20)	(13)
Three or more	2.20	1.55	1.06	1.09	.76	.70	.33	.58
	(100)	(30)	(17)	(39)	(4)	(17)	(6)	(9)

[a] The stake in conformity index was constructed by dichotomizing three items: "Do you like school?"; index of achievement orientation; and index of intimacy of communication with father. The ordering in the table was obtained by weighting the items in the order listed.

Findings like these have before been reported in the literature on delinquency. The McCords report that in the good neighborhood the cohesiveness of the home has little effect on delinquency; that among those from cohesive homes the neighborhood has no effect on the proportion convicted of crimes. When the home is noncohesive *and* the neighborhood poor (that is, "contains a delinquent subculture"), the proportion convicted of crimes is very high.[25] Likewise, Erdman B. Palmore and Phillip E. Hammond show that what they call measures of *legitimate* and *illegitimate* opportunity interact in their effects on delinquency.[26]

[25]William McCord and Joan McCord, *Origins of Crime* (New York: Columbia University Press, 1959), p. 86.
[26]Erdman B. Palmore and Phillip E. Hammond, "Interacting Factors in Juvenile Delinquency," *American Sociological Review*, XXIX (1964), 848–854. As conceptualized by Palmore and Hammond, legitimate opportunities would be equivalent to what are here called stakes in conformity, and illegitimate opportunities would be equivalent to "criminogenic influences."

Conclusion

It is hard to disagree with Bordua that "the key theoretical problem in the literature on lower-class, urban, male delinquency [is] the problem of the relationship of personal characteristics and associational patterns." [27] In fact, there is no reason why we cannot say that "how much feathering precedes how much flocking" is the key theoretical problem in the field of delinquency.

Our theory (and research procedure) has led us to emphasize feathering rather than flocking. We began this chapter, in fact, by pushing our theory to its extreme and denying significance to friendship patterns. In the face of data obviously to the contrary, we backed into the position that both sets of variables are important and both theoretical traditions are wrong insofar as they deny validity to each other. A wise man could have predicted this outcome. But we are not seeking such wisdom. Let us, then, look again at what the data in this chapter, and elsewhere, have to say about the interplay between personal characteristics and associational patterns in the causation of delinquency.

First, contrary to subculture theories and "countless mothers," the gang only rarely recruits "good" boys and, when it does manage to recruit them, only rarely induces them to commit delinquent acts.[28] There is a very strong tendency for boys to have friends whose activities are congruent with their own attitudes. Boys with a large stake in conformity are unlikely to have delinquent friends, and even when a boy with a large stake in conformity does have delinquent friends, the chance that he will commit delinquent acts is relatively low. In my judgment, the evidence strongly supports the view that the boy's stake in conformity affects his choice of friends rather than the other way around.

Second, the idea that delinquents have comparatively warm, intimate social relations with each other (or with anyone) is a romantic myth. Others have focused exclusively or directly on this issue, with the same results.[29] And this is not, I think, a case of

[27] David J. Bordua, "Some Comments on Theories of Group Delinquency," *Sociological Inquiry*, XXXII (1962), 258.
[28] Cf. Cohen, *Delinquent Boys*, pp. 135–136.
[29] Edward Rothstein, "Attributes Related to High Social Status: A Comparison of the Perceptions of Delinquent and Non-Delinquent Boys," *Social*

contradictory results from research with equal claim to validity. The "evidence" for the cohesiveness of delinquents is in many cases simply an assertion on the part of the investigator. In other cases, it is an inference from hard but ultimately irrelevant data. (We are here defining cohesiveness as mutual attraction or respect. If cohesiveness is defined by the frequency or duration of interaction among group members, the "cohesiveness" of the delinquent gang is no doubt often impressive.) [30]

The link between cohesiveness and the commission of delinquent acts is a critical theoretical and empirical issue. The fact that delinquent gangs are not cohesive is consistent with the finding that the less cohesive the gang, the greater its involvement in delinquency.[31] Yet this does not end the matter. There is built-in tension between such facts and "flocking" theories in general, where, as we have seen, "cohesiveness" tends to be synonymous with "ability to influence" or, on the individual level, "be influenced." Although they present much evidence in favor of the view that the delinquent gang is not cohesive, Short and Strodtbeck report correlations indicating that gang boys who see themselves as loyal, polite, helpful, religious, and obedient, and *not* as mean, troublesome, tough, or cool, are *more likely* to engage in what they call conflict activities—individual fighting, group fighting, carrying concealed weapons, assault. They interpret these findings as indicating that such boys are "especially vulnerable to the group process." [32] Although the statement that gang boys who see themselves as kind, helpful, soft, and polite are more likely to carry weapons and to beat, kick, and scratch others has good claim to plausibility within the group-pressure tradition, the statement that boys who carry weapons and who beat, kick, and scratch others are more likely to see themselves as kind, helpful, soft, and polite has little claim to plausibility within any tradition, with the possible

Problems, X (1962), 75–83. See also Short and Strodtbeck, *Group Process,* pp. 243–244.

[30] Malcolm W. Klein and Lois Y. Crawford, "Groups, Gangs, and Cohesiveness," *Journal of Research in Crime and Delinquency,* IV (1967), 63–75. See also Chapter X, below.

[31] Short and Strodtbeck, *Group Process,* chapters 8 and 9; Leon R. Jansyn, Jr., "Solidarity and Delinquency in a Street Corner Group," *American Sociological Review,* XXXI (1966), 600–614. Solomon Kobrin, Joseph Puntil, and Emil Peluso, "Criteria of Status Among Street Groups," *Journal of Research in Crime and Delinquency,* IV (1967), 98–118. See also Table 50.

[32] *Group Process,* pp. 176–177.

exception of abnormal psychology. Yet if we accept the first statement we must also accept the second, since they are identical.

Should we accept the first statement? I see no reason why we
should not. In fact, in several respects the present data support the
findings of Short and Strodtbeck on this point. Among boys in the
present sample who are likely to be members of delinquent gangs,
those who see themselves as leaders and those who *disagree* with
the statement, "Sometimes I think I am no good at all," are more
likely to have committed assault than followers and those who
have doubts about their own goodness.

The issue for now is how such results should be interpreted.
Do we accept the gang boy's self-perceived virtues as real and build
an explanation of his behavior on them? Or do we question these
virtues and build our explanation of his behavior on the fact that
he holds such self-perceptions in the face of evidence to the contrary? The latter approach, it seems to me, is more likely to bear
fruit.[33]

If members of delinquent gangs tend to have in common a
low stake in conformity, if their relations with each other tend to
be cold and brittle, still the data presented here leave much room
for the operation of group processes in the production of delinquent acts. The boy with delinquent friends is unusually likely to
have committed delinquent acts, especially when his ties to conventional society are weak to begin with. In fact, the present findings, as well as those of past research on this topic, may be summarized as follows: (1) The child with little stake in conformity is
susceptible to prodelinquent influences in his environment; the
child with a large stake in conformity is relatively immune to these
influences. (2) The greater the exposure to "criminal influences,"
the greater the difference in delinquent activity between high- and
low-stake boys. Although these criminal influences are beyond the
reach of control theory, group-process theories are forced to work
with material supplied them by the weakening of social controls.

[33] See Robert A. Gordon, "Social Level," especially p. 52.

Chapter IX
Commitment to Conventional Lines of Action

Insofar as social control is inherent in the organization of a society, deviation automatically jeopardizes one's chances of success in that society.[1] In order for such a built-in system of regulation to be effective, actors in the system must perceive the connection between deviation and reward and must value the rewards society proposes to withhold as punishment for deviation. If, for any reason, a person loses his motivation to strive for conventional goals, he is to that extent free to commit deviant acts without "normal" concern for the consequences.

In this chapter, then, we examine those stakes in conformity that are built up by pursuit of, and by a desire to achieve, conventional goals. The stance toward aspirations taken here is virtually opposite to that taken in strain theories, where conventional aspirations are typically seen as a source of motivation to delinquency. Here, in contrast, such aspirations are viewed as constraints on delinquency, since it is assumed that rather than being a means of realizing conventional aspirations delinquency is, if anything, a means of precluding their attainment.

The adolescent may be located on three career lines, all of which are interrelated, all of which have different beginning points, and all of which are surrounded by conventional evaluations of appropriateness with respect to timing and by conventional evaluations of success or failure. These career lines are the educational, the occupational, and, for want of a better term, the passage to adult status.

[1] S. F. Nadel, "Social Control and Self-Regulation," *Social Forces*, XXXI (1953), 265–273.

The Passage to Adult Status

In the ideal case, the adolescent simultaneously completes his education, begins his occupational career, and acquires adult status. He is thus continuously bound to conformity by participation in a conventional game. However, given the age requirements of the occupational system, many adolescents in effect complete their education without at the same time being able to begin their occupational careers. Being no longer tied to an educational career, they become in one sense adults; yet, being free of an occupation, they remain in one sense children. Whatever the process advanced to explain the resulting changes, the adolescent caught in this situation tends to develop attitudes and behave in ways "appropriate" only to an adult;[2] his structural position at the same time guarantees him the freedom appropriate only to a child. The consequence is a high rate of delinquency.

Premature completion of an educational career implies many things, not the least important of which is the status of the occupation one will eventually enter. In contemporary American society, manual labor or a low-status white-collar occupation is the eventual fate of most of those not going on to higher education. The premature completion of an educational career is thus accompanied by delayed entrance into a low-status occupation. The adolescent caught in this situation should see the period between the two careers as one of relative ease and pleasure. He is free to enjoy some of the privileges of adulthood without being burdened by work and family responsibilities. This period is, as he sees it, and will always see it, the "happiest time of his life." As Table 53 shows, this brand of happiness goes hand in hand with delinquency: the adolescent who sees high school and the years immediately following as a period of relative happiness is most likely to commit delinquent acts during this period.

[2] For an explanation of the adoption of such adult attitudes and behavior in terms of the validation of self-identity, as well as for a good deal of data on the correlates of claims to adult status, see Arthur L. Stinchcombe, *Rebellion in a High School* (Chicago: Quadrangle, 1964), especially Chapter 5. See also Carl Werthman, "The Functions of Social Definitions in the Development of Delinquent Careers," *Juvenile Delinquency and Youth Crime*, The President's Commission on Law Enforcement and Administration of Justice (Washington: USGPO, 1967), pp. 159–166.

Table 53 / Self-Reported Delinquency by Happiest Period of Life
(in percent)

Self-Reported Acts	"What period of your life do you think will turn out to have been the happiest part of your life?"		
	Junior High School or Before	High School to Age Twenty	After Age Twenty
None	67	48	63
One	16	28	23
Two or more	16	23	14
Totals	99	99	100
	(103)	(516)	(554)

Although these data suggest difficulties with explanations of delinquency based on "acute discontent" or "extreme frustration," they do not necessarily mean that those who see the high school period as one of relative happiness are happier than those who see some other period of life as promising greater rewards; they do not mean that those committing delinquent acts are happier than those not committing them. On the contrary, those whose happiest days are in high school are probably less happy than those who look forward to better days.[3] These data do suggest, however, that adult privileges without adult responsibilities provide some compensation to those whose prospects are relatively bleak.

The adult activities presumably providing these compensations are, among others, smoking, drinking, dating, and driving.[4]

[3] As a somewhat casual test of this hypothesis, I examined the association between the period of expected greatest happiness and the students' liking of school. Those who expect their adult years to be the happiest are most likely to like school. By period of greatest expected happiness, the percentages liking school are: junior high, 37 (103); senior high to age twenty, 43 (519); after age twenty, 49 (557). I have no explanation for the fact that those who see their junior high and childhood years as the period of greatest happiness are also relatively unlikely to have committed delinquent acts. It is not that they are more likely to be in junior high school, since the relation shown in Table 53 holds when the effects of year in school are removed.

[4] Sometimes referred to as the "automobile-alcohol-sex combination" and used largely to explain middle-class delinquency. See Ralph W. England, Jr., "A Theory of Middle Class Juvenile Delinquency," Journal of Criminal Law, Criminology and Police Science, L (1960), 535-540. England assumes that middle-class children have a "typically lengthened period of ambiguous status compared with working class youngsters" because they begin working later.

Students who expect little formal education are more likely to engage in these practices (Table 54). These "adult" activities, then, are at least in part indicative of lack of commitment to the educational system; they reflect the fact that adulthood has been prematurely obtained—or claimed—by the adolescent. He engages in these activities to validate his claims to adulthood, claims originating in "completion" of his educational career.

Table 54 / Percent Smoking, Drinking, and Dating
by Expected Education

Education Expected	Smokes	Drinks	Dates [a]
Less than college	40 (212)	37 (212)	17 (212)
Some college	28 (353)	33 (353)	7 (353)
College graduation	13 (641)	16 (641)	5 (641)

[a] Twice a week or more.

What are the links between adult activities such as smoking, drinking, driving, and dating, and the commission of delinquent acts? The "adult status" perspective suggests these relations are spurious: because the student has lost his commitment to education, he feels required to demonstrate his adulthood and is at the same time free to commit delinquent acts. Expression of claims to adult status and delinquency thus have the same causes.

There are serious difficulties with this view, the most important of which is that claims to adult status are more strongly related to delinquency than are commitments to the educational system.[5] If a presumed causal variable is less strongly related to delinquency than one of its side effects, the relation between the "side effect" and delinquency cannot be shown to be spurious by holding the causal variable constant.

The alternative is to argue that lack of commitment to education leads to expression of claims to adult status, which in turn leads to delinquency. This causal configuration may be more con-

Stinchcombe's data (Rebellion, Chapter 5) suggest, at least for adolescents in school, that the reverse is true, since the lower-class child in school is engaged in an activity that is likely to be irrelevant to his future. In any case, the important differences with respect to ambiguity of status stem from differential commitment to education and the social class distinction is artificial and misleading.

[5] Stinchcombe, ibid., p. 130.

sistent with the data, but has problems of its own: claims to adult status are expressed in *behavior* such as smoking, drinking, dating. Specification of the links between these acts and delinquency is difficult, since we no longer accept the idea that they—at least drinking and smoking—can be causes of delinquency.[6] One possibility remains: claims to adult status may be seen as an *orientation* toward adult activities which may or may not be expressed in actual indulgence in these activities. If the child claims the *right* to smoke, drink, date, and drive a car, he is more likely to commit delinquent acts, and the link between this orientation and the commission of delinquent acts is explicable within the context of a control theory. To claim the right to act contrary to the wishes of adults is to express contempt for "their" expectations, which, as we have repeatedly stressed, is to free oneself for the commission of delinquent acts.

Table 55 provides evidence that whether smoking is taken as equivalent in etiological significance to the tattoo, as a starting point for the development of a delinquent self-image, or as an indicator of premature claims to adult status, it is a potent predictor of delinquent activity, and the earlier it is begun the more likely the child is to commit delinquent acts. Among those who began smoking before they were thirteen years old, almost half had committed two or more delinquent acts in the year prior to administration of the questionnaire, while among those who do not smoke, only one in eight had committed as many delinquent acts.

An item used in Chapter VII (see Table 37) to measure feelings about the scope of the schools' legitimate authority ("It is none of the school's business if a student wants to smoke outside the classroom") bears directly on the question of claims to adult

[6] Smoking is as extinct as the tattoo in the literature on delinquency, even though at one time the connection between smoking and unconventional conduct was considered obvious: "The victims of the cigarette habit are in danger of joining the ranks of the criminals, for the habit controls them, and its undermining effect on character is known to those who have given attention to the subject" (Hannah Kent Schoff, *The Wayward Child* [Indianapolis: Bobbs-Merrill, 1915], pp. 7–8). Given the attitudes of adults toward children who smoke, the idea that smoking causes delinquency may not be as far-fetched as the utter lack of references to smoking in the modern literature on delinquency suggests. Smoking by the very young provides a highly and continuously visible symbol of immoral character and may thus serve as a foundation of labeling, both by the child himself and by significant others. For development of a labeling theory of delinquency, see Frank Tannenbaum, *Crime and the Community* (Boston: Ginn, 1938), especially pp. 3–22.

Table 55 / Self-Reported Delinquent Acts by Age at Which
Cigarette Smoking Began
(in percent)

| | "Do you smoke cigarettes?" | | | |
Self-Reported Acts	Yes, Began Before 13	Yes, Began 13–15	Yes, Began After 15	No
None	25	32	48	65
One	27	36	24	23
Two or more	48	32	28	12
Totals	100 (154)	100 (117)	100 (29)	100 (952)

status.[7] Since we have raised the question of the relative importance of behavioral and attitudinal indicators of premature adult
status, the simultaneous effect of these variables is shown in Table
56.

Table 56 suggests that the behavioral indicator, smoking, is a
better predictor of delinquent activity than the attitudinal mea-

Table 56 / Percent Committing One or More Delinquent
Acts by Smoking and Attitude Toward School's Authority
Over Smoking

| "It is none of the school's business if a student wants to smoke outside the classroom." | Smoke? | |
	Yes	No
Strongly agree	80 (143)	49 (107)
Agree	59 (73)	41 (170)
Undecided	64 (34)	31 (140)
Disagree	59 (17)	35 (171)
Strongly disagree	59 (32)	31 (363)

sure, even though the attitudinal measure is independently related
to delinquency. All of which suggests that premature adulthood
may result in delinquent activity without ideological justification—
the behavior may lead directly to delinquency and it may lead to
delinquency by way of its effect on attitudes toward adult expectations.

The number of boys in the sample who report drinking is

[7] And was so used by Stinchcombe, Rebellion, pp. 103–133.

virtually the same as the number who report smoking (301 and
305, or 24 percent), but drinking is more strongly related than
smoking to delinquency. (Very few students begin drinking as
early as they begin to smoke, but the age at which drinking begins
appears to have no effect on one's delinquency potential.)

Dating is considered appropriate for adolescents, and it is

Table 57 / Percent Committing One or More Delinquent
Acts by Index of Involvement in Adult Activities

Index Score [a]					
0	1	2	3	4	5
25	40	61	62	65	78
(535)	(270)	(73)	(149)	(17)	(154)

[a] If the student smokes or drinks, he was given a score of 2 on the index.
If he dates, he was given a score of 1. The scores on the index may thus be
interpreted as follows: 0 = Does not smoke, drink, or date; 1 = Dates but
does not drink or smoke; 2 = Smokes or drinks, but does not date; 3 =
Smokes or drinks, and dates; 4 = Smokes and drinks, but does not date;
5 = Smokes, drinks, and dates.

accordingly engaged in by a much larger portion of the sample (52
percent). Many discussions of delinquency suggest that dating
should reduce delinquency by virtue of the fact that the adolescent
is thereby involved in a conventional activity and his opportunities
for delinquency are reduced. Nevertheless, it is established that
early heterosexual activity is predictive of low subsequent social
status, and that such activity is indicative of a claim to adult
status.[8] The child committed to education presumably delays entrance into the dating game and thereby prolongs his adolescence.
As the lack of commitment hypothesis would suggest, dating too is
strongly related to delinquent activity.[9]

The picture is fairly clear, then, that students who smoke,
those who drink, and those who date are more likely to commit
delinquent acts. Combining these items into an index of involvement in adult activities produces Table 57, which shows that the
effects of these activities is cumulative—the more the boy is in-

[8] Stinchcombe, *Rebellion*, pp. 116–123.
[9] Thirty-one percent of the 639 nondaters and 57 percent of the 528 daters
have committed delinquent acts. The age at which the boy begins dating is
not as important in predicting his delinquent activity as is the frequency with
which he dates.

volved in adult activities, the greater his involvement in delinquency.

Three questions were asked about automobiles: "Do you own
a car?" "Do you drive a car you don't own?" And, "How important is having a car to you?" Again, as predicted by the adult status
hypothesis, car ownership, car driving, and felt importance of a car
are all related to delinquent activity. The magnitude of these relations is illustrated in Table 58, where it is shown that the more
important an automobile is to the student, the more likely he is to
have committed delinquent acts.

Table 58 / Self-Reported Delinquent Acts by Importance
of an Automobile
(in percent)

Self-Reported Acts	"How important is having a car to you?"				
	Everything	Very Important	Fairly Important	Not Very Important	Unimportant
None	44	47	56	62	77
One	28	30	25	26	14
Two or more	28	24	19	12	10
Totals	100	101	100	100	101
	(89)	(302)	(407)	(253)	(162)

Table 58 also indicates that many students attach considerable importance to an automobile. About one-third consider having (presumably owning or having access to) a car at least very
important; another third consider a car fairly important. But for
present purposes, the significant fact is that as emphasis on an
automobile increases, the likelihood that one has committed delinquent acts also increases.

The automobile, then, like the cigarette, the bottle of beer,
and the date, signifies that the boy has put away childish things.
Such activities are often considered indicative of involvement in or
attachment to a "teenage culture," a culture that contrasts sharply
with the dominant adult culture. But to emphasize the contrast is
to compare *future* manual laborers and lower white-collar workers
with (somewhat stuffy) adult *professionals* and *executives*.[10] Ac-

10 As does Talcott Parsons; see his "Age and Sex in the Social Structure
of the United States," in *Essays in Sociological Theory* (New York: The
Free Press, 1954), pp. 89–103.

tually, the symbols adopted by these boys are better seen as the symbols of manhood dominant in the class they are to enter. To emphasize the similarity between youth and adult culture is to lose some of the tension those emphasizing dissimilarity have built into their explanations of delinquency, but the discrepancy between the adolescent's self-conception and his treatment by adults who do not recognize his claims to adult status is sufficient to explain his sullenness, his "recalcitrance to the pressure of [middle-class] adult expectations and discipline." [11] And no special motivational force is required to explain his delinquent acts: to withdraw from an educational career is not to retire from life.

Commitment to Education

> Delinquents in Haulburg had high middle-class aspirations. . . . Jackie, aged twenty-one years, continued to express an interest in going to medical school and becoming a surgeon, although he had not gone to college or even completed high school.[12]

> "I mean, if something comes up and I can't finish school, I'm gonna go to college. I don't care what comes up." [13]

At least since Merton's "Social Structure and Anomie," aspirations have played a large part in explanations of delinquent behavior. In their simplest form, the hypotheses stemming from Merton's work are opposite to those emerging from a control perspective. Irving Spergel, for example, suggests: "Delinquents may be under more direct and greater pressure from ambitious and upwardly mobile parents or from parents who are particularly dissatisfied with their own status in life, and nondelinquents may have been less baldly and forcefully exposed to general cultural pressures for success." [14] From the Mertonian perspective, a solu-

---

[11] Parsons, *Ibid.*, p. 92. For a research study reporting conclusions opposite to those of Parsons and other adolescent "storm and stress" theorists, see Frederick Elkin and William A. Westley, "The Myth of Adolescent Culture," *American Sociological Review*, XX (1955), 680–684. Both those in favor of and those opposed to the "adolescent culture" concept tend to forget the fact of variation among adolescents in the extent to which they do or do not rebel against adult authority. Both views thus have a mythical quality.

[12] Irving Spergel, *Racketville, Slumtown, Haulburg* (Chicago: The University of Chicago Press, 1964), p. 99.

[13] A male Negro student in Richmond, quoted in Alan B. Wilson, "Educational Consequences of Segregation in a California Community," mimeographed, Survey Research Center, Berkeley, 1966, p. 60.

[14] *Racketville, Slumtown, Haulburg*, pp. 94–95.

tion to the problem of delinquency would be somehow to bring the adolescent's aspirations into line with his realistic expectations, to synchronize what he wishes to be with what he can be, given his limited academic competence and/or social structural obstacles. From the perspective of control theory, such "cooling out" would remove a major element of social control, leaving the adolescent all the more free to commit delinquent acts.[15]

Table 59 / Percent Committing One or More Delinquent Acts by Educational Aspirations,[a] by Race

Educational Aspirations	White Boys		Negro Boys	
	Self-Reported Acts	Official Acts	Self-Reported Acts	Official Acts
Less than college	56 (172)	33 (181)	56 (231)	47 (248)
Some college	47 (240)	23 (246)	51 (145)	38 (155)
College graduation	40 (825)	14 (837)	38 (315)	36 (328)

[a] The item is: "How much schooling would you like to get eventually?"

As the quotations at the beginning of this section suggest, there are many problems in measuring the intensity of aspirations. In the present case, however, the problem is not serious, since the higher the aspiration the less likely the child is to be delinquent, and it is not necessary to convert weak and unrealistic aspirations into the motive force behind delinquent behavior. As Table 59 makes clear, the higher the student's educational aspirations, whether he be white or Negro, the less likely he is to commit delinquent acts (by both the self-report and official measures).

Aspiration levels in the sample are high and compare with previous research in this area.[16] Forty-five percent of the Negro

[15] Strain theorists of course rarely advocate this solution to the discrepancy between aspirations and expectations, advocating instead the removal of barriers to opportunity. Durkheim, in contrast, tended to stress the moral value of poverty (Emile Durkheim, Suicide [New York: The Free Press, 1951], especially pp. 246–254).

[16] James F. Short, Jr., and Fred L. Strodtbeck, Group Process and Gang Delinquency (Chicago: University of Chicago Press, 1964), p. 111; Ralph H. Turner, The Social Context of Ambition (San Francisco: Chandler, 1964), pp. 42–44. For an analysis of sources of educational aspirations in the present data, see Wilson, "Educational Consequences of Segregation," Chapter 8.

boys and 66 percent of the white boys in the analyzed sample want to graduate from college. Unfortunately for the anomie hypothesis, however, educational expectations in the sample are virtually as high as aspirations (even among Negroes). If we take such minor discrepancies as the difference between a desire to graduate from college and the expectation of attaining only some college as sufficient to produce delinquency, 19 percent of the white boys may be

Table 60 / Percent Committing One or More Delinquent Acts by Educational Aspirations and Educational Expectations

| | Self-Reported Acts | | |
| | Educational Aspirations | | |
Educational Expectations	College Graduate	Some College	Less than College
College graduate	39 (607)	— (6)	— (5)
Some college	42 (174)	44 (196)	— (12)
Less than college	58 (29)	63 (33)	56 (151)

| | Official Acts | | |
| | Educational Aspirations | | |
Educational Expectations	College Graduate	Some College	Less than College
College graduate	12 (616)	— (6)	— (6)
Some college	18 (177)	18 (200)	— (12)
Less than college	13 (29)	49 (35)	33 (159)

classified as suffering from a condition of anomie. If we divide aspirations and expectations between college and no college, only 5 percent desire more education than they expect to get. Frustrated educational aspirations therefore cannot be an important antecedent of delinquency in the present sample. Even if true, then, the anomie hypothesis with respect to educational aspirations is largely irrelevant, there being insufficient variation on the independent variable to account for more than a small fraction of the variation in delinquency.

Yet the issue of frustrated aspirations is of such theoretical significance that it cannot be dismissed merely by pointing to the small portion of the sample whose aspirations appear to be frustrated. In Table 60 we examine the joint effects of educational aspirations and expectations. On the basis of Table 60, it is safe to say that discrepancies in educational aspirations and expectations are not important in the causation of delinquency for two reasons: few boys in the sample have aspirations greatly in excess of their expectations; and, *those boys whose aspirations exceed their expectations are no more likely to be delinquent than those boys whose aspirations and expectations are identical.*

The solid relation between educational expectations and delinquency evident in Table 60 recalls a question raised some time ago: Why, if social class is related to the variables presumably causing delinquency, is social class itself unrelated to delinquency? Much research shows that the higher the family's socioeconomic status, the more likely the child is to expect to attain higher education. The present data are no exception (Table 61).

Table 61 / Percent Expecting to Graduate from College by Father's Education

College Graduate	Some College	High School Graduate	Less than High School Graduation
79	59	45	30
(290)	(186)	(531)	(326)

Father's education is strongly related to educational expectations. Educational expectations are reasonably strongly related to delinquency. Yet, as has been shown, there is no relation between father's education and delinquency in the present sample. What accounts for the zero relation between father's education and delinquency? In an attempt to answer this question, we examine the relation between father's education and delinquency within groups whose educational expectations are the same (Table 62).

The two groups in the sample with the highest rates of delinquency are sons of college graduates not expecting to graduate from college. If these boys had committed delinquent acts at the same rate as boys with equivalent educational expectations, there would be a weak but consistent negative relation between father's education and delinquency in the sample as a whole.[17]

[17] The average number of delinquent acts per boy for the four groups separated on the basis of father's education would be (from less than high school to college graduate): .86, .73, .70, and .67.

Table 62 / Average Number of Self-Reported Delinquent
Acts by Educational Expectations and Father's Education

Father's Education	Educational Expectations		
	Graduate College	Some College	No College
College graduate	.61	1.20	1.23
	(229)	(45)	(16)
Some college	.59	.86	.83
	(110)	(55)	(21)
High school graduate	.55	.81	.98
	(240)	(178)	(113)
Less than high school graduation	.66	.86	1.05
	(100)	(128)	(98)

These results are similar to findings reported by Stinchcombe.
In his sample, the sons of lower middle-class parents doing poorly
in school were more likely to be "rebellious" than the sons of
working-class parents doing equally poorly in school. This helped
account for the fact that the lower middle-class children were as
likely to be rebellious as the working-class children in the sample
as a whole.[18]

Stinchcombe in effect turned strain theory on its head and
argued that the middle-class boy, not the lower-class boy, doing
poorly in school suffers from a discrepancy between aspirations and
expectations and is thus forced into delinquency. Table 62 appears
to support Stinchcombe's argument. (The empirical relation is
trivial, as it was in Stinchcombe's data. However, it is customary at
this point to note that the relation has theoretical significance.) [19]
Father's education is probably a better measure of pressure to
succeed than an item asking what the student would like to do,
since the college-educated father is highly likely to desire at least as
much education for his son. Thus it would be possible to argue on
the basis of Table 62 that most middle-class parents are able to
protect their children from delinquency by assuring them access to
higher education; that, however, if for any reason (perhaps because the child is not academically qualified) the middle-class par-

[18] Rebellion, pp. 134–169.
[19] This custom is pernicious. We should note that the empirical relation
has significance for theory. Theories should choke rather than thrive on such
relations.

ent is unable to assure access to higher education, his emphasis on such education returns to haunt him: his child is more likely to be delinquent than the child who has not been led to value something he cannot have. In effect, then, the advantages enjoyed by the middle-class parent are cancelled by disadvantages, and there is no overall relation between social class and delinquency.

Stinchcombe used father's occupation rather than education, and grade-point average rather than educational expectations. Since grades and father's occupation are available in the present data, and are related to each other and to delinquency in the same manner as in Stinchcombe's data, let us see if his finding is directly replicable in the present sample (Table 63).

Table 63 / Average Number of Self-Reported Delinquent Acts by Grade-Point Average in English and Family Status

Family Status	Grade-Point Average—English		
	0–49	50–79	80–99
Lower	.92 (83)	.67 (94)	.57 (66)
Semi-skilled and skilled manual	1.06 (127)	.70 (148)	.62 (135)
White collar	1.23 (36)	.98 (52)	.60 (55)
Professional	.92 (42)	.79 (61)	.59 (128)

Although Table 63 does not show the effect as clearly as Table 62, if Stinchcombe's procedure is followed and the line drawn between white-collar and manual workers, the results are similar: middle- and lower middle-class children doing poorly in school are more likely to be delinquent than working-class children doing equally poorly in school. The differences are very small, but again they appear to help explain the lack of an overall relation between social class and delinquency.

When data agree with a strain hypothesis, such a hypothesis is likely to be more persuasive than alternative hypotheses that also fit the data. In the present case we could give this relation to strain theory without serious damage, since the effect of the apparent strain is very small and applies only to a small minority of the sample (between 5 and 18 percent, depending on the measure used and the definition of "high-expectation" classes). Once again, however, the logic of strain theory is so removed from that of control theory that we should not grant it a victory without examining alternative hypotheses congruent with control theory logic.

One such hypothesis is that these results are statistical or social artifacts. Suppose, let us say, that some causal variable has the same effect on delinquency within each social class. Further suppose that those lowest on this variable are most likely to be delinquent. Now, within any given social class, *the larger the proportion* we take from the low end of the causal variable, *the lower the rate of delinquency.* Thus some method of statistical classification or social selection which isolates the lowest 21 percent of the sons of college graduates and the lowest 70 percent of the sons of those not finishing high school (see Table 61) might very well show a higher rate of delinquency among the sons of college graduates—even though they are no more likely to be delinquent than the sons of those with less education having the same values of the causal variable. (Note that at this point there is no reason to question the validity of the measure of delinquency. We add little to the strength of the claim that a discrepancy between felt parental expectations and actual academic achievement is the cause of the relatively high rate of delinquency by showing that these boys are more delinquent by other measures.)

Instead of attempting to determine whether the positive relation between social class and delinquency among those doing poorly in school and among those not expecting to graduate from college is spurious, let us examine data bearing directly on the parental pressure hypothesis. The students were asked whether their parents wanted them to go to college. If we combine responses to this question with educational expectations, we get evidence bearing directly on the hypothesis that high parental expectations combined with low actual expectations produces pressure resulting in delinquency.

Straightforward interpretation of Table 64 is impossible because parental pressure and educational expectations interact in their effects on delinquency. In order to make sense of such interactions, it is necessary to question the apparent meaning of the indicators or the quality of the data. Nevertheless, the major implication of the parental pressure hypothesis is certainly disconfirmed by Table 64. Among those *not* planning to graduate from college, the greater the apparent parental pressure to attend col-

Table 64 / Average Number of Self-Reported Delinquent
Acts by Parental Pressure and Educational Expectations

"How much education do you expect to get?"	"Do your parents want you to go to college?"		
	They Insist	Very Much	Other [a]
No college	.52 (30)	1.02 (87)	1.08 (140)
Some college	.68 (56)	.84 (283)	.99 (91)
College graduation	.66 (218)	.56 (444)	.39 (30)

[a] This includes: "I think they want me to go but we don't talk about it"; "They don't care one way or the other"; "No, they don't want me to go"; and "Don't know." Over half of those in this category responded, "I think they want me to go."

lege, the lower the rate of delinquency. It may be, to question the indicator, that among those with relatively small expectations parental "pressure" is actually parental "interest," and that the boys are simply basing their expectations on a realistic evaluation of their own interests and abilities. In any event, undue parental pressure does not appear to account for the high delinquency rate of those whose educational expectations are limited.

If the parental pressure hypothesis is to find any support in these data, it must come from an unlikely source: from among those who expect to graduate from college. In this group, the greater the apparent parental pressure, the higher the rate of delinquency. Rather than speculate on the meaning of this finding, I will report the outcome of further analysis within the group expecting to graduate from college. Among those getting good grades (the majority of those expecting to graduate from college), the relation again reverses—that is, the greater the apparent parental pressure, the lower the rate of delinquency. Among those whose grades are not so good, the greater the apparent parental pressure, the higher the rate of delinquency. And we have again uncovered a small group whose delinquency could be interpreted as resulting from a condition of strain. I am forced to agree with Stinchcombe: "Almost always there were some results that could be tentatively interpreted as supporting the [strain] hypothesis, provided enough *ad hoc* assumptions and interpretations were made." [20]

[20] *Rebellion*, p. 156.

Educational expectations are more strongly related to delinquency than educational aspirations, reflecting perhaps a greater reality component in the former.[21] For that matter, the concept of commitment itself implies that the person has something *invested* in a line of activity: the mere wish to be "something or somebody" is not enough to affect behavior seriously unless the person supports or has supported his words with deeds. The value system the strain theorist sees as feeding the ranks of delinquency also suggests more than that the individual idly aspire to wealth, fame, or success. It may *say* "Be a king in your dreams," but it frowns on dreamers. Thus the unemployed twenty-one-year-old high school dropout who "aspires" to be a surgeon represents not the embodiment of these values, but their absence. The test is not that a man have lofty ambitions, but that he strive mightily. And by this test there is undoubtedly greater variation in the extent to which the values have been "internalized" or the "cultural goal" maintained than is true at the level of verbalized "success aspirations."

Those committed to educational success as evidenced by current efforts should be least likely, according to control theory, to commit delinquent acts. Several items in the questionnaire tap this kind of commitment. For example, "I try hard in school" and "How important is getting good grades to you personally?" both suggest commitment to education at least partially independent of educational aspirations,[22] and they are certainly more relevant to current activities than such aspirations. Since a third item, "Whatever I do, I try hard," is strongly related to the school achievement items, it was combined with them to produce an index of achievement orientation. Table 65 shows the relation between achievement orientation and self-reported delinquency. It is clear from this table that the ambitious, the strivers, are much less likely than the nonambitious to have committed delinquent acts.

[21] See James F. Short, Jr., "Gang Delinquency and Anomie," *Anomie and Deviant Behavior*, ed. Marshall B. Clinard (New York: The Free Press, 1964), pp. 108–111. Short's data show that educational adjustment is more strongly related to delinquency than are educational aspirations. They also show that educational aspirations are negatively related to delinquency, regardless of educational adjustment.

[22] In fact, in the present sample, those expecting less than a college education have a slightly higher average achievement orientation than those expecting some college (as opposed to those expecting to graduate from college).

The data in this chapter could be taken as showing that boys who reject the education game and desire instead the accouterments of success within the lower-class style of life are most likely to become delinquent, as suggested by a Cloward–Ohlin hypothesis.[23] Cloward and Ohlin hypothesize that the boy who desires material success but not the middle-class life style is more likely to be delinquent than the boy who desires neither. If education is the means to the middle-class style of life, and if "cars" and "dames" are symbols of material success within the lower-class culture, then

Table 65 / Self-Reported Delinquency by Achievement Orientation
(in percent)

Self-Reported Acts	Index of Achievement Orientation						
	0	1	2	3	4	5	6
None	26	46	55	57	69	75	80
One	27	27	26	29	22	15	10
Two or more	46	27	19	14	9	10	10
Totals	99	100	100	100	100	100	100
	(91)	(184)	(226)	(247)	(241)	(100)	(50)

these data suggest that delinquents are boys who reject the former and desire the latter.[24]

This conclusion is unacceptable, however, since it suggests two things antithetical to control theory logic: (1) that the truly non-aspiring are less likely to be delinquent than those who maintain an interest in a quasi-legitimate goal (materialistic success); (2) that delinquency is a means to a quasi-legitimate goal and that the desire to reach this goal produces delinquency. It is difficult to disentangle the Cloward–Ohlin hypothesis from the adult status hypothesis, according to which, it will be recalled, the boy rejects education, takes up the symbols of adult status (cars and dames),

[23] Richard A. Cloward and Lloyd E. Ohlin, Delinquency and Opportunity (New York: The Free Press, 1960), pp. 94–97.

[24] Short and Strodtbeck have shown that delinquents and nondelinquents evaluate elements of the middle-class life style equally highly. For example, they all tend to think that "working for good grades in school" is a good thing. At this level, then, the Cloward–Ohlin hypothesis is false. However, when, as in the present case, we get closer to the boys' actual commitment to these values, the differences between delinquents and nondelinquents are large. See Group Process, pp. 47–76.

and becomes a delinquent: both predict the same relations between the two kinds of aspirations and delinquency. The difference enters with respect to the meaning of the relation between adoption of lower-class success symbols (symbols of adult status) and delinquency.

There is, to be sure, some difficulty in the operationalization of aspirations of "success within the lower-class life style." As Bordua has commented: "If they [lower-class boys] aspire to large (how large?) incomes *within* the style of the lower-class life they clearly aspire to the impossible and, indeed—except through some

Table 66 / Percent Committing Two or More Delinquent Acts by Purpose of Job

"The only reason to have a job is for money."				
Strongly Agree	Agree	Undecided	Disagree	Strongly Disagree
32	26	18	17	6
(98)	(239)	(242)	(476)	(193)

type of crime—the almost unimaginable. They seem to be as much the victims of misinformation as of injustice." [25] If the Cloward–Ohlin theory is taken on their own terms, we should attempt to find boys who aspire to wealth but not to education and compare them with boys who aspire to neither wealth nor education. (True to the strain theory tradition, some legitimate—in this case quasi-legitimate—aspiration is behind delinquent behavior.) Unfortunately, no measure of income aspirations is available on the present questionnaire. Tangential measures of the relative importance of life style as opposed to income, however, appear to support the Cloward–Ohlin hypothesis. Boys agreeing with the statement, "The only reason to have a job is for money," are more likely to be delinquent than those disagreeing with this statement (Table 66).

Once again, however, this relation would obtain if money

[25] David J. Bordua, "Sociological Perspectives," *Social Deviancy Among Youth, The Sixty-Fifth Yearbook of the National Society for the Study of Education,* ed. William W. Wattenberg (Chicago: University of Chicago Press, 1966), pp. 78–102.

were a universal aspiration that remains when other aspirations are stripped away. The important test of the Cloward–Ohlin as opposed to the control theory hypothesis involves a comparison of the delinquency rates of those who desire money only with those who, in effect, desire nothing very badly.[26] The item used in Table 66 ("The only reason to have a job is for money") seems a reasonable measure of "crass materialism." What can we use to measure the second dimension of the Cloward–Ohlin typology, the strength of the desire for money? A second measure of ambition, one not tied to education, is available. Students agreeing to the statements: "You should not expect too much out of life" and "An easy life is a happy life," and who see money as the only reason for having a job, cannot be said to be strongly motivated toward either the middle-class life style or toward wealth; students disagreeing with these statements come very close to fitting the Cloward–Ohlin picture of the delinquent: they want wealth more than other things, and whatever they want, they want with some force. Is the latter or the former more likely to be delinquent (Table 67)? [27]

In three of the four family-status groups, the delinquency rate is lower among ambitious seekers of money. In the group lowest in family status, although the relation between ambition and delinquency is in the direction predicted by the Cloward–Ohlin hypothesis, the difference is minuscule. Given three differences in

[26] The "corner boys," according to Cloward and Ohlin, "are not strongly oriented toward social mobility in any sphere" and are, as a result, less likely to be delinquent than those desiring material success (*Delinquency and Opportunity*, p. 97). Insofar as these distinctions are useful and meaningful, control theory would suggest that those not oriented to any kind of social mobility would be most likely to be delinquent.

[27] As in most of the tests of control versus some version of strain theory involving three variables, I know the marginal relations in advance of running the three-variable tables. And, as usual, I know that the strain theory is predicting a "specification" in which the original relation *reverses* in one of the partials. It is not that my operationalizations stack the cards against these theories, but that they explicitly theorize such reversals. The strain theorists would undoubtedly grant that in general the higher the aspiration the lower the delinquency rate; they would also grant that in general the higher the expectation the lower the delinquency rate. Thus the hypothesis that, among those with little expectations, the higher the aspiration the higher the delinquency rate, is a hypothesis which states that, among some sub-group, the relation between some variable and delinquency is opposite to that found in the population as a whole.

Table 67 / Average Number of Self-Reported Delinquent
Acts by Ambition and Family Status—Among Those
Agreeing That "The Only Reason to Have a Job
Is for Money"

	Family Status			
Ambition	Lower	Semi-Skilled and Skilled Manual	White Collar	Professional
High	1.03 (24)	.76 (53)	.58 (19)	.87 (28)
Low	.98 (48)	.86 (78)	1.44 (28)	1.16 (21)

the direction opposed to the hypothesis, and one comparison (admittedly the crucial one) showing virtually no difference, the Cloward–Ohlin hypothesis may be said to be, as judged by the present data, false.[28]

Commitment to a High-Status Occupation

In contemporary American society, higher education is virtually a necessary condition for a high-status occupation. As the experience of lower-class persons and Negroes shows, however, higher education is by no means a sufficient condition for such occupations.[29] (This fact is poorly communicated to Negro youth, who are likely to see attainment of a "good" education as more difficult than attainment of a "good" job.) In the context of present concerns, the distinction between educational and occupational aspirations is not critical: either should inhibit delinquent activity, since the higher the aspiration, whether educational or occupational, the greater the perceived cost of such activity.

We proceed, then, directly to the strain hypothesis that high occupational aspirations coupled with low occupational expectations generate pressure resulting in delinquency (Table 68).

As was true with respect to educational aspirations, the proportion of students whose occupational aspirations exceed their expectations is small: frustrated occupational ambition cannot be

[28] Cloward and Ohlin do not intend their theory to account for delinquent acts anywhere in the class structure. It is designed to account for lower-class, urban, gang delinquency. Even so these data are relevant to the theory, and their implications for the theory should, I think, be spelled out.

[29] Seymour Martin Lipset and Reinhard Bendix, Social Mobility in Industrial Society (Berkeley: University of California Press, 1959), pp. 91–101.

Table 68 / Average Number of Self-Reported Delinquent
Acts by Desired and Expected Occupation

	Job Desired		
Job Expected	Professional	White Collar	Manual
Professional	.66 (565)	— (22) [a]	— (14) [a]
White collar	.53 (34)	.71 (118)	— (16) [a]
Manual	.90 (65)	.93 (32)	.97 (243)

[a] Aspiration-expectation logic suggests that many of the cases in these cells represent response errors, since a student who wants a low-status occupation should be able to get it. Since the occupational questions were relatively complicated, the errors suggested here, few as they are, misrepresent the overall quality of the data.

an important cause of delinquency in the present sample. As was also true with respect to educational aspirations, but is even clearer in the present case, *the higher the aspiration, the lower the rate of delinquency, regardless of the student's expectations.* The data are again opposite to the prediction stemming from strain theory.

And, once again, some strain theories are not directly falsified by data such as those shown in Table 68. Cloward and Ohlin, for example, repeatedly affirm that the explanation the person advances for his failure to attain his goal is crucial in determining the reaction that ensues. If he blames himself, the system remains unchallenged, and he is not likely to turn to delinquency. If, however, he perceives (more or less correctly) that the fault lies in social forces over which he has no control, he becomes alienated from the system, rejects its normative patterns, and turns to delinquency.[30]

Many items on the questionnaire deal with the student's perception of the obstacles between him and his desired occupation. If we turn again to the Negro boys, we find items offering a direct contrast between blaming the social system and blaming one's self for failure, especially in light of a specification offered by Cloward and Ohlin: "The efforts of reformers to expose discriminatory practices actually furnish such persons with further justification for withdrawing sentiments in support of the legitimacy of the established norms and free them to attribute legitimacy to alternative

[30] *Delinquency and Opportunity,* pp. 112, 117–118.

norms which may be both legally and morally proscribed by the dominant system." [31]

The Negro boy convinced of his own competence and convinced that racial discrimination will prevent him from attaining his goals is, according to this hypothesis, a prime candidate for delinquency. His anticipated failure stems not from personal shortcomings, but from injustice. At another extreme,[32] the Negro

Table 69 / Average Number of Delinquent Acts by Perceptions of Racial Discrimination and Personal Incompetence as Potential Obstacles to Occupational Success— Negro Boys Only

	"Do you think that any of the following things will keep you from getting the kind of job you want to have eventually?"		
"Am Not Smart Enough"	Racial Discrimination		
	Yes	Maybe	No
Yes	.88 (48)	.89 (58)	.65 (45)
Maybe	.89 (43)	.83 (156)	1.00 (51)
No	.81 (43)	.91 (147)	.82 (155)

boy convinced of his own incompetence and unaware of racial discrimination has no one to blame but himself. He has no excuse for violating the rules of a society prepared to give him all he has earned.

In Table 69, the average number of delinquent acts committed by Negro boys prepared to blame themselves but not racial discrimination for occupational failure is .65; the corresponding average for boys blaming racial discrimination rather than themselves is .81. The general thrust of the results of this test is not, however, in a direction favorable to the Cloward–Ohlin hypothesis. In general, it does not matter whether the boy blames himself or the social system for potential failure; ascription of blame is essentially unrelated to the commission of delinquent acts.

[31] Delinquency and Opportunity, p. 122.
[32] As with any typological independent variable, at least four types are possible and each requires a subtheory. Cloward and Ohlin imply that the "both" and the "neither" cells are empty, that the lower class boy either blames himself or the system.

Conclusion

These data are at odds with sociological theories constructed on the assumption that frustrated aspirations *provoke* delinquency. Discrepancies between the student's hopes and expectations are either unrelated to delinquency or are related in the direction opposite to that which these theories lead us to expect. We have followed several possible routes of escape for the strain theorist, but, as in Chapter VII, none of them takes us anywhere. Whatever the conventional aspiration and whatever the object of blame for failure, the picture of the delinquent as a striver, either in word or in deed, simply does not fit the data.

It can be argued that the lower educational and occupational aspirations of delinquents represent a "defensive downgrading" of aspirations, that ideally they would still prefer higher education to high school and a profession to manual labor. Thus, in this view, there is still a discrepancy between what the student would "really" like and what he actually expects to have. This argument is plausible when delinquents have lower aspirations than nondelinquents and both groups are equally confident their aspirations will be realized.[33] It cannot survive, however, when those boys whose *stated* aspirations exceed their expectations are less likely to be delinquent than boys with equivalent expectations and lower aspirations, as is true in the present data.[34]

At the same time, there can be little doubt that the educational and occupational expectations of delinquents tend to be low.[35] We have emphasized the fact that a low-status future is not jeopardized by delinquency, that adolescents whose prospects are bleak are to that extent free to commit delinquent acts. Although consistent with much thinking and research, this view and even the data supporting it probably exaggerate the distant future as a factor in the prevention of delinquency. Actually, measures of general achievement orientation, of the student's desire to do well

[33] Martin Gold, *Status Forces in Delinquent Boys* (Ann Arbor: Institute for Social Research, 1963), pp. 162–173.

[34] See also James F. Short, Jr., in *Anomie and Deviant Behavior*, ed. Clinard, pp. 111–113.

[35] Short, *ibid.*; Delbert S. Elliott, "Delinquency and Perceived Opportunity," *Sociological Inquiry*, XXXII (1962), 216–227.

in current activities, are more strongly related to delinquency than his hopes, plans, and prospects for the future. Aspirations and expectations without foundation are probably much like belief in a life after death. There may be logical or theological links between these imagined future states and present behavior, but these links are often too weak to withstand the demands of everyday life.[36]

[36] See Travis Hirschi and Rodney Stark, "Hellfire and Delinquency," a paper presented at the annual meetings of the Pacific Sociological Association, San Francisco, 1968. Comparison of educational expectations with belief in a life after death overstates the case for the weakness of worldly expectations. Such expectations do, in the present data, affect delinquency when the effects of academic competence and performance and achievement orientation are removed. Again, however, achievement orientation with an emphasis on present activities is strongly related to delinquency when the effects of expectations are removed.

Chapter X
Involvement in Conventional Activities

Of the elements of the bond to conventional society, involvement in conventional activities is most obviously relevant to delinquent behavior. The child playing ping-pong, swimming in the community pool, or doing his homework is not committing delinquent acts. The obviousness of this picture of "wholesome" activity as incompatible with delinquent activity lies behind many delinquency prevention projects. Yet reaction to this view in the scientific literature is as strong as the claim that work and recreation would reduce delinquency is obvious.

> As a preventive, "keeping youth busy," whether through compulsory education, drafting for service in the armed forces, providing fun through recreation, or early employment, can, at best, only temporarily postpone behavior that is symptomatic of more deep-seated or culturally oriented factors.[1]

> . . . the fact that most delinquencies occur during the leisure time of children does not in itself reveal *anything* about the basic causation of delinquency. . . . To suggest that a boy will not be a delinquent because he plays organized ball is no more valid than to say that he will not play ball because he is a delinquent.[2]

Research designed to evaluate the thesis that "idle hands are the devil's workshop," that the fundamental approach to curing delinquency involves "getting the kids off the streets" has rarely produced evidence for the effectiveness of such programs.[3] Yet in

---

[1] William C. Kvaraceus and Walter B. Miller, *Delinquent Behavior: Culture and the Individual* (Washington: National Education Association, 1959), p. 39.

[2] Milton L. Barron, *The Juvenile in Delinquent Society* (New York: Alfred A. Knopf, 1954), p. 183. Emphasis added.

[3] U. S. Department of Health, Education, and Welfare, *Report to the Congress on Juvenile Delinquency* (Washington: USGPO, 1960), p. 21.

theoretical statements, in practical programs, and in the common sense, the idea of involvement remains central to much thinking about the causation and prevention of delinquency. In this chapter I shall attempt to determine the extent to which such faith is justified.

A Methodological Problem

In control theories, the end of the trail for delinquency is usually marked by the point at which the person marries or goes to work. In observational accounts of gang life, the boy is often removed from delinquent activities by work or heterosexual activity. Practical approaches stress the same pattern: ". . . if I were forced to select a single approach that struck me in my travels as coming closer to a whole solution [to the problem of delinquency] than any other, it could be summed up in the four-letter word [work]." [4]

With respect to heterosexual activity, we have already seen the positive relation between dating and delinquency. Let us look now at the relation between employment and delinquency (Table 70).

The relation between working and delinquency shown in

Table 70 / Self-Reported Delinquency by Employment While Attending School
(in percent)

Self-Reported Acts	Currently Working for Pay	
	Yes [a]	No
None	53	60
One	26	24
Two or more	22	16
Totals	101	100
	(668)	(595)

[a] Fifty-five percent of the working boys work less than six hours a week. The number of hours the boy works is unrelated to his delinquency.

This report concludes that provision of recreational facilities would not reduce the delinquency rate.

[4] Roul Tunley, Kids, Crime and Chaos (New York: Dell Publishing Co., 1962), p. 258.

Table 70 is weak. Boys who work while attending school are only slightly more likely to have committed delinquent acts than boys without jobs. With respect to dating, the relation is stronger. Boys who date are considerably more likely to have committed delinquent acts than boys who do not. The strength of these relations, however, is not the problem. The problem is that both relations are in the direction *opposite* to that predicted by an involvement hypothesis. Working and dating should remove opportunities to commit delinquent acts; they should, at least to some extent, have the same effect as "work and marriage" at the attainment of adulthood. They do not appear to have such an effect.

These variables illustrate how hard it is to disentangle measures of "involvement" from other aspects of the social bond. As I have shown in Chapter IX, boys who date are less likely to be committed to higher education; it is easy to suggest that this difference might swamp differences between daters and nondaters with respect to opportunities to commit delinquent acts, if any.[5] The problem is equally difficult where the zero-order relation is in the direction predicted by an involvement hypothesis. The fact that a student truants, for example, tells us more about him than that he enjoys hours free of conventional involvements not enjoyed by other boys. Although such freedom is often taken as the crucial link between truancy and delinquency, there is evidence that the increased opportunity to commit delinquent acts resulting from truancy probably accounts for little of its effect on delinquency.[6]

Time-Consuming Work, Sports, Recreation, Hobbies

When we turn to those conventional activities that devour many of the adolescent's leisure hours, the problems of the in-

---

[5] Controls for achievement orientation and educational expectations do not, however, remove the relation between dating and delinquency.

[6] In these as in other data, truancy is very strongly related to delinquency (see Table 8, p. 63). Although I do not think the relation between truancy and delinquency need be tautological, I have found it difficult to deal with, as have other investigators. For one thing, it behaves much like any other indicator of delinquency—the variables that predict truancy are much like those that predict the number of illegal acts the boy has committed. As a result, it is possible to treat truancy as a measure of attachment, commitment, or involvement.

volvement hypothesis appear to be more than methodological. Television, newspapers, magazines, comic books; basketball, football, baseball; hobbies and work around the house account for much of the leisure time of the boys in the sample. Yet measures of time spent in these activities are for all intents and purposes individually and therefore collectively unrelated to the commission of delinquent acts.[7]

Something is wrong with our theory. The difficulty, it seems, is that the definition of delinquency used here is not the definition that makes the involvement hypothesis virtually tautological. When Cohen, for example, says the delinquent gang "makes enormous demands upon the boy's time," [8] he is of course not saying that delinquency as here defined takes an enormous amount of the boy's time. In fact, as defined, delinquency requires very little time: the most delinquent boys in the sample may not have devoted more than a few hours in the course of a year to the acts that define them as delinquent. Since this is so, it might be necessary to account for almost all the time available to the boys in the sample to find differences in conventional involvements that account for delinquent activity.[9] Involvement would then be interesting only as a limiting case.

What tricked us into rather naïve acceptance of a straightforward involvement hypothesis (see Chapter II) is the idea that "delinquency" is a more or less full-time job, a common enough idea in delinquency theory but highly inappropriate when applied to an explanation of delinquent acts. Most "conventional" activities are neutral with respect to delinquency; they neither inhibit nor promote it. We might account for much involvement in automobile accidents simply in terms of exposure—in terms of hours on the road—but time spent on the job is quite easily seen as irrelevant, even though persons involved in sedentary work are *not* having automobile accidents.

We must consider, then, *what* the child is doing, and assidu-

[7] The more time the boy spends watching television, reading romance magazines and comic books, or playing games, the more likely he is to have committed delinquent acts. These relations are, however, very weak.

[8] Albert K. Cohen, "Middle-Class Delinquency and the Social Structure," *Middle-Class Juvenile Delinquency*, ed. Edmund W. Vaz (New York: Harper and Row, 1967), pp. 203–207.

[9] This suggests the difficulties encountered by prevention programs that rely directly on time-consuming activities as a means of reducing the delinquency rate, when delinquency is measured by the commission of delinquent acts.

ously avoid the idea that doing "something"—anything—is better than, that is, inhibitive of, the commission of delinquent acts.

Analysis of involvement in conventional activities will thus parallel previous analysis of attitudinal commitments to conventional success goals. Such activities are presumably in large part consequences of such commitment; the analysis which follows may then be taken as illustrative of the process by which conventional commitments prevent delinquency.

Involvement in School-Related Activities

The school does more than prepare students for the future. It acts also as a holding operation; it attempts to engross and involve students in activities that are or may be essentially irrelevant to their occupational futures. If it succeeds, the student's delinquency potential may be less than would be expected from his status prospects: the boy destined to be a carpenter may become involved in academic work *as though* it were important for his future. If it fails, the opposite discrepancy between aspirations and delinquency may be produced: the boy who wants to be a doctor may treat school *as though* it were irrelevant to this occupational goal.[10]

Evidence of involvement in school is traditionally measured by time spent in and concern for homework. Several indicators of attention to homework are available on the questionnaire. All are reasonably strongly related to the commission of delinquent acts, as Table 71 illustrates.

Table 71 / Percent Committing One or More Delinquent Acts by Time Devoted to Homework

Time Spent on Homework per Day			
One and One-Half Hours or More	One Hour	One-Half Hour	Less than One-Half Hour
34	48	52	64
(593)	(361)	(199)	(117)

[10] Cohen suggests that the alleged general weakening of standards has made it possible for even the boy with middle class aspirations to take it easy during his public school career. According to Cohen, this may account for the alleged increase in middle-class delinquency.

There are, to be sure, many ways to interpret the relation between time devoted to homework and delinquency. For example, such investment of time and energy affects the student's performance in school, and may thus operate on delinquency through its effects on attachment and commitment to the school. To investigate this possibility, we examine the relation between time devoted to homework and delinquency with school performance held relatively constant (Table 72).

Table 72 / Average Number of Self-Reported Delinquent
Acts by Time Devoted to Homework and Average Grade
in English

Time Devoted to Home-work per Day (Hours)	Average Grade in English		
	0–49	50–79	80–99
Less than one-half	1.39 (54)	1.04 (32)	1.47 (24)
One-half	1.03 (60)	1.10 (81)	.79 (30)
One	.88 (95)	.89 (110)	.76 (103)
One and one-half or more	.88 (95)	.62 (174)	.41 (247)

Homework is related to delinquency at all grade-point average levels. While time spent on homework of course affects school performance, its effect on delinquency is not accounted for by its effect on such performance. (Grade-point average, in contrast, appears to be less strongly related to delinquency the less time devoted to homework, which is consistent with Cohen's notion that the easier it is for him to do well in school, the more likely the "middle-class" [that is, the academically competent, high aspiring] student is to be delinquent.)

Involvement in "Working-Class Adult" Activities

The classic picture of the delinquent, if not of the adolescent in general, is that of a boy looking for "something to do." At least relative to adults, adolescents possess much leisure time. If they cannot occupy this leisure time in meaningful ways, they are likely, it seems to follow, to engage in delinquent activities, if only because such activities offer a measure of excitement. The total row in Table 73 is suggestive of the extent of the problem of boredom among adolescents in general. About three-fourths of the boys in the sample at least sometimes feel they have nothing to do. The more often the boy feels he has nothing he wishes to do, the more likely he is to commit delinquent acts. The relation, however, is relatively weak, with only those who often feel unoccupied being unusually likely to commit delinquent acts.

Table 73 / Percent Committing One or More Delinquent Acts by Feelings of Boredom

"Do you ever feel that 'there's nothing to do'?"			
Often	Sometimes	Rarely	Never
51	43	40	38
(313)	(619)	(246)	(78)

What are the sources of a sense of boredom among adolescents? Previous argument suggests that lack of involvement in the school and lack of commitment to education release the adolescent from a primary source of time-structuring. He has nothing to do but wait for the attainment of adulthood. As would be expected, then, involvement in school work is negatively related to a sense of boredom (Table 74).

Table 74 / Percent Often Feeling "There's Nothing to Do" by Time Spent on Homework

Time Spent on Homework per Day			
One and One-Half Hours or More	One Hour	One-Half Hour	Less than One-Half Hour
19	26	29	33
(659)	(381)	(200)	(125)

Being to some extent a recurring obligation, homework should act to limit involvement in a variety of activities conducive to delinquency. For example, it restricts involvement with peers, especially with respect to those activities designed to "kill time" or to demonstrate masculinity or adultness (Table 75). Boys who spend much time talking with friends and/or riding around in a

Table 75 / Time Talking with Friends and Riding Around
in a Car by Time Devoted to Homework

	Time Spent on Homework per Day			
Item	One and One-Half Hours or More	One Hour	One-Half Hour	Less than One-Half Hour
Percent talking to friends nine hours or more a week	6	8	12	24
Percent riding around in a car three hours or more a week	26 (659)	36 (381)	40 (200)	47 (125)

car are likely to commit delinquent acts (Table 76). Among those
who spend five or more hours a week riding around in a car, the
proportion having committed a delinquent act is more than twice
the proportion among those who spend no time in this activity.

Since time spent on homework is strongly related to the commission of delinquent acts and to leisure variables also related to
the commission of delinquent acts, its effect on delinquency may
occur by way of its effect on leisure activities conducive to delin-

Table 76 / Percent Committing One or More Delinquent
Acts by Time Spent Riding Around in an Automobile

"How many hours a week do you spend riding around in a car?"				
None at All	Less than One	One–Two	Three–Four	Five or More
28 (174)	35 (356)	44 (282)	53 (195)	59 (220)

quency, or it may be that these leisure activities are only spuriously
related to the commission of delinquent acts. However, Table 77
suggests that neither of these configurations is consistent with the
data. Each of the measures of involvement is independently related to delinquent activity.

Regardless of time devoted to homework, boys who ride
around in a car are more likely to commit delinquent acts than

Table 77 / Self-Reported Delinquency by Selected Leisure
Activities and Attitudes

Variable	Marginal Relations		Partial Regression Coefficients	
	Sample Number	Estimated Mean	Raw	Normalized
Time spent on homework				.20
One and one-half hours	659	.55	−.18	−.08
One hour	381	.81	+.01	.00
One-half hour	200	1.00	+.18	+.06
Less than one-half hour	125	1.49	+.62	+.15
Nothing to do				.08
Often	323	1.02	+.16	+.06
Sometimes	669	.70	−.05	−.02
Rarely	284	.70	−.04	−.01
Never	89	.67	−.08	−.02
Time talking with friends				.07
Less than one hour	359	.60	−.07	−.03
One–two hours	381	.69	−.05	−.02
Three–four hours	292	.80	+.05	+.02
Five–eight hours	216	.87	+.02	+.01
Nine hours or more	117	1.32	+.21	+.05
Time riding in car				.17
None	191	.47	−.24	−.07
About one hour	399	.55	−.17	−.07
One–two hours	322	.78	+.03	+.01
Three–four hours	217	.91	+.09	+.03
Five or more hours	236	1.26	+.35	+.12

($R = .33$)   Number of Cases $= 1,365$

those not engaging in this activity. The feeling of boredom and
the amount of time spent talking to friends, however, are only
weakly related to delinquent activity when the effects of the other
variables are removed. This is presumably expectable, since riding
around in a car is one solution to the problem of having nothing to
do; [11] and talking with friends and riding around in a car are
largely one and the same activity.

There is again evidence, then, that two types of leisure activities are important in the causation of delinquency. As was suggested also by data analyzed in Chapter IX, the two types of
activities cluster around the school-education and the working-class-

[11] The common idea that delinquency is itself a solution to the problem
of boredom thus finds only very weak support in these data.

adult poles. (Further evidence for the automobile centeredness of the working-class-adult cluster is provided by a strong relation between the patronization of drive-in restaurants and delinquency.) The myriad activities of adolescents that have no apparent connection to either of these clusters (television, nonacademic reading, sports, hobbies) are generally unrelated to delinquency.

Involvement in school-related activities inhibits concern with and involvement in "working-class-adult" activities, but the latter is not simply the complement of the former. Boys who smoke, drink, date, ride around in cars, find adolescence "boring" and so on, are more likely to commit delinquent acts than boys who do not have these attitudes and do not engage in these activities, *regardless* of commitment to education and involvement in school-related activities.[12] It is suggestive in this regard that both white and Negro boys who see themselves as "well-built" (as opposed to fat, skinny, or just average), are more likely to have committed delinquent acts.[13] There are routes to "premature adulthood" other than through disenchantment with the school.

[12] See especially tables 56 and 77.

[13] The Gluecks' delinquents were much more likely than their nondelinquents to be "muscular," "masculine," or "mesomorphic" (Sheldon and Eleanor Glueck, *Unraveling Juvenile Delinquency* [Cambridge, Mass: Harvard University Press, 1950], pp. 183–197). Since such findings are perfectly consistent with and provide evidence for some sociological explanations of delinquency, it is unfortunate that they tend to be dismissed on the grounds that "physique" is not a sociological variable..

Chapter XI

Belief

Conflicting claims, vague and shifting definitions, and limited empirical data have left in their wake deep and abiding confusion about the place of beliefs in the causation of delinquency. This in spite of the fact that beliefs are the major variables in most sociological explanations of delinquent behavior.[1]

Theories in the cultural deviance tradition suggest that in committing his acts the delinquent is living up to the norms of his culture. These theories usually suggest the existence of beliefs that positively require delinquent acts. With Merton as an exception, most strain theorists borrow this assumption from cultural deviance theory. That is to say, the strains which eventually produce delinquency are seen as leading to delinquency by way of adoption or invention of a set of beliefs which justify the delinquency.[2] In the pure strain theory, no such assumption is required or, for that matter, warranted. In fact, Merton suggests that a condition of strain will have two outcomes: in the short run, people will simply violate the rules in which they believe; in the long run, the rules themselves will erode away, and there will occur a "situation erroneously held by the utilitarian philosophers to be typical of society, a situation in which calculations of personal advantage and fear of punishment are the only regulating agencies." [3]

As suggested earlier, control theorists have not taken a uniform position on this question. To some, beliefs appear to be the

---

[1] David Matza, *Delinquency and Drift* (New York: Wiley, 1964), p. 19; James F. Short, Jr., and Fred L. Strodtbeck, *Group Processes and Gang Delinquency* (Chicago: University of Chicago Press, 1964), p. 47.

[2] The theories I have in find here which straddle the strain and cultural deviance traditions are those of Albert K. Cohen (*Delinquent Boys* [New York: The Free Press, 1955] and Richard A. Cloward and Lloyd E. Ohlin (*Delinquency and Opportunity* [New York: The Free Press, 1966]). Cohen's paper, "The Sociology of the Deviant: Anomie Theory and Beyond" (*American Sociological Review*, XXX [1965], 5–14), is the most explicit recent attempt to combine in one statement all the key assumptions of these two theoretical traditions.

[3] Robert K. Merton, *Social Theory and Social Structure* (New York: The Free Press, 1957), p. 157.

key independent *variable:* delinquency results when the norms have not been internalized.[4] To others moral concerns are irrelevant and/or unimportant: for one thing, they are more or less *constant* throughout the society; for another, they do not have much impact on delinquency even if they are present.[5] Yet a third view on this problem is detectable within the control theory tradition. The relevant beliefs are more or less universally held within the society, but are variably "neutralized" or explained away.[6]

Control theorists are, to be sure, in agreement on one point (the point which makes them control theorists): delinquency is not caused by beliefs that require delinquency but is rather made possible by the absence of (effective) beliefs that forbid delinquency. In this sense they concur with part of the argument of Merton and other anomie theorists: normlessness, and not a system of norms, is at the root of nonnormative behavior.

Now, if the place of beliefs in these theories is clear at an abstract, general level, we may turn to the difficult question: Which beliefs are important in the causation or prevention of delinquency? In general, three sets of beliefs have been stressed by delinquency theorists: middle-class, lower-class, and criminal. We shall examine the relations between each of these sets of beliefs and delinquency.

Values Relative to Law and the Legal System

The beliefs most obviously relevant to delinquency are those bearing on the goodness or badness of delinquent behavior as such. Sutherland's theory, which we may take to be the forerunner of theories that rely on *criminal* values as the major explanatory construct, exhibits a carefully constructed ambiguity about the

[4] Albert J. Reiss, Jr., "Delinquency as the Failure of Personal and Social Controls," *American Sociological Review*, XVI (1951), 196–207. In theories relying on the internalization of norms, it is often not clear whether a person will say that he does or does not accept the norms. Presumably there are ways of determining whether internalization of norms has taken place independent of norm-violating behavior: otherwise, such theories are mere tautology.

[5] Scott Briar and Irving Piliavin, "Delinquency, Situational Inducements, and Commitment to Conformity," *Social Problems*, XIII (1965), 38–39.

[6] Matza, *Delinquency and Drift*, especially pp. 59–62.

nature of these values: "In some societies an individual is surrounded by persons who invariably define the legal codes as *rules
to be observed*, while in others he is surrounded by persons whose
definitions are favorable to the violation of the legal codes." [7]

This statement is consistent with three separate views of the
values that contribute to criminal conduct: 1) some groups define
legal codes as rules not to be observed (an oppositional subculture); 2) some groups define legal codes simply as contingen-
cies of action (an amoral subculture); 3) some groups are essentially mindless of legal codes but positively encourage behavior
which has as a by-product the violation of law (an autonomous
culture).

All three of these views are represented in current delinquency theory, with the view that delinquency is based on an
oppositional subculture most closely identified with Sutherland's
theory. Tests of this theory often simply compare the friendship
patterns of delinquents and nondelinquents. When the delinquents are shown to have associated more frequently with delinquents, it is assumed that they have somehow acquired attitudes
and values favorable to the violation of law, and that the theory is
therefore confirmed. But what these attitudes and values are is not
stated.[8]

In their attempt to specify the content of the "definitions
favorable to violation of law," Sykes and Matza assume that the
delinquent is bound to the conventional order and must somehow
find a way to neutralize "internal and external demands for conformity." [9] The "techniques of neutralization" which result free
the actor for the commission of delinquent acts, but by no means
require delinquent behavior. We follow the view that the definitions favorable to violation of law are definitions which merely free
the actor for delinquency, but we argue that the conditions which
for Sykes and Matza create the necessity for such definitions (the
child's ties to the conventional order) make explanation of their
adoption unduly difficult. For the fact is, the more strongly the

[7] Edwin H. Sutherland and Donald R. Cressey, *Principles of Criminology*,
7th ed. (Philadelphia: Lippincott, 1966), p. 81. Emphasis added.
[8] E.g., James F. Short, Jr., "Differential Association and Delinquency,"
Social Problems, IV (1957), 233–239.
[9] Gresham M. Sykes and David Matza, "Techniques of Neutralization,"
American Sociological Review, XXII (1957), 666.

child is tied to the conventional order, the less likely he is to be able to invent and use techniques of neutralization. Conversely, the weaker his ties to the conventional system, the less he needs to neutralize moral restraints, and the more likely he is to do so, for the simple reason that attachment to a system and belief in the moral validity of its rules are not independent.[10]

In other words, we take the view that definitions favorable to violation of law are rooted in the absence or weakness of intimate relations with other persons, especially in most cases the parents. The person closely attached to his parents is rewarded for conformity by the approval and esteem of those he admires. If such attachments are absent, there is no reward for conformity and only weak punishment for deviation. Lack of concern for the reactions of such persons as parents generalizes as a lack of concern for the approval of persons in positions of impersonal authority. The child who does not need the love and approval of his parents will tend not to need the love and approval of impersonal others, and will thus be free to reject the normative pattern "they" attempt to impose.[11] The beliefs that arise or are adopted under these conditions will tend to reflect and in some sense to rationalize the position of the unattached: the only reason to obey rules is to avoid punishment.

The chain of causation is thus from attachment to parents, through concern for the approval of persons in positions of authority, to belief that the rules of society are binding on one's conduct. All persons in society are assumed to be more or less "exposed" to definitions favorable to violation of law; whether these definitions are accepted largely depends upon the extent to which they are congruent with the person's attitudes and experience vis-à-vis conventional society.[12]

We have seen the effects of attachment to parents and

[10] "Faith is not uprooted by dialectic proof; it must already be deeply shaken by other causes to be unable to withstand the shock of argument" (Emile Durkheim, Suicide [New York: The Free Press, 1951], p. 169).

[11] Talcott Parsons, The Social System (New York: The Free Press, 1951), especially pp. 264, 279.

[12] Differential association theorists seem to argue that the concept of differential association was in fact devised to deal with the question of differential receptivity to cultural definitions favorable to violation of law. If they wish to call the process of learning to hate one's father "differential association" or "assimilation of a part of a culture complex," they are of course free to do so.

teachers; Table 78 shows an equivalent relation between "respect for the police" and delinquent behavior. Given the similarity between this relation and those shown earlier for parents and teachers, it seems reasonable to conclude that lack of respect precedes delinquent acts and does not simply follow from contact with the police. Nevertheless, the strong relation between this item and official delinquency [13] suggests the possibility that actual contact with the police may account for the relation, that the causal ordering may be opposite to that assumed. We therefore reexamine the relation between self-reported delinquency and respect for the police among those reporting *never* having been picked up by the police and having no official record (Table 79). (Among white boys, it will be recalled, police records were found for 16 percent of those reporting never having been picked up by the police, but only a handful of this 16 percent could be said to have provided "bad" information.)

Table 78 / Self-Reported Delinquent Acts and
Respect for the Richmond Police
(in percent)

Self-Reported Acts	"I have a lot of respect for the Richmond police."				
	Strongly Agree	Agree	Undecided	Disagree	Strongly Disagree
None	71	62	46	42	34
One	17	25	32	26	21
Two or more	12	13	22	33	45
Totals	100	100	100	101	100
	(273)	(496)	(325)	(98)	(89)

Control of variables consequent to the dependent variable frequently leads to uninterpretable and/or misleading results. However, in the case of delinquent acts, the slippage between commission and detection is sufficiently great that Table 79 is, I think, meaningful. And it shows that the relation between respect for the police and the commission of delinquent acts is not wholly a consequence of the fact that delinquent acts lead to contact with the police and that this contact somehow results in the lessening of respect.

[13] Eleven percent of those strongly agreeing and 40 percent of those strongly disagreeing with this item have police records.

Attitudes toward law are "affectively neutral." One does not love or hate the law; the law does not react to praise or blame one's actions. But, as we have argued, there is no necessary discontinuity between attitudes toward persons and attitudes toward the law.[14] Lack of respect for the police presumably leads to lack of respect for the law, just as contempt for the ignorant and the foolish leads to "contempt" for the laws designed to protect the ignorant and the foolish from exploitation. It is thus no accident

Table 79 / Self-Reported Delinquent Acts and Respect for the Richmond Police—Those Having No Police Record and Reporting Never Having Been Picked Up by the Police (in percent)

| Self-Reported Acts | "I have a lot of respect for the Richmond police." | | | | |
	Strongly Agree	Agree	Undecided	Disagree	Strongly Disagree
None	80	73	58	62	61
One	15	20	30	25	18
Two or more	5	7	12	13	20
Totals	100	100	100	100	99
	(224)	(360)	(196)	(32)	(33)

that a factor analysis of the attitudinal data in the present study suggests that the following items tap the same dimension: "Suckers deserve to be taken advantage of." And, "To get ahead, you have to do some things which are not right." And it is no accident that there is a correlation of .39 between an index made up of these items and responses to the item, "It is alright to get around the law if you can get away with it."

When the only thing that stands between a man and violation of the law are considerations of expediency, for him the state of anomie has arrived. He has accepted a definition favorable to the violation of law; he is by no means constrained to violate the law, but he is free to violate the law if it appears that it would be to his advantage to do so (Table 80). Few items or indexes thus far reported are more strongly related to delinquency than the

[14] Rap Brown, the SNCC leader arrested July 26, 1967, on federal charges of inciting to riot, illustrated the connection very well when he said: "I hate you Honkies, and I am [therefore] not bound by your laws."

item in Table 80. There is variation in the extent to which boys believe they should obey the law, and the less they believe they should obey it, the less likely they are to do so.

Table 80 / Self-Reported Delinquency by Attitude Toward the Law
(in percent)

| Self-Reported Acts | "It is alright to get around the law if you can get away with it." | | | | |
	Strongly Agree	Agree	Undecided	Disagree	Strongly Disagree
None	31	32	46	55	71
One	29	23	25	30	20
Two or more	41	45	29	15	9
Totals	101	100	100	100	100
	(49)	(93)	(219)	(493)	(426)

Belief in the moral validity of the law is consistently related to the measures of attachment and commitment discussed earlier: the child with little intimate communication with his parents, the child who does not like school, the child who is unconcerned about the opinion of teachers, the child who has little respect for the police, the child who feels little desire for success in conventional terms, is unlikely to feel that the demands of law are binding on his conduct.[15] The "demands of conformity" are perhaps heard, but those making the demands are not respected, and the punishment they propose to mete out is not considered serious.

If definitions explicitly favorable to the violation of law spring from lack of attachment and commitment to conventional institutions, then it may be that these attachments and commitments account for the relation between beliefs and delinquency—it may be that the beliefs are *only* rationalizations of one's position vis-à-vis conventional society. We have claimed earlier that these beliefs should have an independent effect on delinquency, that although they often reflect the absence of stakes in conformity, they affect

[15] For example, belief that it is all right to get around the law if one can get away with it is correlated −.24 with achievement orientation, −.24 with intimacy of communication with the father, and −.21 with liking school. The simultaneous effects of the remaining items and belief in the moral validity of law are shown in Table 81.

delinquency in their own right. In Table 81 we therefore examine the simultaneous effects of several attachment items and the belief that the law should be honored only when it is dangerous not to honor it.

Table 81 illustrates that "respect for the law" is strongly related to the commission of delinquent acts regardless of respect for its agents and regardless of ties to conventional adults. (It also shows that attitudes toward persons may be favorable to the violation of law without being transformed into beliefs more or less consistent with these attitudes, that the delinquent, like most people, has not necessarily created an ideological system that accounts for and is consistent with his behavior.)

Table 81 / Delinquency by Attachment to Father, Respect for Impersonal Authority, and Acceptance of the Normative System

Variable	Zero-Order Correlations (r)	Partial Regression Coefficients	
		Raw	Normalized
Attachment to father	−.26	−.12	−.17
Respect for police	−.28	−.16	−.15
Concern for teachers' opinion	−.23	−.16	−.10
Alright to get around law	+.32	+.23	+.21
(R = .42) Number of Cases = 1,282			

Evidence that the delinquent is relatively likely to be free of concern for the morality of his actions, as Table 80 shows, is at the same time evidence for many apparently contradictory statements about the extent to which he recognizes and accedes to the demands of conventional morality. For example, the statement by Sykes and Matza, that ". . . many delinquents *do* experience a sense of guilt or shame, and [that] its outward expression is not to be dismissed as a purely manipulative gesture to appease those in authority" [16] finds some support in this table. After all, 62 percent of those committing delinquent acts do not agree that it is all right to get around the law if one can get away with it. These boys

[16] "Techniques of Neutralization," pp. 664–665.

have violated laws which they apparently accord legitimacy and moral validity.[17]

Nevertheless, as concern for the morality of delinquent acts declines, the greater the likelihood they will be committed. In fact, among those committing two or more delinquent acts, a minority defends law-abiding behavior as a matter of principle. If we assume that boys commiting two or more delinquent acts in the present sample are, on the whole, much less "delinquent" than those on whom sociological theory has traditionally focused, then theories based on the assumption of considerable potential guilt would appear to be unwarranted.

Table 81 suggests further reasons for doubting the assumption that delinquents experience considerable guilt: those boys committing delinquent acts even though they accept the law as something that *should* be obeyed are relatively unlikely to have close ties to their parents and are unlikely to respect impersonal authority. Thus the expectation of guilt or shame that arises from their allegiance to the law is to some extent negated by their lack of concern for the opinion of other persons, a concern that is itself an important source of "conscience."

The belief that the claims of law are not binding on one's conduct may be seen as a master "technique of neutralization." Boys holding this belief are free to commit delinquent acts. Yet, as mentioned, many boys committing delinquent acts believe that the claims of law *are* binding, and are not in this general sense free to commit delinquencies. Let us then look at beliefs that may free the boy in specific instances for delinquency but which do not necessarily imply general rejection of the claims of the normative system.

Techniques of Neutralization

Sykes and Matza have proposed that ". . . much delinquency is based on what is essentially an unrecognized extension of defenses to crimes, in the form of justifications for deviance that are

---

[17] The distinction between the legitimacy and moral validity of norms is found in Max Weber's The Theory of Social and Economic Organization (New York: Oxford University Press, 1947), pp. 124–126. Weber' distinction is murky, as is its subsequent use in the literature of delinquency. (See especially Cloward and Ohlin, Delinquency and Opportunity, pp. 16–20).

seen as valid by the delinquent but not by the legal system or the society at large." [18] Indicators of most of the "justifications for deviance" proposed by Sykes and Matza are available on the present questionnaire. Several items were in fact designed explicitly to measure the extent to which these techniques are part of the boy's ideological system.

Denial of responsibility. It is frequently alleged that a belief in determinism frees one from responsibility for one's actions. Whether or not the conclusion follows from the premise, it is unrealistic to expect most high school students to be aware of the subtleties of the free will–determinism argument: "It may also be asserted [by delinquents] that delinquent acts are due to forces outside of the individual and beyond his control such as unloving parents, bad companions, or a slum neighborhood. In effect, the delinquent approaches a 'billiard ball' conception of himself in which he sees himself as helplessly propelled into new situations" (p. 667).

Table 82 / Percent Committing One or More Self-Reported Delinquent Acts by Belief in Individual Irresponsibility

"Most criminals shouldn't really be blamed for the things they have done."				
Strongly Agree	Agree	Undecided	Disagree	Strongly Disagree
51	51	48	44	39
(49)	(105)	(177)	(503)	(449)

While it may be possible to overlook the logical problems in the link between determinism and irresponsibility when assigning a belief in such a link to delinquents, operationalization of such constructs is not easy. However, if "many delinquents seem to show a surprising awareness of sociological and psychological explanations of their behavior" (p. 667), and if they further link these explanations with a doctrine of individual irresponsibility, they should be able to see the implications of the statement:

[18] "Techniques of Neutralization," p. 666. All page references in this section of the text are to this source.

"Most criminals really shouldn't be blamed for the things they have done." Table 82 shows the relation between responses to this statement and the commission of delinquent acts.

Only 12 percent of the students in the sample agree that criminals are somehow not to be blamed for their actions. Those accepting the statement are slightly more likely to have committed delinquent acts, but the overwhelming majority (71 percent) of students committing delinquent acts disagree with it.

The delinquent may of course develop a " 'billiard ball' conception of himself" without at the same time denying that he is responsible for his actions, or without generalizing his own predicament to a justification for criminals in general. Another item related to denial of responsibility is then: "I can't seem to stay out of trouble no matter how hard I try."

Table 83 / Percent Committing One or More Delinquent Acts by Helplessness to Avoid Trouble

"I can't seem to stay out of trouble no matter how hard I try."				
Strongly Agree	Agree	Undecided	Disagree	Strongly Disagree
63	66	49	44	25
(46)	(104)	(176)	(621)	(251)

The student agreeing that he cannot stay out of trouble no matter how hard he tries cannot be accused of being overly possessed with the idea that he is the captain of his soul. As Table 83 shows, students with this attitude toward self-determination are considerably more likely than those rejecting it to have committed delinquent acts. This item, then, would seem to confirm one aspect of the denial of responsibility thesis.

Such an item could be construed as a report about past behavior, as a generalization from experience as well as or rather than an attempt to justify one's actions. The apparent methodological difficulty with this and several other techniques of neutralization, both at the level of on-the-spot observation and in the analysis of survey data, is that they may appear only *after* the delinquent act(s) in question has been committed. They may thus be seen as after-the-fact rationalizations rather than before-the-fact neutralizations. The question boils down to this: Which came first, the delinquent act or the belief justifying it?

To my mind, the assumption that delinquent acts come before justifying beliefs is the more plausible causal ordering with respect to many of the techniques of neutralization. It is in fact in many cases difficult to imagine how the boy could subscribe to the belief without having engaged in delinquent acts. But these considerations do not require that we reject such "neutralizing" beliefs as causes of delinquency. On the contrary, since a boy may commit delinquent acts episodically over an extended period of time, there is every reason to believe that neutralizations in some sense resulting from the earlier acts are causes of later acts. In fact, if we reject, as we do here, the idea that the delinquent develops a set of beliefs that positively require delinquent behavior, then the development of a series of neutralizing beliefs is exactly what we mean by the "hardening" process that presumably occurs at some point in a delinquent "career."

Denial of injury. Sykes and Matza note that the delinquent may define his acts as not really causing anyone serious harm: the car was only borrowed, the smashed property was a result of boyish mischief, and so forth. This technique of neutralization, which they call "denial of injury," was measured by the straightforward item: "Most things that people call 'delinquency' don't really hurt anyone" (Table 84).

Table 84 / Percent Committing One or More Delinquent Acts by Perceived Seriousness of Delinquency

"Most things that people call 'delinquency' don't really hurt anyone."				
Strongly Agree	Agree	Undecided	Disagree	Strongly Disagree
72	55	43	38	31
(78)	(232)	(432)	(376)	(164)

The relation in Table 84 is reasonably strong. Those who believe that most delinquent acts are not serious are much more likely to have committed them. The origins of this belief and its link to delinquent behavior can of course not be clarified by examination of the actual seriousness of delinquent acts or by determining whether they "really" hurt anyone. In fact, one implication of this relation (and of the technique of neutralization it supports) is undoubtedly misleading—that is, the boy must somehow convince himself that his acts are harmless to others before he can engage in them. In fact, apparent concern for injury is probably better seen as lack of concern for the victim; otherwise, the origin of this belief is inexplicable.[19] In the last analysis, then, "denial of injury" is probably very close to "denial of the victim," the next technique to be discussed, and one whose origins and consequences are more readily grasped.

Denial of the victim. Several items examined in other contexts might well serve as indicators of the technique of neutralization Sykes and Matza term "denial of the victim." "Suckers deserve to be taken advantage of" is an excellent example. At a general level, in fact, it might be said that the entire control theory of delinquency is based on the premise that those who feel that others are not "worthy" of the respect implied in observance of the law are just those who make others their victims. For this reason, the failure of the item designed as a measure of "denial of the victim" to predict delinquency is particularly surprising (Table 85).

Opinions about the relative culpability of the auto thief and the careless car owner are peculiarly neutral with respect to criminal activity. The fact that almost two-thirds of the white boys in the sample agreed that the car owner was as much to blame as the thief led me to investigate a blunder hypothesis. The hypothesis

19 Much sociological thought has been devoted to the link between the ability to perceive the suffering of others and status inequality (or social distance). Tocqueville, for example, explains the rise of humanitarianism as a consequence of democratization; and Ross argues that status inequality renders impotent the natural sentiment of sympathy as a source of social control. Usually, of course, we think of these inequalities as affecting the ability of those in positions of power to sympathize with those more likely to be suffering, but there is no reason to think that those of low status are any better able to "take the role of the other" when the "other" is not one of them. In these terms, campaigns for a get-tough-with-delinquents policy are the middle-class equivalent of delinquency. (For a summary of Tocqueville's argument, see Robert K. Merton and Robert A. Nisbet, eds., *Contemporary Social Problems*, 2nd ed. [New York: Harcourt, Brace and World, 1966], pp. 8–10. See also Edward A. Ross, *Social Control* [New York: Macmillan, 1920], pp. 23–26.)

Table 85 / Percent Committing One or More Delinquent Acts by Feeling That the Victim of Theft Is Equally Responsible

"The man who leaves the keys in his car is as much to blame for its theft as the man who steals it."				
Strongly Agree	Agree	Undecided	Disagree	Strongly Disagree
44 (391)	42 (461)	49 (131)	46 (211)	37 (102)

was disconfirmed. (In fact, investigation reveals that white boys are the group in the sample least likely to agree with the statement. At the other extreme, 83 percent of Negro girls say the owner is as much to blame as the thief.)

Although responses to this item are for all practical purposes unrelated to the many measures of delinquency, there is one exception: the official measure of auto theft is fairly strongly related to opinions about the relative culpability of the owner and the thief—in the direction opposite to that shown by every other measure of delinquency. The few boys in the sample with official records for auto theft (among those completing the questionnaire, there were 11 white and 28 Negro boys) know that the man leaving the keys in his car is not equally to blame. No car owners shared their cells.[20]

We should not leave "denial of the victim" on a negative note, however, since the idea underlying this technique is central to social control theory, and we have seen too much evidence previously of the close connection between contempt for potential victims and delinquency to doubt that this belief is an important neutralizer of social controls. Why did the operationalization of the concept in this case fail? The answer, it appears, is that the item is overly intellectual; it tells us nothing about the respondent's attitude toward the victim. If the statement were rephrased as "The *sucker* who leaves his keys in his car is as much to blame

20 Given the number of boys arrested for auto theft, the correlations are in fact very strong (for Negroes, $r = .11$; for whites, $r = .06$). Incidentally, the present data do not support the idea that auto thieves are a "favored group." See William W. Wattenberg and James Balistrieri, "Automobile Theft: A 'Favored-Group' Delinquency," *American Journal of Sociology*, LVII (1952), 575-579.

for its theft as the man who steals it," there is little doubt that responses would be strongly related to the commission of delinquent acts.[21]

Condemnation of the condemners. Once again, empirical specification of one of the Sykes and Matza techniques, "condemnation of the condemners," reveals the similarity between the attitudes they suggest as favorable to the violation of law and the attitudes isolated by the analysis of the social bond in which we have engaged. Any measure of the extent to which a boy is willing to condemn police, teachers, and parents will very much resemble the measures we have used as indicators of "attachment." For example, it is easy to see the bearing of many items used previously on such statements as: "Police, it may be said, are corrupt, stupid, and brutal. Teachers always show favoritism and parents always 'take it out' on their children" (p. 668). Even so, an item specifically designed to measure the extent to which this technique has been adopted provides a fair test of the hypothesis.

Table 86 / Percent Committing One or More Delinquent Acts by Perceptions of Equability of Police Treatment

"Policemen try to give all kids an even break."				
Strongly Agree	Agree	Undecided	Disagree	Strongly Disagree
35 (260)	42 (460)	39 (255)	55 (194)	58 (117)

The belief that policemen do not treat all kids the same or do not treat all kids fairly is, to be sure, somewhat weaker than the belief that policemen are "corrupt, stupid, and brutal." Yet this relatively mild condemnation of the police is moderately strongly related to the commission of delinquent acts (Table 86).

A fifth technique of neutralization discussed by Sykes and Matza, "the appeal to higher loyalties," cannot be directly tested with the present data. However, it is probably fair to say that previous data question the phrasing if not the assumption underly-

[21] Sixty-seven percent of those strongly agreeing with the statement "Suckers deserve to be taken advantage of" and only 32 percent of those strongly disagreeing with the statement have committed delinquent acts.

ing Sykes and Matza's description of this technique. If the delinquent is caught in a conflict between "the claims of friendship and the claims of law," it is important to recognize that the claims of neither are as strong for delinquents as they are for high-stake boys. Whereas Sykes and Matza say "The delinquent is unusual, perhaps, in the extent to which he is able to see the fact that he acts in behalf of the smaller social groups to which he belongs as a justification for violations of society's norms" (p. 669), the data presented earlier suggest that the delinquent is unusual in that he acts in behalf of his group in spite of the fact that to him they are not worth the sacrifice.[22]

Lower-Class Norms, Values, Beliefs

Among those focusing on beliefs favorable to the violation of law, no one has been more explicit than Walter B. Miller in rejecting the idea that these beliefs merely make delinquency possible. He argues that there is a lower-class culture in the United States having as members or "directly influencing" as much as 60 percent of the population.[23] This culture is a set of values, beliefs, norms, and practices which automatically leads its members to violation of the law. The primary motivational support for illegal activities in this segment of the population derives, according to Miller, "from a positive effort to achieve what is valued within [the] tradition, and to conform to its explicit and implicit norms." [24]

Miller's conclusions are based on "thirteen worker years" of contact with corner groups in the slums of Boston. Many of his observations have been supported by data presented earlier: for example, those committing delinquent acts are unlikely to be explicitly committed to "official" legal or moral norms; they place less emphasis on achievement in the conventional sense of that term; they are more likely to see themselves as pawns of fate; and

[22] For a test of the neutralization hypothesis (in which no attempt is made to isolate indicators of specific techniques) with results similar to those reported here, see Richard A. Ball, "An Empirical Exploration of Neutralization Theory," *Criminologica*, IV (1966).

[23] Walter B. Miller, "Lower Class Culture as a Generating Milieu of Gang Delinquency," *Journal of Social Issues*, XXIV (1958), 5–19.

[24] *Ibid.*, p. 19. All of the summaries and quotations that follow in this section are from this source.

they are more likely to be concerned that they be defined by others as adults.[25]

If Miller's observations and the data of the present study are in many ways consistent, the interpretation he offers differs radically from that offered here. For present purposes, then, we shall concentrate on Miller's interpretation of the meaning and origin of the attitudes and values of delinquents.

We begin with his assertion that lower-class culture "is a distinctive tradition many centuries old with an integrity of its own" (p. 19). If the word "culture" means anything, and if the phrase "lower-class culture" means anything, then: (1) members of the lower class should be more likely than members of other classes to adhere to the tenets of their culture; and (2) membership and participation in, and acceptance of the culture should be at least to a large extent independent of personal or individual characteristics. If these conditions are not met, some noncultural explanation of what is called lower-class culture would appear to be required.

Social Class and Lower-Class Culture

We must begin the discussion of lower-class culture by recalling that in the present data there is, in terms applicable to Miller's theory, no relation between social class and delinquency. This finding cannot be dismissed on the grounds that the present sample is inappropriate as a means of testing the theory. If from 40 to 60 percent of Americans are "directly influenced" by lower-class culture, and if the "hard core" lower-class group encompasses 15 percent of the population, then it would be stretching the limits of plausibility to suggest that the present sample does not include substantial numbers of lower-class persons, as they are defined by Miller. (The family-status typology occasionally used in the past contains a substantially populated "lower" category that extends up

[25] On the other hand, some of Miller's observations are refuted by the present data. The delinquent gang is not marked by a "high level of intergroup solidarity"; gang members are not, in terms of personal competence, the most "able" members of the community. Furthermore, and at a somewhat different level, there is no basis for concluding that the "female based household" is at the root of, or that it is even related to, the values and norms that Miller sees as somehow deriving from it (see Appendix A, pp. 242–243).

the class ladder only as far as steadily employed laborers.) If lower-class culture "explicitly supports" or "implicitly demands" the commission of illegal acts, members of this culture should certainly have a higher rate of delinquency than nonmembers. If they do not have a higher rate of delinquency, which they do not, then it may be that "lower-class culture" is fairly evenly distributed through the social structure. Let us examine this possibility.

Miller describes lower-class culture in terms of what he calls its "focal concerns." These are, according to Miller, trouble, toughness, smartness, autonomy, fate, and excitement. I shall explicate the concept of focal concerns in the process of testing Miller's suggestion that these concerns are in some way peculiar to the lower class.

Trouble. Trouble, Miller argues, is one of the dominant, if not *the* dominant, concerns of lower-class culture. If this simply means that lower-class people are more likely than middle-class people to get into trouble, then it is simply a restatement of what was initially to have explained. One statement in Miller's discussion of trouble involves an implicit comparison, however, and is thus subject to test: "Expressed desire to avoid behavior which violates moral or legal norms is often based less on an explicit commitment to 'official' moral or legal standards than on a desire to avoid 'getting into trouble,' e.g., the complicating consequences of the action" (p. 8).

The implications of this statement are clear. The member of the lower-class culture has *and expresses* an attitude of expediency toward the law (which, after all, is not of his making). He is, therefore, less likely than the middle-class person to feel that one should obey the law simply because it is the law, because it embodies moral values which he shares with its framers. We have previously examined an item which measures just such attitudes, and which we have shown to be strongly related to the commission of delinquent acts. Are responses to this item related to social class (Table 87)?

The answer to our question, for all practical purposes, is "No." The overwhelming majority of the members of the lowest class in our sample will not agree that the "complicating consequences" of law violation are the major justification for law-

Table 87 / Percent Agreeing "It Is All Right to Get Around the Law If You Can Get Away With It," by Family Status

	Family Status		
Lower	Semi-Skilled and Skilled	White Collar	Professional
12 (350)	13 (558)	12 (194)	9 (297)

abiding behavior, and the proportion expressing disdain for the law in the lowest class is only very slightly greater than the proportion expressing such disdain in the highest class in the sample.

Toughness. It has been suggested that Miller would reject findings like those shown in Table 87 as merely showing that lower-class children will verbally express allegiance to an "official ideal" which they do not *really* believe.[26] Perhaps fortunately no good purely verbal indicator of concern for toughness is available on the questionnaire. For behavioral indicators, however, we may turn to two sources: self-reports and police records on fighting, or assault (Table 88).

We may, for purposes of argumentation, admit that Table 88 is consistent with the Miller thesis that concern for toughness or masculinity is more prevalent in the lower than in the middle class, when behavioral indicators are taken as the criterion. Behavioral indicators, however, merely beg the question with respect to the existence of a lower-class culture, since presumably such differentials in behavior prompted the search for an explanation in the beginning.[27]

[26] Robert A. Gordon, James F. Short, Jr., Desmond S. Cartwright, and Fred L. Strodtbeck, "Values and Gang Delinquency,: A Study of Street-Corner Groups," *American Journal of Sociology,* LXIX (1963), 109–128.

[27] Miller's study is open to the criticism that he has described rather than explained delinquent behavior. As with all such attempts to stay close to the data, to take what people say and do on the spot as evidence of what they think or mean, there is as much danger of misinterpretation as there is in the analysis of survey data. Thus, for example, Miller asserts that "the concept of performing semi-magical rituals so that one's 'luck will change' is prevalent; one hopes that as a result he will move from the state of being 'unlucky' to that of being 'lucky'" (*ibid.,* p. 11). I have seen such rituals performed many times, but I know no one who believes for a moment that such rituals are efficaceous.

Table 88 / Percent Ever Committing Assault,
by Family Status

Assault	Family Status			
	Lower	Semi-Skilled	White Collar	Professional
Self-Reported [a]	43	43	47	34
	(355)	(560)	(199)	(303)
Official [b]	7	4	2	1
	(365)	(571)	(204)	(303)

[a] "Not counting fights you may have had with a brother or sister, have you ever beaten up on anyone or hurt anyone on purpose?" (This item was used as part of the self-report delinquency index.)

[b] In collecting data from the police departments, I tabulated offenses involving force and violence separately. Nine penal code offenses were included: for example, assault with a deadly weapon, simple assault, resisting arrest.

Smartness. A third focal concern of lower-class culture is "smartness." This characteristic or trait, as manifest in an ability to gain one's ends "through a maximum use of mental agility and a minimum use of physical effort," is, again according to Miller, highly valued in lower-class culture. Persons whose lives are affected by concern for smartness tend to classify people into two categories, the sharp operators on the one hand and the suckers on the other. Since the ideal is for the sharp operator to take what he can from the sucker, it follows according to the precepts of this culture that the sucker gets what is coming to him.

Table 89 does not dispute the fact that many persons feel that those not "smart" enough to protect themselves are "legitimate targets of exploitation." It does however dispute the idea that the con-man philosophy is unusually strong among members of the lower class.[28]

Table 89 / Percent Agreeing That "Suckers Deserve to be Taken Advantage of," by Family Status

Family Status			
Lower	Semi-Skilled	White Collar	Professional
20	20	20	17
(263)	(427)	(164)	(245)

[28] Weak evidence in favor of the thesis that concern for "smartness" is a trait of the lower classes is provided by the fact that 30 percent of Negro boys agree with the statement in Table 89.

Autonomy and adultness. Miller's description of the lower-class focal concerns centered around autonomy sounds very much like the description of "premature claims to adult status" discussed in Chapter IX. The lower-class boy, in Miller's view, is especially concerned—at least overtly—to show that he is free of external authority. As part of this concern, he emphasizes his freedom to drink, drive, and, in general, to be seen as grown up. One of the consequences of this concern is, as was also suggested in Chapter IX, a high rate of involvement in delinquent activities. Again, the question is whether this phenomenon should be seen as a class phenomenon or as a consequence of rejection of the educational system. Table 90 summarizes several items relevant to this question.

Table 90 / Family Status and Selected Adult-Status Items

Item	Family Status			
	Lower	Semi-Skilled	White Collar	Professional
Percent agreeing they don't like to be criticized by adults	58	55	55	53
Percent drinking away from home	23	27	26	24
Percent considering a car very important	37	33	28	23
	(263)	(427)	(164)	(245)

Tabulations not shown offer good evidence that the face content of the item, "I don't like to be criticized by adults," is not misleading. Students agreeing with the statement are more likely to be concerned about their own adulthood by other measures. The relevance of drinking to claims of autonomy and adulthood is obvious. Yet neither of these items is related to family status.

One item in Table 90, interest in automobiles, shows a moderate relation in the direction predicted by the Miller hypothesis. The lower the status of the child, the more likely he is to consider a car important. As suggested earlier, however, interest in automobiles is an aspect of "teenage culture" often associated with *middle-class* rather than lower-class adolescents. Howard L. and Barbara G. Myerhoff say, for example, that in their observations of middle-class "gangs," "No subject dominated the conversation as much as the car, which seemed an object of undying, one might say morbid, fascination." It is tempting to see a solution to the "discrepancy" between the present findings and the Myerhoffs' observations in the sentence which follows their description of the middle-class adolescent's fascination with the automobile: "The majority of girls and boys owned their own cars and virtually all had access to a car, usually a late model." [29] It may be, then, that the middle-class children in the present sample evince relatively little interest in automobiles because they take them for granted.

All of which implies that middle-class adolescents are "really" as interested in cars as lower-class adolescents and that the Miller hypothesis is therefore false, even though the data appear to say otherwise. But good evidence against an hypothesis cannot come from data supporting it. On the basis of what we have seen, we can only conclude that lower-class boys *are* more likely than middle-class boys to be interested in automobiles.

The question, then, is: Why? Differential Aptitude Test verbal scores are more highly predictive of interest in automobiles than is family status. Forty-one percent of the lowest fifth and only 17 percent of the highest seventh on verbal ability report being "very interested" in cars. Among the bottom three-fifths on this measure of verbal ability, the relation between family status and interest in automobiles disappears: the academically incompetent son of a professional or executive is as likely to be interested in automobiles as the academically incompetent son of a laborer. (Among the top two-fifths in verbal ability, the negative relation between family status and interest in cars is even stronger than that shown in Table 90.) The fact that the relation between family status and interest in cars depends upon the student's academic ability makes a simple summary of these data difficult. Nevertheless, they do suggest that the automobile is valued to the extent that things of greater value are unavailable, that this aspect of "lower-class culture" reflects a culture of deprivation, not a culture separate from but equal to that of middle-class society in the eyes of its members. This point is, I think, more clearly established in the section which follows.

[29] Howard L. and Barbara G. Myerhoff, "Field Observations of Middle Class 'Gangs,'" *Middle-Class Juvenile Delinquency,* ed. Edmund W. Vaz (New York: Harper and Row, 1967), p. 121.

Fate. It is a sociological commonplace that the lower classes are more likely than the middle classes to be present oriented. They are less likely than middle-class persons to make long-range plans, feeling that such planning is essentially futile. Fate will bring what it will, and man is essentially powerless to alter it. That such a view should emerge when men are without resources to affect their future seems perfectly expectable. That such a view should affect one's willingness to engage in delinquent acts has been made plausible by theory discussed earlier; [30] that it is in fact related to the commission of delinquent acts has also been shown (see tables 82 and 83).

Once again, then, we encounter a case in which the attributes of the lower class are also the attributes of delinquents. Since lower-class boys are, according to Miller's observations and according to general sociological theory, more likely to believe in fate and since boys believing in fate are more likely to be delinquent, then, it seems to follow, lower-class boys are more likely to be delinquent. Where, then, is the theoretical chain broken? Are lower-class boys no more likely to believe in fate?

Table 91 suggests that, once again, the two-variable relations are in the predicted direction: the lower the status of the father's occupation, the more likely the child is to believe that he is essentially powerless to control his destiny. Miller's observations on the acceptance of fate by lower-class boys are weakly confirmed. Lower-class boys are more likely to feel that "their lives are subject to a set of forces over which they have relatively little control" (p. 11).

The issue is whether acceptance of such beliefs is rooted in culture or in social structure, whether the feeling that one is powerless arises from objective powerlessness or is transmitted by one's culture, regardless of one's power in some objective sense. George Orwell says that when he was penniless, he found it impossible to plan beyond the next meal. Orwell had presumably not been raised in a culture in which the concept of man as a pawn of magical powers predominated, yet he found himself acting as though he accepted such beliefs.[31] Although most adoles-

---

[30] See the earlier discussion of Sykes and Matza's technique of neutralization, "denial of responsibility."

[31] George Orwell, *Down and Out in Paris and London* (New York: Avon Publications, n.d.); originally published in 1933.

Table 91 / Percent Rejecting Fatalistic Statements,
by Father's Occupation

| | Father's Occupation | | | |
Statement	Semi-Skilled	Skilled	White Collar	Professional
"What is going to happen to me will happen, no matter what I do."	52 (332)	53 (425)	50 (165)	69 (307)
"There is no sense looking ahead since no one knows what the future will be like."	53 (352)	59 (416)	61 (169)	73 (305)
"A person should live for today and let tomorrow take care of itself."	58 (337)	56 (425)	60 (167)	63 (311)

cents may not have to worry about food, all are not equally endowed with the resources that allow them to exercise control over their destiny. Some are competent in academic things, and thus possess a highly marketable currency; others are incompetent in things academic, and thus have limited power to plan for the future. Do these differences affect one's willingness to accept whatever fate has to offer (Table 92)?

The answer to our question is: Very much indeed. The relation between Differential Aptitude Test verbal scores and rejection of the view that the person cannot and therefore should not at-

Table 92 / Percent Rejecting Fatalistic Statements,
by Differential Aptitude Test Verbal Scores

| | DAT Scores | | | |
Statement	0–9	10–19	20–29	30 and above
"What is going to happen to me will happen, no matter what I do."	37 (240)	50 (505)	63 (341)	80 (182)
"There is no sense looking ahead since no one knows what the future will be like."	36 (249)	52 (508)	70 (329)	80 (185)
"A person should live for today and let tomorrow take care of itself."	38 (245)	52 (510)	71 (341)	74 (181)

tempt to influence his own future is much stronger than the relation between family status and these views.

It may be, then, that the effect of class position on fatalism is a consequence of its effects on academic competence or personal ability, such that no class differences occur when such competence is held constant. If so, this would, in my opinion, be a serious blow to the "lower-class culture" argument. (If class differences survive, it would of course by no means clinch the "culture" argument, since the resources available to children of the middle class are considerably greater than those available to children of the lower class, and they could thus affect attitudes about the manipulability of the future irrespective of personal ability and irrespective of the existence of a culture that encourages or discourages the view that the future is manipulable.) But let us examine the data in Table 93 which bear directly on the question.

Within two categories of Differential Aptitude Test verbal scores, there is no relation between family status and responses to the item, "What is going to happen to me will happen, no matter what I do." In the remaining two categories, the difference between the sons of professionals and the sons of laborers is reduced to about one-half its original size.

The original differences by family status in the proportion rejecting the statement "There is no sense looking ahead since no one knows what the future will be like" persist in three of the four aptitude test categories. The small original relation between family status and "A person should live for today and let tomorrow take care of itself" disappears, however, when aptitude test scores are held more nearly constant (in fact, the tendency is for the relation to reverse). On all three measures the slightly more talented son of a lower- or working-class father is more likely to reject the doctrine of fate than the slightly less talented son of a middle- or upper middle-class father.

On the whole we can say, then, that with respect to several aspects of lower-class culture, there are no differences between lower-class and middle-class children; that with respect to others, lower-class children are only slightly more likely than middle-class children to accept the attitudes and values of their own culture. Even when the latter is true, however, the academically incompetent middle-class child is much more likely than the academically

Table 93 / Percent Rejecting Fatalistic Statements, by Family
Status and Differential Aptitude Test Verbal Scores

"What is going to happen to me will happen, no matter what I do."

Differential Aptitude Test Verbal Score	Family Status			
	Semi-Skilled	Skilled	White Collar	Professional
0–9	38	34	40	48
	(66)	(92)	(26)	(25)
10–19	56	48	43	58
	(124)	(196)	(69)	(71)
20–29	63	63	59	71
	(72)	(119)	(45)	(81)
30 and above	—a	81	81	80
	(18)	(49)	(30)	(74)

"There is no sense looking ahead since no one knows what the future
will be like."

Differential Aptitude Test Verbal Score	Family Status			
	Semi-Skilled	Skilled	White Collar	Professional
0–9	33	35	46	50
	(57)	(88)	(22)	(24)
10–19	55	57	51	49
	(118)	(177)	(68)	(65)
20–29	64	73	57	84
	(69)	(112)	(44)	(76)
30 and above	—a	67	82	91
	(18)	(49)	(28)	(74)

"A person should live for today and let tomorrow take care of itself."

Differential Aptitude Test Verbal Score	Family Status			
	Semi-Skilled	Skilled	White Collar	Professional
0–9	39	43	32	42
	(57)	(88)	(22)	(24)
10–19	61	52	61	42
	(118)	(177)	(68)	(65)
20–29	77	74	66	70
	(69)	(112)	(44)	(76)
30 and above	—a	71	80	80
	(18)	(49)	(28)	(74)

aToo few cases for stable percentages.

competent lower-class child to accept the norms, beliefs, and practices of the lower class. The ease with which middle-class children absorb "lower-class" beliefs, and the ease with which they are discarded or ignored by lower-class children forces us to conclude that if "lower-class culture" is "many centuries old," it is only because powerlessness and deprivation are older. If they were to disappear, lower-class culture would quickly die. And there would be no one to mourn its passing.

Middle-Class Values

We conclude this discussion of the place of beliefs in the causation of delinquency by recalling some of the many relations between acceptance of what are called middle-class values and delinquency (or nondelinquency). High educational and occupational aspirations, high achievement orientation, and so on, are all predictive of nondelinquency. These findings, to be sure, are in accord with almost all theories of delinquency. They are not, however, at least on the surface, in accord with some recent and carefully conducted empirical research.

One of the items in a test by Robert A. Gordon and his colleagues of Cohen's, Cloward and Ohlin's, and Miller's theories requires that the subjects rate "someone who works for good grades at school" on favorable-unfavorable and smart-sucker dimensions. This image, according to the authors, was evaluated equally highly by all groups in their sample.[32] The hypotheses stemming from Cohen, Cloward and Ohlin, and Miller with respect to the delinquent's attitude toward middle-class values were not supported by the data. Delinquents were as likely as nondelinquents, lower-class boys were as likely as middle-class boys, and Negroes were as likely as whites to hold that it is a good, smart thing to work for good grades in school. Now look at Table 94.

According to Table 94, the greater the value the student places on grades, the less likely he is to be delinquent. If "good grades" represent a middle-class value, then these data support theories that take rejection of middle-class values as an intervening link

[32] Gordon et al., "Values and Gang Delinquency"; reprinted in Short and Strodtbeck, Group Process, pp. 47–76. Six groups, Negro and white gang, Negro and white lower-class, and Negro and white middle-class boys, were compared.

Table 94 / Self-Reported Delinquency by Importance of
Good Grades
(in percent)

Self-Reported Acts	"How important is getting good grades to you personally?" [a]			
	Very Important	Somewhat Important	Fairly Important	Completely Unimportant
None	64	53	44	21
One	23	28	24	21
Two or more	13	20	32	58
Totals	100	101	100	100
	(674)	(409)	(176)	(38)

[a] This item has appeared earlier as part of the index of achievement motivation, Chapter IX, p. 178.

between some independent variable and delinquency. These and earlier findings could thus be taken as inconsistent. But they are of course not necessarily inconsistent. We have here measured the student's "values" at a different level, at a level that is obviously more relevant to delinquency than is the level of the abstract general principle. For that matter, there is much indirect evidence in the present data to the effect that the delinquent and the nondelinquent evaluate middle-class images equally highly (see especially the material on respect for peers in Chapter VIII). In fact, on the basis of the present data, we have every reason to think that the boy for whom grades are personally unimportant believes that the boy pursuing good grades is taking a path preferable to his own.

Chapter XII

A Look Back

We began by contrasting strain, control, and cultural deviance perspectives on delinquency. Throughout the book, I have emphasized my belief that their assumptions are basically incompatible. Before I summarize what the data have had to say about each of these perspectives, let us look for a moment at their origins.

The early sociologists in this country were openly moralistic. In deciding whether a given act should be praised or condemned, they simply drew upon their own sense of the rightness of things, secure in the belief that all would agree with them.[1] They tended to ascribe one evil to other evils, to assume that if one thing had gone wrong, other things must have gone wrong to bring it about.[2] Many explicitly assumed that crime results from the failure of society to tame and control man's animal nature. Theirs were essentially control theories; strain and cultural deviance theories are reactions to the kind of theory I have espoused here.

The strain theorist retains the assumption of moral consensus implicit in the earlier theorist's faith in his own judgment, but he rejects the view that the motivation to deviance is given in human nature. On the contrary, he argues, men desire to conform and will do so unless forced to do otherwise by the pressure of unfulfilled but legitimate desires. This shift in focus was heralded when, in 1938, Kingsley Davis pronounced a fallacy the belief that evil causes evil, that all that is deplorable in American society has its roots in equally deplorable home and community conditions.[3] In

---

[1] Edwin M. Lemert, *Social Pathology* (New York: McGraw-Hill, 1951), pp. 3–16. See also C. Wright Mills, "The Professional Ideology of Social Pathologists," *American Journal of Sociology*, XLIX (1942), 165–180.

[2] Albert K. Cohen, "Multiple Factor Approaches," *The Sociology of Crime and Delinquency*, ed. Marvin E. Wolfgang et al. (New York: Wiley, 1962), pp. 77–80.

[3] Cohen (*ibid.*) attributes the naming of the "evil-causes-evil fallacy" to Davis and cites the following paper, in which, as far as I can determine, the phrase does not appear, although the critique of moralistic thinking is similar

that same year, Robert K. Merton suggested that "That great American virtue, 'ambition,' promotes that great American vice, deviant behavior." [4] Since this reaction, many students of deviant behavior have attempted to demonstrate that good causes evil, that vice is, or often is, a product of virtue.

The reaction of the cultural deviance theorist was, in one sense, more fundamental. He focused on the assumption implicit in earlier theories that there is one and only one standard of good and desirable conduct in American society (the standard of the theorist, that is, of the middle class). It is not so, he argued: there are many groups and subgroups in American society. To learn the standards of one's own group may put one automatically in conflict with the standards of the larger society. Thus the idea that societies may fail in the task of socialization, and the search for causally important individual differences between criminals and noncriminals were thrown out as relics of an older, moralizing age. Since crime is learned, the cultural deviance theorist said, the processes behind "crime" are as positive and moral as those behind any form of learned behavior.

In my view, strain theory suffers most from the data presented. Time and again, every theory based on the assumption of strain has run into difficulty. In some cases, to be sure, the tests are not definitive, and strain theory can save itself by falling back on its own ambiguities. Such tenacity for life is not a virtue in a theory; it is in fact a defect. Good theories, it is generally agreed, challenge the data and thus expose themselves to the risk of failure. Where it has been possible to extract predictions from strain theory and subject them to direct test, the data have often failed to support the prediction.

Strain theories are class theories. In most cases, they begin by assuming a strong relation between social class and delinquency. The trouble for these theories thus begins with the failure of social class to be importantly related to delinquency. Although they can survive a zero relation between class and delinquency by focusing on the variables presumably affected by social class, the failure of the original prediction is cause for alarm, since it questions the basic theorem upon which they are constructed.

to that advanced later by Cohen: Kingsley Davis, "Mental Hygiene and the Class Structure," *Psychiatry*, I (1938), 55–65.
  [4] Robert K. Merton, *Social Theory and Social Structure* (New York: The Free Press, 1957), p. 146.

Since strain theories rarely have anything to say about the family, the parental relations findings may appear irrelevant to them. But they are not irrelevant. The consistent strain theory assumes the delinquent's relations with his family are as "good" as those of the nondelinquent, that the delinquent is initially bound to the conventional order and must be forced by discrimination or lack of opportunity to depart from the forms of conduct deemed acceptable by conventional society. Yet the parental relations findings indicate that he is not so bound to the conventional system.

By the same token, the delinquent's acceptance of neutralizing beliefs suggests that unusual pressure is not required to explain his delinquent acts. Given his freedom from the bonds of belief and attachment, there is no barrier to be overcome, and theories that assume such a barrier start from an assumption contrary to fact.

The findings about the family and moral beliefs suggest that a strain theory is unnecessary. Many specific findings cited throughout this study suggest that the alleged sources of strain are not related to delinquency anyway. The delinquent is not a person convinced in the face of discrimination of his own ability; he does not blame the social system rather than himself for his failures; he does not aspire with some force to material things while rejecting the middle-class life style.

In general, the values, aspirations, and goals the strain theorist uses to produce pressure are related to delinquency in the direction opposite to that he predicts when realistic expectations are held constant. The greater one's acceptance of conventional (or even quasi-conventional) success goals, the less likely one is to be delinquent, regardless of the likelihood these goals will some day be attained.

Unfortunately for this theoretical tradition, then, the "evil-causes-evil fallacy" is not a fallacy,[5] and the paradoxical conversion of virtue into vice makes better reading than theory. It is not true that ambition leads to crime; on the contrary, ambition reduces the chances of crime. It is not true that the adolescent is likely to be delinquent to the extent that he cares about conventional things; on the contrary, the less he cares, the more likely he is to

[5] The moral assumptions underlying a theory are of course irrelevant to the question of its truth or falsity. If the assumption that evil causes evil "works," it is better than a good causes evil assumption that does not.

be delinquent. Conflicts between aspiration and realistic expectation may account for much mental anguish in some segments of the population, but they do not account for the commission of delinquent acts by adolescents. Thus the theories of delinquency growing from the strain reaction to earlier and admittedly highly moralistic theorizing have a decided defect: they are not consistent with the data.

Theories stemming from the cultural deviance perspective are more difficult to test than strain theories. In the beginning I suggested that predictions stemming from cultural deviance and control theories would have to be considered one at a time, since at a general level they are much alike. Yet they do focus on rather different material. Matza has said: "The major contribution of sociology to the understanding of deviance has consisted of two fundamental insights. First, persistent deviance typically is not a solitary enterprise; rather, it best flourishes when it receives group support. Second, deviance typically is not an individual or group innovation; rather, it has a history in particular locales." [6] These insights are contributions of cultural deviance theory; they do not stem from theories emphasizing strain or the absence of social controls. We must, I think, grant the validity of these insights. At the same time, however, we must see that they are often sources of misunderstanding about the causes of delinquency. Matza offers us a clue about why they have tended to lead us astray: "The conformity of delinquents to the unconventional standards of their peers —their minimal capacity to behave civilly—is no embarrassment to sociological theories of delinquency. On the contrary, it is their point of departure." [7]

The capacity of delinquents to behave civilly is to cultural deviance theory what social class is to strain theory; it is, as Matza says, the point of departure. The cultural deviance theorist, however, has more difficulty disavowing his past than does the strain theorist, because the truth of more of what he says is dependent upon the validity of his starting point. The assumptions that all groups are more or less equal in their ability to command the loyalty and affection of their members; that delinquent groups are as cohesive as nondelinquent groups; that failure in a conventional

[6] David Matza, Delinquency and Drift (New York: Wiley, 1964), p. 63.
[7] Ibid., p. 26.

group increases the likelihood that one will search for and find interpersonal success in an unconventional group—these assumptions pervade the work of the cultural deviance theorist.

Yet the data on these points are clear: the interpersonal relations among delinquents are not of the same quality of warmth and intensity as those among nondelinquents; failure in one group decreases the likelihood that one will find intimate personal relations in some other group; delinquents do not possess the skills requisite to the argument that they are somehow the finest products of their own culture.

The argument that criminal influences must intervene if any child is to become delinquent, that criminality is not an invention of the individual, also stems from the cultural deviance theorist's point of departure. We have on several occasions tested this argument. In every case, the conclusion is the same: the absence of control increases the likelihood of delinquency regardless of the presence of group traditions of delinquency. Although social support, to be sure, increases the likelihood that delinquent acts will be committed, the view that the child must somehow be taught crime in intimate, personal groups greatly overstates the case.

In simplest terms, cultural deviance theory assumes that cultures, not persons, are deviant. It assumes that in living up to the demands of his own culture, the person automatically comes into conflict with the law. We have devoted much attention to the question of whether deviant cultures actually exist in American society. The first test of this thesis involved the effects of attachment to lower-class parents, on the premise that if lower-class culture is different from that of the society as a whole, attachment to members of this culture would have effects different from those of attachment to persons belonging to the conventional culture. The evidence suggests that the effects of attachment are the same in all class segments of the population: the stronger the attachment, the less likely the child is to be delinquent. This proposition appears to hold true even if the "others" to whom one is attached are themselves delinquent, a strong argument for the view that all accept conventional patterns of conduct as ultimately desirable.

The second test of this thesis involved the social distribution of values, beliefs, or norms. A set of values has been ascribed by cultural deviance theorists to the lower class. It was found that class, as measured by father's occupational or educational status, was only weakly and erratically related to possession of the values described; that, on the other hand, differences in academic competence among students were very strongly related to these "lower-class" values. The implications are clear: the values in question are available to all members of American society more or less equally; they are accepted or rejected to the extent they are consistent or inconsistent with one's realistic position in that society. They are not, in other words, "class" values in the sense that they are transmitted by a class culture.

In short, the data suggest, there are no groups of substantial proportions in American society that positively encourage crime in the sense that those belonging to the groups in question would prefer their children to follow their own rather than a conventional way of life. In fact, on the basis of the data presented here, it appears there are no groups of substantial proportions in American society whose values are neutral with respect to crime. The beliefs and values that feed delinquency are not peculiar to any social class or (nondelinquent) segment of the population.

The control theory I have advocated does not escape unscathed. The first difficulty it encountered was the companionship factor, the importance of which was underestimated in the initial statement of the theory and in the preparation of the data collection instrument. There are group processes important in the causation of delinquency whose automatic operation cannot be predicted from the characteristics of persons.

The theory underestimated the importance of delinquent friends; it overestimated the significance of involvement in conventional activities. Both of these miscalculations appear to stem from the same source, the assumption of "natural motivation" to delinquency. If such natural motivation could legitimately be assumed, delinquent friends would be unnecessary, and involvement in conventional activities would curtail the commission of delinquent acts.

In other words, failure to incorporate some notions of what delinquency does *for* the adolescent probably accounts for the failure of the theory in these areas. Notions about the centribution delinquent activities make to the person's self-concept or self-esteem would also seem to be necessary in accounting for much of the potency of the adult-status items, such as smoking, drinking, dating, and driving a car. The control theory as stated here can take us some way toward understanding these relations, but much remains unexplained. I am confident that when the processes through which these variables affect delinquency are spelled out, they will supplement rather than seriously modify the control theory, but that remains to be seen.

All three of the perspectives I have discussed share a common interest. They are all concerned to know why some people do and some do not commit deviant acts. This concern itself is increasingly coming under attack. Howard S. Becker has written:

> What laymen want to know about deviants is: why do they do it? . . . What is there about them that leads them to do forbidden things? Scientific research has tried to find answers to these questions. In so doing it has accepted the common-sense assumption that there is something inherently deviant (qualitatively distinct) about acts that break . . . social rules. It has also accepted the common-sense assumption that the deviant act occurs because some characteristic of the person who commits it makes it necessary or inevitable that he should. Scientists do not ordinarily question the label "deviant" when it is applied to particular acts or people but rather take it as given. In so doing, they accept the values of the group making the judgment.[8]

What Becker and other critics want to know is: why do they do it? What is there about some criminologists that leads them to ask, "Why do they do it?" In asking these questions, the critics accept the common-sense assumption that there is something inherently suspect about those who disagree with them; they accept the common-sense assumption that evil ideas have evil roots. What are the evil roots of concern for the causes of crime?

> What sources inform the values and judgments on which the foundation of criminological science erects its superstructure of research? Prominent among the public opinion makers in this field are the articulate lawmen. The following cites a sampling of quotations collected from the speeches of J. Edgar Hoover, director of the Federal Bureau of Investigation: "Criminals are

[8] Howard S. Becker, Outsiders (New York: The Free Press, 1963), pp. 3–4. See also Richard R. Korn, ed., Juvenile Delinquency (New York: Crowell, 1968), pp. 1–11; and David Matza, Delinquency and Drift (New York: Wiley, 1964), pp. 11–12.

not just criminals. They are: 'Scum from the boiling pot of the underworld,' 'public rats,' 'lowest dregs of society,' 'scuttling rats in the ship of politics,' 'vermin in human form,' etc." [9]

We could complete the circle, and ask: why do they do it? What is there about the critics of criminology that leads them to ask why some ask, "Why do they do it?" [10] If it is because they are more concerned with "killers who command armies, . . . robbers who steal elections, . . . [and] the unhungry who fatten on food taken from the not-yet-born," [11] then so be it. I wish them success in their endeavor. I hope they find they can ask why men do things they do not like without denying the humanity we all share. Whether they can or cannot, they may rest assured that I, for one, will not judge the quality of their answer by the laudability of their motives.

[9] Korn, ed., *Juvenile Delinquency*, p. 8. Korn's quotation is from Harry Elmer Barnes and Negley K. Teeters, *New Horizons in Criminology* (Englewood Cliffs, N.J.: Prentice-Hall, 1951), p. 454.

[10] For an answer to this question, see Alvin W. Gouldner, "The Sociologist as Partisan: Sociology and the Welfare State," *American Sociologist*, III (1968), 103–116.

[11] Korn, ed., *Juvenile Delinquency*, p. 11.

Reference Matter

Appendix A

Some Traditional Variables and Delinquency

The structural variables upon which delinquency research has traditionally focused have been largely ignored in the text. Since these variables may on occasion provide a plausible alternative explanation to results reported in the text, since they are of continuing interest to sociologists, and since in some cases I have devoted much analysis to them, the results with respect to some of them are reported here.

Age

With most operational definitions of delinquency, a positive relation between age and delinquency is forced, regardless of the age range of the sample. Thus most studies are concerned to remove rather than to study the effects of age. In the present case, no such relation is a necessary consequnce of the operational definition of delinquency, since acts committed more than a year prior to the administration of the questionnaire are forgotten. Because of the dropout problem, the decline in delinquent activity among eleventh and twelfth graders evident in Table A-1 cannot be taken as direct evidence of "maturational reform." The fact that dropouts tend to be delinquent, however, strengthens the inference that delinquent activity increases until about age fifteen.[1]

If it is true, as a recent investigation has suggested,[2] that the delinquent activity of dropouts declines *after* they have left

[1] For a study using a time-bound measure of delinquency and reporting findings similar to these, see John P. Clark and Eugene P. Wenninger, "Socio-Economic Class and Area as Correlates of Illegal Behavior among Juveniles," *American Sociological Review*, XXVII (1962), 826–834.

[2] Delbert S. Elliott, "Delinquency, School Attendance and Dropout," *Social Problems*, XIII (1966), 307–314.

school, there is reason to believe the age-specific delinquency rate
for dropouts is much like that for the in-school population. Be this
as it may, there is little doubt that middle adolescence is the
period of maximum delinquent activity, a fact with theoretical
significance that is out of proportion to the magnitude of the
empirical relation.

Table A-1 / Self-Reported and Official Delinquent Acts
by Grade [a]
(in percent)

Self-Reported Acts	Grade					
	7	8	9	10	11	12
None	64	57	57	51	54	53
One	19	26	26	27	23	29
Two or more	16	17	17	22	23	18
Totals	99	100	100	100	100	100
	(222)	(216)	(258)	(262)	(223)	(122)

Official Acts	Grade					
	7	8	9	10	11	12
None	84	85	79	79	80	83
One	9	8	9	12	13	10
Two or more	7	7	12	9	7	8
Totals	100	100	100	100	100	100
	(223)	(221)	(263)	(270)	(232)	(126)

[a] Grade and age show the same trends in delinquent activity.

Although the relation between age and delinquency did not
require that it be controlled in the analysis, I on several occasions
included it to put the analysis on a familiar footing [3] and in hopes
of accounting for the small relation that does obtain.

Attitudes toward and relations with parents do not affect the
relation between age and delinquency. "Growing away from the
parents" is thus not an explanation of the (small) relation in

[3] None of the traditional "background variables" not controlled by exclusion was sufficiently strongly related to delinquency to require that it be
controlled in examining the relations between other variables and delinquency. This has had the effect of removing the markers upon which sociological discussions of delinquency often depend.

Table A-1. On the other hand, removing the effects of adult-like attitudes and activities causes the relation to reverse rather markedly (see especially Chapter IX). This is perfectly consistent with impressionistic evidence that the "old child" (sissy?) is least likely and the too-young man is most likely to be delinquent.

Mother's Employment

The relation between mother's employment and delinquency (Table A-2) is not particularly strong, but the linearity of the relation, from full-time employment to part-time to housewife, suggests that some aspect of direct supervision and not some characteristic of the mother or of the child accounts for the relation.[4]

Table A-2 / Self-Reported Delinquency by Mother's Employment
(in percent)

	Mother's Employment		
Self-Reported Acts	Full-Time	Part-Time	Housewife
None	50	56	63
One	30	27	21
Two or more	20	17	16
Totals	100	100	100
	(362)	(189)	(538)

Nye controlled many of the obvious background variables such as socioeconomic status, mother's education, and number of children in the family, and found that the relation between mother's employment and delinquency persisted.[5] In the present data, the

[4] The Gluecks found that children whose mothers worked "sporadically" were more likely to be delinquent than those whose mothers worked regularly and were thus led to the conclusion that characteristics of the mother other than her employment led to the high rate of delinquency among the children of the sporadically working. Maccoby's reanalysis of the Gluecks' data suggests, however, that differences in supervision completely account for the relation between mother's employment and delinquency in the Gluecks' sample. See Sheldon and Eleanor Glueck, "Working Mothers and Delinquency," *Mental Hygiene* (July 1957), pp. 327–350; and Eleanor E. Maccoby, "Effects Upon Children of Their Mothers' Outside Employment," *A Modern Introduction to the Family*, ed. Norman W. Bell and Ezra F. Vogel (New York: The Free Press, 1960), p. 523.

[5] Actually Nye reports that the relation became statistically nonsignificant. However, a relation is still present and the loss of statistical significance may well have resulted from the loss of cases entailed in Nye's control procedures

Table A-3 / Self-Reported Delinquency and Mother's
Employment with Selected Antecedent and Intervening
Variables Controlled

| Variable | Marginal Relations | | Partial Regression Coefficients | |
	Sample Number	Estimated Mean	Raw	Normalized
Mother's employment				
Full-time	281	.86	+.10	+.04
Part-time	160	.74	.00	.00
Housewife	468	.66	−.06	−.03
Family status				
Lower	163	.66	−.12	−.04
Semi-skilled and skilled manual	370	.80	+.02	+.01
White collar	146	.84	+.13	+.04
Professional	230	.63	−.02	−.01
Parents met friends				
All	598	.66	−.02	−.01
Some	311	.88	+.04	+.02
Mother's supervision			−.24	−.20
Attachment to mother [a]			−.15	−.20
Number of siblings at home			+.03	+.04
Time spent sitting around with friends			+.05	+.07
Time spent riding around in car			+.10	+.14
Age			+.01	+.01

Number of Cases = 909   Mean, total sample =.74   (R = .42)

[a] The index of attachment to parents is described in Chapter VI, p. 92.

relation between mother's employment and delinquency persists
when the obvious antecedent variables *and* variables that analysis
suggests could interpret the relation are controlled (Table A-3).

Table A-3 poses difficulties for obvious explanations of the
relation between mother's employment and delinquency. It is not
that the child is less likely to be supervised; it is not that he is
more likely to feel estranged from his mother; it is not that he is

rather than from reduction in the strength of the relation. (Nye does not
show the original relation.) F. Ivan Nye, *Family Relationships and Delinquent Behavior* (New York: Wiley, 1958), pp. 53–59. Nye considers the
loss of direct control as a result of mother's employment obvious and makes
no attempt to interpret the relation even though many measures of direct
control were available to him.

more likely to engage in delinquency-producing activities with his friends. Something more subtle accounts for the relation. The following is a possibility.

There is reason to think that geographical proximity is an important element in social control. Men apparently feel safer about their peccadilloes the farther they are removed from the ultimate source of sanctions. Thus the mother two blocks away may be more potent as a source of conscience than a mother four miles away, even though the objective probability of detection is unchanged. There is impressionistic evidence, for example, that high school students on trips to neighboring cities, and businessmen or professionals attending out-of-town conventions, are more likely to engage freely in delinquent activities in these settings *even though* they are with the only persons who could and would act as informers on their home territory.

Size of Family and Ordinal Position

Like mother's employment, size of family is an empiricist's dream. The results of research on this question have been remarkably consistent, showing that as family size increases, the likelihood of delinquency increases. Table A-4 illustrates that the present data are no exception: children from large families are more likely than children from small families to have committed delinquent acts.

Explanations of this relation are virtually as numerous as the studies reporting it:

> The size of the delinquent's family . . . seems to have interested nearly all investigators; but it would hardly be argued that this was a direct cause of delinquency. Its significance (if it has any), must lie in its association with other factors such as social status, intelligence, or overcrowding.[6]

> In relation to size of family, it is reasonable to conclude that greater crowding of the home meant increased competition on the part of the children for parental attention, more likelihood of emotional strain, tension, friction, and less privacy, with resulting sexual and other emotional trauma.[7]

[6] Barbara Wootton, *Social Science and Social Pathology* (New York: Macmillan, 1959), p. 84.

[7] Sheldon and Eleanor Glueck, *Unraveling Juvenile Delinquency* (Cambridge, Mass.: Harvard University Press, 1950), p. 120.

Family sociologists have come to believe that interaction and emotional involvement are more intense in smaller families. . . . Closer parent-child affectional ties should, in turn, result in more effective indirect controls and, perhaps, more effective internalization as well.[8]

Much of this speculative activity seems, however, to have been for naught. According to the present data, none of these interpretations is true. The relation between size of family and delinquency is untouched by controls for affectional ties to and interaction with parents; it persists when the effects of these variables *and* parental supervision are removed (see Chapter VI). For

Table A-4 / Self-Reported Delinquency by Number of
Children in Family
(in percent)

Self-Reported Acts	Number of Children						
	1	2	3	4	5	6	7+
None	67	61	56	54	52	50	51
One	19	24	28	20	29	27	20
Two or more	14	15	16	26	19	23	29
Totals	100	100	100	100	100	100	100
	(91)	(342)	(333)	(231)	(120)	(66)	(90)

that matter, since the number of children at home is less predictive of delinquency than total number of children in the family, the supervision hypothesis is easily ruled out. (The much weaker relation between number of siblings at home and delinquency is incidentally shown in Table A-3).

Overcrowding cannot explain the relation, since measures of crowding in the home are, in the present sample, unrelated to delinquency. The academic achievement hypothesis is plausible, since size of family *is* related to academic achievement and academic achievement is related to delinquency. Once again, however, the relation survives control for a variety of academic achievement variables.[9]

[8] Nye, *Family Relationships*, p. 37.
[9] Alan B. Wilson, "Educational Consequences of Segregation in a California Community," mimeographed, Survey Research Center, Berkeley, 1966, p. 62.

When data are available, a table is usually presented showing the effects of another family structure variable, ordinal position or birth order. The results of research have not been as consistent with respect to the effects of birth order, but the recent and better studies all show that the middle child is most likely to commit delinquent acts, as do the present data (Table A-5).[10]

There are also apparently many good reasons why only, eldest, and youngest children should be less likely than middle children to commit delinquent acts. All have exclusive relations with parents. The eldest child has, in addition, a position of responsibility. The middle child, in contrast, simply receives less attention from his parents.[11] Another good reason for the greater delinquency potential of middle children, and one too often overlooked by delinquency researchers in the past, is that the families of middle children are, on the whole, larger than those of children occupying other structural positions.

Table A-5 / Self-Reported Delinquency by Birth Order
(in percent)

Self-Reported Acts	Birth Order			
	Only Child	First-Born	Middle	Last-Born
None	67	59	51	58
One	19	24	27	23
Two or more	14	17	22	19
Totals	100	100	100	100
	(91)	(399)	(436)	(339)

And, indeed, when we control for family size, the relation between ordinal position and delinquency becomes highly erratic, suggesting that the statistical artifact explanation of the small [12] original relation is superior to those explanations based on assumed personality differences resulting from variations in role definition and/or in the quality and intensity of parent-child relations.

[10] See Nye, *Family Relationships*, p. 37; William McCord and Joan McCord, *Origins of Crime* (New York: Columbia University Press, 1958), p. 118; Sheldon and Eleanor Glueck, *Unraveling*, p. 120.

[11] These explanations are from Nye, *Family Relationships*, p. 37, and the McCords, *Origins of Crime*, p. 118. Neither Nye nor the McCords control for number of children in the family.

[12] It should be noted that this relation is as large as those reported elsewhere.

The Broken Home

The fact that the proportion of boys in institutions from broken homes is considerably greater than the proportion of boys in the general population from broken homes is beyond dispute. That this difference increases at each stage of the adjudication process is also reasonably firmly established. The juvenile court "has [and acts on] information available not only on the offense but also on the child and his family, assembled by social workers or

Table A-6 / Self-Reported Delinquency by Men Living at Home, by Race
(in percent)

Self-Reported Acts	"Do any of these men live at your home now?" [a]					
	White			Negro		
	Real Father	Step Father	None	Real Father	Step Father	None
None	58	50	59	54	45	53
One	25	21	25	25	23	27
Two or more	17	29	17	20	32	20
Totals	100	100	101	99	100	100
	(957)	(100)	(114)	(397)	(95)	(152)

[a] Possibilities excluded from the table were "foster father" and "guardian," which together account for very few students in the sample.

probation officers attached to the court." [13] The self-report technique quickly revealed that the differences in behavior between children from broken and unbroken homes did not justify the great emphasis placed on this factor in common-sense explanations of delinquency.

There is no dearth of boys from broken homes in the present sample: 21 percent of the white boys and 44 percent of the Negro boys are not living with their real fathers. Yet only those living with step- or foster-fathers are more likely than children from "intact" homes to be delinquent (Table A-6).[14]

[13] Ruth Shonle Cavan, Juvenile Delinquency (Philadelphia: Lippincott, 1962), p. 233.
[14] With respect to official delinquency, the pattern is reversed for both Negroes and whites. Boys living with their step-fathers are no more likely

The figures in Table A-6 are consistent [15] with recent research on the relation between the broken home and self-reported delinquency. They show only a very weak relation favoring the intact home. Yet the "broken-homes-cause-delinquency" hypothesis is so firmly ingrained in the common sense that data like those presented here cannot be expected seriously to weaken it.[16]

Conclusion

Delinquency research is repeatedly accused of being, on the one hand, atheoretical, and, on the other, "inconclusive and inconsistent." Yet the relations between the traditional variables and delinquency in the present data are very much like those revealed by previous research. Among the better studies of delinquency, then, inconsistency is not, in my opinion, a serious problem. The empirical findings on delinquency fluctuate much less widely than the statements made about them.

The inconclusiveness of delinquency research is curiously tied to its alleged lack of theory. There is no lack of explanations of the relations revealed by research. At one level, at least, there has been, if anything, too much theory and too little testing of theory. It is very easy to construct plausible interpretations of the relations between the traditional variables and delinquency; it is, on the other hand, as I have found many times, very difficult to construct an interpretation that works. (This is not a complaint about lack of data. In most cases the data appear to be perfectly adequate for testing the interpretation.) If research on the structural determinants of delinquency is to increase our understanding, it is going to have to take a much more aggressive and skeptical stance to-

than boys living with their real fathers to have been picked up by the police, while those boys living in fatherless homes are more likely to have a police record. Among white boys, 17 percent of those living with their real father or step-father and 26 percent of those without a father have police records. Among Negro boys, the percentages are 39 and 46, respectively.

[15] Both Nye (Family Relationships, p. 44) and Robert A. Dentler and Lawrence J. Monroe ("Social Correlates of Early Adolescent Theft," American Sociological Review, XXVI [1961], 733–743) report that the relations they observe are not significant. However, since the relations they found were much like that shown in Table A-6, "consistency" refers to the relation and not to the level of significance.

[16] There is a relation between the broken home and delinquency. The problem is that the relation is, compared to the expectation, very weak.

ward its own theories. Taken together, all of the variables discussed in this section do not explain much of the variance in delinquency; and the criterion should be statistical rather than theoretical, for the fact is that we do not know why they are related to delinquency.

Appendix B
A Note on Techniques of Analysis

Attachment to or awareness of the standards of multivariate statistical techniques by one addicted to tabular analysis produces undue amounts of dissimulation and an abiding sense of sin. Although there are many ways to reduce the strain produced by this discrepancy between methodological ideal and research practice, none is entirely satisfactory.

Since any hypothesis developed and defended by the use of tabular material is subject to direct test by the use of more complex analytic techniques, an obvious solution is to use both methods of analysis, one as a check on the other. The problem here is that a hypothesis developed and defended at some length by the use of tabular material may fail when subjected to more complex analysis. The solution to this "problem" is well known: the hypothesis is rejected and previous argument in its favor abbreviated, revised, or discarded. Unfortunately, the testing of such hypotheses by regression analysis [1] is not straightforward, and the "failure" of the hypothesis may be due to misuse of the testing procedure rather than to lack of agreement with "the facts." It is common practice in tabular analysis, for example, to buttress one's argument by showing the effects of more than one indicator of the independent variable. If all measures of this independent variable are then included in a regression analysis, none may appear to have much effect on the dependent variable,[2] and previous argument

[1] The program used in the present analysis, developed by Alan B. Wilson, allows use of both nominal and continuous independent and dependent variables. Depending upon the types of variables used, it is equivalent to multiple regression, nonorthogonal analysis of covariance, or discriminant function analysis. See Alan B. Wilson, "Educational Consequences of Segregation in a California Community," mimeographed, Survey Research Center, Berkeley, 1966, pp. 115–119.

[2] See Robert A. Gordon, "Issues in the Ecological Study of Delinquency," American Sociological Review, XXXII (1967), 931–934.

will appear to have been erroneous, that is, the effects of the variable will appear to be largely spurious. In tables 26 and 27 (pp. 103–104), for example, "intimacy of communication" appears to have only a very weak effect on delinquency at least partly because two measures of intimacy of communication are included in the analysis.

This misuse of the technique is well known and in principle easily corrected: the analysis is repeated using one relatively pure measure of the variable in question. In many cases, however, the apparent falsification of an earlier hypothesis will occur as an incidental by-product of analysis not designed specifically to test it. In tables 26 and 27, the analysis was designed to allow comparison of multiple correlations, for which purpose no damage is done and something in fact gained by inclusion of redundant measures of independent variables. By the same token, if one is attempting to show that a given variable, say, delinquency of companions, is spuriously related to delinquency, it makes sense to introduce many possible antecedent variables. When the effort fails, as it does in Table 51 (p. 156), the total effect of the "antecedent" variables is underestimated: part of their effect is through what turns out to be an intervening variable, and part is through each other.[3]

In most cases, then, I have not used regression analysis as a means of checking assertions based on or implied by the tabular material. I have used it instead for the highly limited object discussed in each case in the text, and straightforward interpretation of the regression results other than those discussed in the text is likely to be unwarranted.

[3] Wilson ("Educational Consequences of Segregation") notes that partial regression coefficients represent the *total* effect of a variable only when antecedent variables are included and intervening variables and variables consequent on the dependent variable are excluded from the analysis (p. 118). This assumes that alternative measures of a given variable have been excluded or that they are equivalent in effect to intervening variables. (The "alternate forms" analogy oversimplifies the problem, since inclusion of several distinct variables at the same "analytic level" will have an equivalent effect.)

Appendix C

Research Instruments

Appendix C-1. High School Questionnaire

Richmond Youth Study
Survey Research Center
University of California, Berkeley

This is part of a study to find ways to make life better for the young people in the Richmond area. In order to plan useful programs we need to know a great deal about your opinions, plans, experiences, and problems.

No one at the school will know how you mark your answers. At the University we will count *how many* students answer questions each way. Your names are on the answer sheets for two reasons. The study is so long that we have to divide it up into parts; later we have to put the different parts for each person back together. In a few years we will want to know if the programs which are planned have helped you or other students.

The questionnaire is quite long, so please work as rapidly as you can. Answer the questions frankly, even if you think there are people who disagree with you. We want your opinions.

If you can't understand a question, or don't want to answer a question, you may skip it. Also most questions have a place where you can mark if you don't know the answer. But please try to answer all you can.

If you can't read a question, raise your hand. The teacher will read words you don't know. If the teacher is busy, mark the number of the question so you can ask later when your teacher is free.

Please answer the questions the way you really feel. We want to know what students think. When you have finished these questions, put your answer sheet in the large envelope which is marked:

Answer Sheets
Richmond Youth Study
Survey Research Center
University of California, Berkeley

No one in the school will look at your answers. They will be taken to the University where they will be punched on IBM cards and counted.

Look at the top of your answer sheet. Your name should be printed on the top line. Be sure you have your own answer sheet and that you are starting with answer sheet number 1.

How to Mark Answers

All of your answers are to be made on the answer sheets with a number 2 pencil. Do not make any marks on this booklet.

Each side of the answer sheet has two empty boxes: a small one, labelled A, in the lower left corner, and a larger one, labelled B, near the top on the right side. You will be asked to write a few numbers or words in these boxes.

All of the rest of the questions are to be answered in the rows which are numbered from 8 through 80 on each side of the answer sheet.

After each question in this booklet, there are several answers. Each answer has a letter, A, B, C, . . . , in front of it. Find the answer to the question which is best for you. Then, on the answer sheet, make a heavy black mark through the letter which stands for the answer you have chosen. Try to fill up the small dotted lines with your pencil mark without marking outside.

Examples

8. Are you a student in school?
    A. Yes   B. No.

Your answer should be "yes." Be sure you are on Answer Sheet 1. Find row 8, and mark out A.

9. What grade are you in?
    A. 7th   D. 10th
    B. 8th   E. 11th
    C. 9th   F. 12th

Mark out the letter for the correct answer on row 9 of your answer sheet.

PART I. SCHOOL

Which of these schools have you attended in the past? (Please write the numbers of all the schools you have been to in the Richmond area in Box A in the lower left hand corner of answer sheet 1.)

Junior and Senior
  High Schools

1. Adams	14. Alvarado	40. Mira Vista
2. De Anza	15. Balboa	41. Montalvin Manor
3. Downer	16. Bayview	42. Murphy
4. El Cerrito	17. Belding	43. Nystrom
5. Ells	18. Broadway	44. Olinda
6. Gompers	19. Cameron	45. Peres
7. Granada	20. Castro	46. Pinole-Hercules #1
8. Helms	21. Coronado	47. Pinole-Hercules #2
9. Pinole-Hercules #1	22. Cortez	48. Potrero
10. Portola	23. Del Mar	49. Pullman
11. Richmond Evening High	24. Dover	50. Rancho
	25. Ellerhorst	51. Riverside
12. Richmond High	26. El Monte	52. Seaport
13. Roosevelt	27. El Portal	53. Serra
	28. Fairmede	54. Sheldon
	29. Fairmont	55. Sobrante
	30. Ford	56. Stege
	31. Grant	57. Stewart
	32. Harding	58. Tara Hills
	33. Hilltop	59. Valley View
	34. Hillview	60. Verde
	35. Kensington	61. Vista Hills
	36. Kerry Hills	62. Washington
	37. Lake	63. Woodrow Wilson
	38. Lincoln	64. Woods
	39. Madera	65. None of the above

NOW FIND ROW 10 ON THE LEFT SIDE OF ANSWER
SHEET 1.

10. In general, do you like or dislike school?
    A. Like it
    B. Like it and dislike it about equally
    C. Dislike it

11. Which of these three things do you think is the *most* impor-
    tant thing that you can get out of school? (Choose only one.)
    A. Job training
    B. Skill in subjects like English and Mathematics
    C. Ability to think clearly

12. How do you rate yourself in school ability compared with
    other students in your school?
    A. Among the best   D. Below average
    B. Above average   E. Among the worst
    C. About average   F. Don't know

13. What kind of grades do you think you are *capable* of getting?
    A. Mostly A's   F. Mostly C's and D's
    B. Mostly A's and B's   G. Mostly D's
    C. Mostly B's   H. Mostly D's and F's
    D. Mostly B's and C's   I. Mostly F's
    E. Mostly C's

14. How important is getting good grades to you personally?
    A. Very important   C. Fairly important
    B. Somewhat important   D. Completely unimportant

15. How important do you think grades are for getting the kind
    of job you want when you finish school?
    A. Very important   D. I have no idea
    B. Somewhat important   E. I don't plan to work when
    C. Unimportant   I finish school

16. Do you have any trouble keeping your mind on your studies?
    A. Often
    B. Sometimes
    C. Almost never

17. Do you finish your homework?
    A. Always   D. Never
    B. Usually   E. We are not given any
    C. Seldom   homework

18. Do teachers check your homework?
    A. Always   C. Sometimes
    B. Usually   D. We are not given any
                                homework

19. On the average, how much time do you spend doing home-
    work outside school?
    A. 3 or more hours a day   E. About ½ hour a day
    B. About 2 hours a day   F. Less than ½ hour a day
    C. About 1½ hours a day   G. We are not given any
    D. About 1 hour a day   homework

20. Do you have any trouble finding a quiet place in which to do
    your homework?
    A. Usually   C. Never
    B. Sometimes   D. I don't do homework

PART II. TEACHERS

---

21. How many of your teachers seem to care about how well you
    do in school?
    A. Almost all   C. A few
    B. Many   D. None

22. What kind of work do most of your teachers seem to expect
    from you?
    A. Excellent work   D. Poor work
    B. Good work   E. They don't seem to care
    C. Fair work

23. Do you care what teachers think of you?
    A. I care a lot
    B. I care some
    C. I don't care much

Do you agree or disagree with the following statements about
school and teachers?

USE THE ANSWERS IN THE BOX ON THE RIGHT
TO ANSWER THESE QUESTIONS.

24. Teachers should give credit for effort.

25. Teachers talk about the kinds of problems which people I know really have.

26. Brains are more important in school than manners.

27. I would do better in schoolwork if teachers didn't go so fast.

28. It is none of the school's business if a student wants to smoke outside of the classroom.

29. Teachers give enough examples to make things clear for me.

30. I feel nervous and tense in school.

31. Many of the things we have to memorize are meaningless.

32. Teachers pick on me.

33. The things we learn in school help me to understand what is going on around me.

34. Teachers use words that I don't know.

35. Teachers understand students.

36. Teachers just want you to be quiet.

37. Most teachers enjoy teaching.

38. Most teachers know their subject.

39. Teachers keep good order in class.

40. Pupils of all races should attend school together.

A. Strongly agree
B. Agree
C. Undecided
D. Disagree
E. Strongly disagree

41. In the last few years, have you had more men or women teachers?
    A. More men
    B. More women
    C. Both about the same
    D. Don't know

NOW GO TO ROW 42 ON THE UPPER RIGHT HAND SIDE OF ANSWER SHEET 1.

42. Would you prefer to have more men or women teachers?
    A. More men
    B. More women
    C. Both about the same
    D. Don't care

43. I would prefer my teachers to be
    A. Negro
    B. Mexican
    C. Oriental (Chinese, Japanese, Korean)
    D. White
    E. Don't care

PART III. SCHOOL ACTIVITIES

Are you active in any school-connected activities like these?

Athletic teams   Musical groups
Cheer leaders   Art and dance clubs
Hobby clubs   Publications
Science clubs   Student government
Service clubs   Honor societies
Future nurses, teachers, . . . Human relations committees

Please write the names of *all* the school-connected activities in which you are active in Box *B* on the upper right hand side of answer sheet 1.

44. Are your friends here at school active in school activities?
    A. Very active
    B. Somewhat active
    C. Not very active
    D. Not active at all
    E. I have no friends at this school

45. Would you say that your group of friends is the "top crowd" at this school?
    A. Yes
    B. Near the top
    C. No
    D. I have no group of friends at this school
    E. I don't know

46. How much do you think most *students* like the group of friends you go with?

A. Very much
B. Fairly well
C. Not much
D. Not at all

E. I have no group of friends at this school
F. I don't know

47. How much do you think most *teachers* like the group of friends you go with?

A. Very much
B. Fairly well
C. Not much
D. Not at all

E. I have no group of friends at this school
F. I don't know

48. Are you one of the leaders in your group of friends?

A. Yes
B. No
C. I have no group of friends at this school

49. Teachers care most about students who are going to college.

A. Strongly agree
B. Agree
C. Undecided

D. Disagree
E. Strongly disagree

50. If you could be remembered here at school for one of the following, which one would you most want it to be?

A. Bright student
B. Athletic star
C. Popular

D. Leader in student government
E. Well dressed
F. Just average

Below is a list of statements that have been used to describe groups of students. Which group does the statement describe best? (Choose one group from the box at the right.)

51. Are often in trouble with the police

52. Run pretty much everything in this school

53. Teachers like them

54. Try hard in school

55. Likely to succeed in life

56. Teachers don't like them

A. Negroes
B. Mexicans
C. Orientals
D. Whites
E. No difference

57. How well do Negro and white students get along in your school?
    A. Very well   C. Not very well
    B. Fairly well   D. Don't know

58. Do Negro and white students mix and talk to each other at your school?
    A. Often
    B. Sometimes
    C. Hardly ever

PART IV. ATTENDANCE AND DISCIPLINE

---

59. During the last year, did you ever stay away from school just because you had other things you wanted to do?
    A. Often   C. Once or twice
    B. A few times   D. Never

60. How did your parents feel about your staying away from school?
    A. I never have stayed away E. They approved
    B. They didn't know about   F. I don't know
       it   G. I am not living with or in
    C. They didn't care   contact with my parents
    D. They disapproved

61. During the last year, did you ever cheat on any class test?
    A. Often   C. Once or twice
    B. A few times   D. Never

62. During the last year, were you ever sent out of a classroom by a teacher?
    A. Often   C. Once or twice
    B. A few times   D. Never

63. Have you ever been suspended from school?
    A. Often   C. Once or twice
    B. A few times   D. Never

64. How did your parents feel about your being suspended?
    A. I never have been suspended
    C. They didn't care
    D. They were angry with me
    B. They didn't know about it
    E. They were angry with the school
    F. I don't know
    G. I am not living with or in contact with my parents

65. Have you ever been picked up by the police?
    A. Never
    B. Once
    C. Twice
    D. Three times
    E. Four or more times

66. Have any of your close friends ever been picked up by the police?
    A. No
    B. One friend has
    C. Two friends have
    D. Three friends have
    E. Four or more friends have
    F. Don't know

67. Have you ever taken little things (worth less than $2) that did not belong to you?

68. Have you ever taken things of some value (between $2 and $50) that did not belong to you?

69. Have you ever taken things of large value (worth over $50) that did not belong to you?

70. Have you ever taken a car for a ride without the owner's permission?

71. Have you ever banged up something that did not belong to you on purpose?

72. Not counting fights you may have had with a brother or sister, have you ever beaten up on anyone or hurt anyone on purpose?

USE THESE ANSWERS NOW

A. No, never
B. More than a year ago
C. During the last year
D. During the last year and more than a year ago

73. What would be the worst thing about getting caught for stealing?
    A. The police might not treat you right
    B. Your parents would be angry
    C. Your friends would look down on you
    D. Don't know

Would you tell the police if you saw these things?

74. A 14-year-old drinking in a bar

75. A man beating his wife

76. Someone stealing a coat

77. A man peddling dope

A. Yes
B. Maybe
C. No

78. Do you ever think of yourself as a "delinquent"?
    A. Never   D. All the time
    B. Once in a while   E. I don't know what the
    C. Often   word means

79. Does anyone else ever think of you as a "delinquent"?
    A. Never   D. All the time
    B. Once in a while   E. I don't know what the
    C. Often   word means

80. Have you ever attended a California Youth Authority (CYA) camp?
    A. Yes
    B. No

NOW TURN YOUR ANSWER SHEET OVER AND BEGIN
WITH ROW 8 ON THE LEFT HAND SIDE OF ANSWER
SHEET 2.

8. Are you on parole?
    A. I am now
    B. Not now, but I have been
    C. No, I never have been

9. Are you on probation?
    A. I am now
    B. Not now, but I have been
    C. No, I never have been

10. Have you ever been roughed up by the Richmond police?
    A. Yes, more than once   D. No, and I don't know
    B. Yes, once   anyone who has been
    C. No, but I know people
         who have been

DO YOU AGREE OR DISAGREE WITH THE FOLLOWING STATEMENTS?

11. The man who leaves the keys in his car is about as much to blame for its theft as the man who steals it.
12. People who break the law are almost always caught and punished.
13. Being sent to juvenile court would bother me a lot.
14. Policemen try to give all kids an even break.
15. Most things that people call "delinquency" don't really hurt anyone.
16. It is alright to get around the law if you can get away with it.
17. Most criminals really shouldn't be blamed for the things they have done.
18. I have a lot of respect for the Richmond police.

> A. Strongly agree
> B. Agree
> C. Undecided
> D. Disagree
> E. Strongly disagree

PART V. BEST FRIENDS

19. Would you like to be the kind of person your best friends are?
    A. In most ways   C. Not at all
    B. In a few ways   D. I have no best friends
20. Do you respect your best friends' opinions about the important things in life?
    A. Completely   D. Not at all
    B. Pretty much   E. I have no best friends
    C. A little

21. Would your best friends stick by you if you got into really bad trouble?

A. Certainly
B. Probably
C. I doubt it
D. Don't know
E. I have no best friends

22. Do the people you think of as your best friends also think of you as *their* best friend?

A. All of them do
B. Most of them do
C. Some do
D. None do
E. Don't know
F. I have no best friends

23. How many people were you thinking of when you answered these questions about your "best friends"?

A. Eight or more
B. Seven
C. Six
D. Five
E. Four
F. Three
G. Two
H. One
I. None

PART VI. LEISURE ACTIVITIES

---

24. Who do you spend *most* of your free time with?

A. By myself
B. With boys
C. With girls
D. With a group of boys and girls
E. With my family
F. With adults outside my family

25. Do you smoke cigarettes? If you do, at what age did you first begin to smoke?

26. Do you drink beer, wine, or liquor away from home? If you do, at what age did you first begin?

27. Do you date? If you do, at what age did you first begin to date?

A. No, I don't
B. Before age 11
C. Age 11
D. Age 12
E. Age 13
F. Age 14
G. Age 15
H. Age 16
I. Age 17
J. Age 18 or after

28. Do you ever feel that "there's nothing to do"?
    A. Often
    B. Sometimes
    C. Rarely
    D. Never

29. How often do you go to the movies?
    A. Three or more times a a week
    B. Once or twice a week
    C. Two or three times a month
    D. About once a month
    E. Less than once a month
    F. Almost never, or never

30. How often do you go out on dates
    A. I don't date
    B. Four times a week or more
    C. Two or three times a week
    D. About once a week
    E. Two or three times a month
    F. About once a month or less

31. Are you going steady, or are you engaged or married?
    A. No
    B. Am going steady
    C. Am engaged
    D. Am married

On the average, about how many hours a day do you spend doing these things?

32. Watching television
33. Reading newspapers or news magazines
34. Reading romance, movie, or teen-ager magazines
35. Reading comic books

A. 4 or more
B. About 3
C. About 2
D. About 1½
E. About 1
F. About ½ or less
G. None

36. How often do you go to drive-in restaurants?
    A. Three times a week or more
    B. Once or twice a week
    C. One to three times a month
    D. Less than once a month
    E. Almost never, or never

How many hours a week do you spend doing these things?

37. Playing a team game (such as football, basketball, or baseball)?

38. Playing an individual sport (such as swimming, cards, pool)?

39. Sitting around talking with friends?

40. Sitting around talking with parents?

A. None at all
B. Less than 1
C. 1–2 hours
D. 3–4 hours
E. 5–6 hours
F. 7–8 hours
G. 9 or more hours

41. Riding around in a car?

NOW GO TO ROW 42 ON THE UPPER RIGHT HAND SIDE OF ANSWER SHEET 2.

42. Reading books for pleasure?

43. Working around the house for your parents?

44. Working at hobbies?

Do you belong to any youth clubs like these?

Belding Teen Club
Charmettes
Chez Mones
Diamond Lacion
Dukes & Debs
Granada Teens
High Pointers
Hi Phi's
Kennedy Teen Club
La Shonettes
Modernistics
Shields Teen Club

Boys' Club
Car or motorcycle clubs
Catholic Youth Organization
Explorer's Club
Greek-Letter Societies
Hi Y
Jacket or Sweater Clubs
Nurses' Aides
Scouts
Y Teens
Young Life

Please write the names of all the clubs you belong to in Box *B* on the upper right hand side of answer sheet 2.

If you belong to any other youth clubs that have not been listed, write them in Box *B* also. (If you need more space, you may write in Box *A* on the lower left hand side of answer sheet 2.)

Now find row 45 on your answer sheet.

45. Do you ever use the public library or any of its branches?
    A. More than once a week   C. Less than once a week
    B. About once a week   D. No

46. Do you own a motorcycle?
    A. Yes
    B. No

47. Do you own a car?
    A. Yes
    B. No

48. Do you drive a car that you don't own?
    A. Yes, my parents' car only   D. More than one car
    B. Yes, a friend's car only   E. No
    C. Yes, some other car only

49. How important is "having a car" to you?
    A. It is everything   D. Not very important
    B. Very important   E. Unimportant
    C. Fairly important

50. What is the longest trip you have taken outside your city?
    A. Have never gone outside the city limits
    B. Have only gone to other Bay Area cities
    C. Have only gone to other cities in California
    D. Have gone outside the State of California

During the last two months did you need any help with these things?

51. Getting a job

52. Doing school work

53. Health

> A. Didn't need help
> B. Needed help and got it
> C. Needed help but didn't get it

54. In general, do you like or dislike school?
    A. Dislike it
    B. Like it
    C. Like it and dislike it about equally

PART VII. ATTITUDES AND OPINIONS

Do you agree or disagree with the following statements?

55. It is hard to tell other people how I feel

56. A person should never stop trying to get ahead

57. What is going to happen to me will happen, no matter what I do

58. I have no really close friends

59. A person should live for today and let tomorrow take care of itself

60. I am not the person I pretend to be

61. I would rather not start something at which I may not be successful

62. Nothing is worth moving away from one's parents

63. People don't seem to realize that my feelings can be hurt

64. In our country, opportunities for success are available to everyone

65. I may seem happy to people, but inside I often feel unhappy

66. Planning is useless since one's plans hardly ever work out

67. To get ahead, you have to do some things which are not right

A. Strongly agree
B. Agree
C. Undecided
D. Disagree
E. Strongly disagree

68. People are always picking on me

69. It is hard for me to talk to people when I first meet them

70. I worry all the time

71. Most people can be trusted

72. I often feel discouraged

73. Whatever I do, I try hard

74. I do not have much to be proud of

75. You should not expect too much out of life

76. I don't like being criticized by adults

77. What is lacking in the world today is the old kind of friendship that lasted for a lifetime

78. I don't approve of dancing

79. I try hard in school

80. Most people don't care what happens to you

A. Strongly agree
B. Agree
C. Undecided
D. Disagree
E. Strongly disagree

SECTION B

This is the second part of the Richmond Youth Study. Be sure that you have the answer sheet which is numbered 3 on one side and 4 on the other side, and that your name is printed on the top of the sheet. All of your answers are to be made on the answer sheets with a number 2 pencil, as before. Do not make any marks in this booklet.

The first few questions are about different kinds of jobs which people have, and jobs they might like to have.

Below is a list of different kinds of jobs. Use this list to answer the questions on the next page. There are four groups of jobs: *manual work*, where you work with your hands, and usually wear jeans or overalls or a uniform; *white-collar work*, where you wear a shirt and tie, or ladies wear dresses; *self-employed jobs*, where you own your own business and don't have a boss; and *other* answers which don't fit in any group.

Letters	Kind of Job	Examples
	Manual Work	
A + F	Domestic	housecleaning, maid, babysitter
A + G	Laborer	construction worker, janitor, helper
A + H	Semi-skilled	machine operator, truck driver
A + I	Craftsman	journeyman carpenter, electrician, machinist
A + J	Foreman	foreman of a work gang, inspector in factory
	White-Collar	
B + F	Semi-skilled	store clerk, mailman, salesman
B + G	Skilled	secretary, bookkeeper, court clerk
B + H	Entertainer	actor, athlete, model
B + I	Professional	doctor, social worker, teacher
B + J	Manager	executive, superintendent, editor, senator

	Self-employed	
C + F	Professional	lawyer, architect, dentist
C + G	Craftsman	carpenter-contractor, jeweler, mechanic
C + H	Merchant	grocery or variety store owner
C + I	Large business	factory or department store owner
C + J	Farmer	owner of farm or ranch
	Other	
D + F	Housewife	taking care of own home—not for pay
D + G	Don't know	
D + H	Don't care	
D + I	None	
D + J	Deceased	

In front of each kind of job on the opposite page there are two letters. To answer the questions about jobs, find the kind of job which is most like the one you are thinking of. On your answer sheet mark out the two letters that are listed in front of that kind of job.

Example

8. Which of these jobs comes closest to describing the kind of of work the school custodian does?

Since a custodian works with his hands and probably wears coveralls or a uniform, this is *manual work.* "Janitor" is one of the examples for *laborer.* So you should mark out the letters A and G in row 8 of your answer sheet 3. Now go ahead and answer questions 9 to 14 the same way.

9. Which of these jobs comes closest to describing the kind of work your father usually does.

10. Which of these jobs comes closest to describing the kind of work your mother does?

11. Which of these jobs comes closest to describing the first full-time job you expect to have after you finish schooling and/or military service?

12. Which of these jobs comes closest to describing the job you *want* eventually?

13. Which of these jobs comes closest to describing the job you really *expect* to have eventually?

14. Which of these jobs comes closest to describing the job your parents most want to see you get after you finish school?

To give us a better idea of your father's job, please write the name of his job in Box *B* near the upper right hand corner of answer sheet 3. Also write a few words to tell what he does on his job.

NOW FIND ROW 15 ON THE LEFT SIDE OF ANSWER SHEET 3. (Mark out one letter only on your answer sheet.)

15. Where were you born?
    A. RICHMOND, California
    B. In the RICHMOND AREA, but not in Richmond
    C. In CALIFORNIA, but not in this area
    D. In the SOUTH (Texas, Oklahoma, Arkansas, Louisiana, Kentucky, Tennessee, Alabama, Mississippi, West Virginia, Virginia, North & South Carolina, Georgia, Florida)
    E. Elsewhere in the United States
    F. Outside of the United States

16. In what size city were you raised during most of your childhood?
    A. On a FARM
    B. In a SMALL TOWN, population under 2,500
    C. In a SMALL CITY, about the size of Richmond
    D. In a LARGE CITY, about the size of Oakland or San Francisco

17. Are you
    A. Negro   D. White
    B. Mexican   E. Other
    C. Oriental (Chinese or   F. Decline to state
       Japanese)   G. Don't know

18. Are your real parents living?
    A. Both living
    B. Only mother living
    C. Only father living
    D. Neither living

19. Up until you were five, were you living with both real parents?
    A. Both   C. Father only
    B. Mother only   D. Neither

USE THE ANSWERS IN THE BOX ON THE RIGHT TO ANSWER THESE QUESTIONS.

20. How many brothers (including half-brothers) do you have?

21. How many of your brothers are living at home with you?

22. How many sisters (including half-sisters) do you have?

23. How many of your sisters are living at home with you?

24. How many of your brothers and sisters are older than you?

A. None
B. One
C. Two
D. Three
E. Four
F. Five
G. Six
H. Seven
I. Eight or more

25. In general, would you say that you are
    A. Skinny   C. Well-built
    B. Fat   D. About average

26. Compared to most people your age, are you
    A. Bigger
    B. Smaller
    C. About the same

27. About how many days have you been absent from school this school year for health reasons?
    A. None   D. 5 to 9
    B. 1 or 2   E. 10 to 14
    C. 3 or 4   F. 15 or more

28. How good is your health?

A. Excellent
B. Quite good
C. Fair

D. Not very good
E. Very poor

29. How many people altogether (including yourself, children, parents, relatives, and boarders) live in your home?

A. 1 person only
   (I live by myself)
B. 2 people
C. 3 people
D. 4 people
E. 5 people

F. 6 people
G. 7 people
H. 8 people
I. 9 people
J. 10 people or more

30. Do you have your own room at home or do you share it?

A. Have my own room
B. Share it with brother(s) only
C. Share it with sister(s) only
D. Share it with brother(s) and sister(s) only

E. Share it with adult(s) only
F. Share it with other(s) only
G. Share it with more than one of these

At your home, are there any of the following?

31. A dictionary

32. A musical instrument

33. A map of the United States

34. A daily newspaper

35. A weekly news magazine

36. Paper and pencils

37. An encyclopedia

38. Paints or crayons

A. Yes
B. No

39. About how many books are there in your home?

A. None
B. 1–5
C. 6–10
D. 11–25
E. 26–50

F. 51–100
G. 101–200
H. 201–500
I. Over 500

40. Do you belong to any of these churches?
    A. African Methodist Episcopal
    B. Assemblies of God
    C. Baptist
    D. Catholic
    E. Church of Christ
    F. Church of God
    G. Church of God in Christ
    H. None of these
    I. Don't belong to any church
    J. Decline to state

41. Do you belong to any of these churches?
    A. Christian Methodist Episcopal
    B. Congregationalist
    C. Episcopalian
    D. Jewish
    E. Lutheran
    F. Methodist
    G. Pentecostal
    H. Presbyterian
    I. None of these
    J. Decline to state

NOW GO TO ROW 42 ON THE UPPER RIGHT HAND SIDE OF ANSWER SHEET 3.

42. On the average, how often do you attend religious services?
    A. Once a week or more
    B. Two or three times a month
    C. Once a month
    D. Only on important holidays
    E. Hardly ever
    F. Never

43. Does your church have special programs for boys or girls your age?
    A. Yes, but I never attend
    B. Yes, and I go sometimes
    C. Yes, and I attend all the time
    D. No, there are no special programs
    E. Don't know
    F. I don't go to any particular church

How does your pastor (minister, priest, rabbi) feel about

44. Dancing?

45. Gambling?

46. Sports?

47. Racial integration?

A. He approves
B. He disapproves
C. He doesn't care
D. I don't know
E. I have no pastor

PART II. YOUR NEIGHBORHOOD

The following statements are often made about neighborhoods. If they were made about your neighborhood, would you agree or disagree with them?

48. People around here keep up their houses and yards.

49. Young people are always getting in trouble

50. There aren't enough places for children to play

51. Many of the men in the neighborhood do not have work

52. A lot of people moving in are running down the neighborhood

A. Strongly agree
B. Agree
C. Undecided
D. Disagree
E. Strongly disagree

53. Most of the families know each other

54. My friends all live in the neighborhood

55. Most people around here don't care what happens to you

56. How many of the people in your neighborhood are of the same race as you?
    A. All
    B. Most
    C. About half
    D. Some
    E. None
    F. Don't know

57. What do most of the fellows you know usually wear in their free time?
    A. Black jeans
    B. Blue jeans
    C. Corduroys
    D. Khakis
    E. Dress pants
    F. Other

58. All in all, how would you describe your neighborhood?
    A. Luxurious   D. Below average
    B. More than comfortable   E. Rundown
    C. Average   F. A slum

59. How does your family compare to other families in the neighborhood?
    A. Much better-off   D. Worse-off
    B. Better-off   E. Much worse-off
    C. About the same   F. Don't know

60. Does your family plan to stay in the neighborhood?
    A. Definitely   D. Definitely not
    B. Probably   E. Don't know
    C. Probably not

61. Do you think your neighborhood will improve or go down in the next couple of years?
    A. Improve   C. Go down
    B. Stay the same   D. Don't know

62. How do you *personally* like your neighborhood as a place to live?
    A. Very much   C. Only a little
    B. Somewhat   D. Not at all

63. When you get to be on your own, would you want to live in a neighborhood like the one you live in now?
    A. Definitely   D. Definitely not
    B. Probably   E. Don't know
    C. Probably not

What do you usually call your part of town? Write the name of your neighborhood in Box A in the lower left hand corner of answer sheet 3.

PART III. WORK AND INCOME

64. How old were you when you got your first job at which you worked for pay at least five hours a week?

    A. I have never had such   F. Age 14
       a job   G. Age 15
    B. Age 10 or before   H. Age 16
    C. Age 11   I. Age 17
    D. Age 12   J. Age 18 or older
    E. Age 13

65. Do you get any spending money for pleasure from your parents?

    A. No, none   E. $4.00 to $5.99 a week
    B. Yes, less than $1.00 a   F. $6.00 to $7.99 a week
       week   G. $8.00 to $9.99 a week
    C. $1.00 to $1.99 a week   H. $10.00 or more a week
    D. $2.00 to $3.99 a week   I. It changes from week to
                                     week

66. Has the Employment Office ever been helpful in getting you a job?

    A. I have never applied   D. Fairly helpful
    B. No, not at all   E. Very helpful
    C. A little

67. On the average, how many hours a week do you work for pay now, while you are attending school?

    A. Not at all   E. 16 to 20 hours
    B. Less than 6 hours   F. 21 to 25 hours
    C. 6 to 10 hours   G. 26 to 39 hours
    D. 11 to 15 hours   H. Full time (40 hours or
                                     more)

68. Do you give your family any of the money you earn?

    A. I don't earn any   D. Half of it
    B. All of it   E. A little
    C. Most of it   F. None of it

IF YOU DO NOT HAVE A JOB NOW, SKIP TO QUES-
TION NUMBER 72 ON PAGE 10.

69. What do you get paid an hour?
 A. Less than 50¢ an hour G. $2.00 to $2.49
 B. 50¢ to 99¢ an hour H. $2.50 to $2.99
 C. $1.00 to $1.24 I. $3.00 or more
 D. $1.25 to $1.49 J. It varies too much to give
 E. $1.50 to $1.74 an average
 F. $1.75 to $1.99

70. Do you plan to keep on working on this same job when you
finish school?
 A. Yes, definitely D. Definitely not
 B. Yes, probably E. Don't know
 C. Probably not

71. How did you find out about your present job?
 A. From members of my family
 B. From other people I know
 C. In some other way

Do you agree or disagree with the following statements about
jobs?

72. My job should allow me to
work with my hands

73. The work I do should change
from day to day

74. The work I do should allow me
to use my own ideas

75. A steady job is more important
than a chance for promotion

76. My job should be easy on the
nerves

77. I want to be able to talk to
other workers on the job

78. My job should allow me to
direct others

A. Strongly agree
B. Agree
C. Undecided
D. Disagree
E. Strongly disagree

79. My job should not have a lot of responsibility

80. My job should not make me move from city to city

A. Strongly agree
B. Agree
C. Undecided
D. Disagree
E. Strongly disagree

NOW TURN YOUR ANSWER SHEET OVER AND BEGIN WITH ROW 8 ON THE LEFT HAND SIDE OF ANSWER SHEET 4.

8. My job should pay well

9. I prefer a job which lets me work at my own speed

10. I would like to work with others

11. At the end of the day I should be able to forget about the job

12. The only reason to have a job is for money

13. My job should not be tiring

14. In my job it should be possible for me always to be learning something new

15. I want to use my own special talents on my job

16. My job should not make me worry

A. Strongly agree
B. Agree
C. Undecided
D. Disagree
E. Strongly disagree

17. I would prefer a job in a large company rather than in a small one

18. I should be able to keep clean at work

19. My job should be outdoors

20. My job should give me a good chance for promotion

21. I want a job in which I can help people

PART IV. ASPIRATIONS AND EXPECTATIONS

Are you worried about any of these things?

22. Knowing what your real interests are

23. Knowing what you will do after high school

24. Knowing what work you are best suited for

25. Deciding whether you should go to college

A. Very worried
B. Somewhat worried
C. Not worried at all

26. Knowing how much ability you really have

27. Finding out how you can learn a trade

28. Being able to find a job after you get out of school

29. Thinking about getting married

30. How often do you think about what you are going to do and be after you get out of school?
    A. Very often   D. Seldom
    B. Often   E. Never
    C. Sometimes

How often have you talked over your future plans with these people?

31. Your mother

32. Your father

33. Other relatives

34. People your age

35. Minister

36. Other adults

A. Often
B. Occasionally
C. Never

37. As you see it now, do you plan to graduate from high school?
   A. Yes, go straight through
   B. Yes, but leave for a while and come back
   C. No

38. How much schooling do you *actually expect* to get eventually?
   A. Some high school
   B. High school graduation
   C. On the job apprenticeship
   D. Trade or business school
   E. Some college or junior college
   F. College graduation (four years)

39. How much schooling would you *like* to get eventually?
   A. Some high school
   B. High school graduation
   C. On the job apprenticeship
   D. Trade or business school
   E. Some college or junior college
   F. College graduation (four years)

40. At what age do you want to get married?
   A. I don't   F. 19
   B. 15 or under   G. 20
   C. 16   H. 21 or over
   D. 17   I. Don't know
   E. 18   J. I am already married

41. Do you think that things will be the same for your children as they are for you?
   A. They will be better   D. Don't know
   B. They will be the same   E. I don't intend to have
   C. They will be worse   children

NOW GO TO ROW 42 ON THE UPPER RIGHT HAND SIDE OF ANSWER SHEET 4.

42. Where do you want to live after you have finished all your schooling?

A. In Richmond, California
B. In this area, outside of Richmond
C. Other areas of Northern California
D. Southern California
E. Elsewhere in the United States
F. Don't know
G. Don't care

43. Among the following things, which one do you think will give you the most satisfaction in your life?

A. My work
B. My future family
C. My friends
D. My hobbies
E. My house
F. My church

44. What period in your life do you think will turn out to have been the *happiest* part of your life?

A. Grade school years
B. Junior high school years
C. High school years
D. Between high school and age 20
E. Age 20 to 30
F. Age 30 to 40
G. Over age 40
H. None of my life has been or will be happy

45. If you could start work in any of the following and get the same income at the start, which would you choose?

A. Government civil service work
B. Working for a *large* business or corporation
C. Working for a *small* business
D. Owning your own business
E. Profession
F. Farming
G. Armed forces
H. Don't know

46. Have you decided on a particular kind of job that you want to aim for when you have finished your schooling?

A. Yes
B. No
C. I don't intend to get a job

In Box A at the lower left hand corner of answer sheet 4, write the name of the job which you want eventually. Please tell us as much about it as you can.

47. At what age did you first decide on this particular job?
   A. Age 10 or earlier
   B. Age 11
   C. Age 12
   D. Age 13
   E. Age 14
   F. Age 15
   G. Age 16
   H. Age 17
   I. Age 18 or more
   J. Don't remember; don't know

48. How sure are you that you will actually get the job you want?
   A. Completely certain
   B. Pretty sure I will
   C. Not too sure
   D. Not sure at all

49. Do you know anyone who has a job like the one you want?
   A. No
   B. Someone in my family
   C. Someone I know well
   D. Someone I know slightly
   E. Someone I don't know personally

How would you feel about taking these jobs?

50. House cleaning

51. Construction worker

52. Truck driver

53. Carpenter

54. Store clerk

55. Bookkeeper

56. Social worker

57. Doctor

A. Would like it
B. Wouldn't mind it
C. Would hate it

Do you think that any of the following things will keep you from getting the kind of job you want to have eventually?

58. Bad grades

59. Racial discrimination

60. Don't know the right people

61. Getting into trouble

62. Am not smart enough

63. Not willing to make the effort

A. Yes
B. Maybe
C. No

64. Lack of money

65. Schools don't give the necessary
training

66. Don't know how to go about it

67. Getting married too soon

68. No job available

69. Poor health

A. Yes
B. Maybe
C. No

How many relatives, not counting your parents, brothers and sisters, are living *at home* with you?

grandmothers   cousins
grandfathers   nephews
aunts   nieces
uncles   other relatives

In Box *B*, in the upper right hand side of answer sheet 4, please write the number of each kind of relative who is living at home with you. Write a number, 0, 1, 2, . . . , in front of each word on the list.

PART IV. ATTITUDES AND OPINIONS

Do you agree or disagree with the following statements?

70. I don't approve of people who drink

71. Everyone in this world is out for himself

72. If you need help it is better to get it from relatives or friends than from public welfare

73. At times I think I am no good at all

74. When a person gets out of school he should leave home

75. Most people who need welfare need it because of things beyond their control

A. Strongly agree
B. Agree
C. Undecided
D. Disagree
E. Strongly disagree

76. I have been happy in my home

77. It is hard for young people without high school diplomas to find good jobs

78. Most people have little respect for those who get welfare assistance

79. I have a lot of trouble controlling my temper

80. I often feel that I just can't learn

A. Strongly agree
B. Agree
C. Undecided
D. Disagree
E. Strongly disagree

SECTION C

This is the last section of the Richmond Youth Study. Be sure that you have the answer sheet that is numbered 5 on one side and 6 on the other side, and that your name is printed on the top of the sheet. All of your answers are to be made on the answer sheets with a number 2 pencil, as before. Do not make any marks in this booklet.

The first questions are about your parents' attitudes and what they do.

PART I. PARENTS

---

8. Who is it that is now acting as a father for you?
   A. My real father, who is living at home
   B. My real father, who does not live at home
   C. My step-father
   D. A foster-father
   E. A grandfather
   F. Other relative
   G. Other adult
   H. No one

9. Who is it that is now acting as a mother for you?
   A. My real mother, who is living at home
   B. My real mother, who does not live at home
   C. My step-mother
   D. A foster-mother
   E. A grandmother
   F. Other relative
   G. Other adult
   H. No one

Please answer these questions by thinking about the persons you checked above. If you checked "no one" do not answer about that parent. You should mark two letters on your answer sheet for each of these questions. First mark A, B, or C for your mother; and then mark F, G, or H for your father.

Example

USE THESE ANSWERS

10. Do your parents eat breakfast with you?
If your mother *usually* does and your father *never* does, you should mark out A for your mother and H for your father in row 10 on answer sheet 5. Go ahead and mark row 10; then go on to row 11.

MARK EACH ROW TWICE. ONCE FOR EACH PARENT.

MOTHER
A. Usually
B. Sometimes
C. Never

FATHER
F. Usually
G. Sometimes
H. Never

11. Do your parents seem to understand you?

12. Do your parents make rules that seem unfair to you?

13. When you don't know why your parents make a rule, will they explain the reason?

14. Do your parents check to see whether you have done what they tell you to do?

15. Do your parents know where you are when you are away from home?

16. Do your parents know who you are with when you are away from home?

17. When you come across things you don't understand, do your parents help you with them?

18. Do your parents ever ask about what you are doing in school?

19. Do your parents get after you to do well in your schoolwork?

20. How often do you work in the garden with your parents?

21. How often do you make household repairs with your parents?

22. How often do you go to sports events with your parents?

23. How often do you watch television with your parents?

24. Do you share your thoughts and feelings with your parents?

25. Have you ever felt unwanted by your parents?
    Do your parents ever punish you in these ways?

26. By slapping or hitting you?

27. By not letting you do things that you want to do?

28. By nagging or scolding you?

29. By telling you that you are hurting their feelings?

30. By calling you bad names?

31. Do your parents ever promise to give you things if you will act right?

32. Do your parents ever explain why they feel the way they do?

33. Do your parents ever tell you that you have mispronounced or misused a word?

NOW USE
THESE ANSWERS

MOTHER
A. Often
B. Sometimes
C. Never

FATHER
F. Often
G. Sometimes
H. Never

34. Does your mother think you work hard enough in school?
    A. No, not hard enough   C. She thinks I work too hard
    B. Yes, about right   D. Don't know

35. Does your father think you work hard enough in school?
    A. No, not hard enough   C. He thinks I work too hard
    B. Yes, about right   D. Don't know

36. If you brought home a good report card, would your parents praise you?
    A. Definitely   D. Definitely not
    B. Probably   E. They don't ask to see my
    C. Probably not   report card
                               F. Don't know

37. If you brought home a good report card, would your parents give you money?
    A. Definitely   D. Definitely not
    B. Probably   E. They don't ask to see my
    C. Probably not   report card
                               F. Don't know

38. Do your parents want you to go to college?
    A. They insist on it   D. They don't care one way or
    B. They want me to go   the other
       very much   E. No, they don't want me to
    C. I think they want me to   go
       go but we don't talk   F. Don't know
       about it

39. Would you like to be the kind of person your mother is?
    A. In every way   D. In just a few ways
    B. In most ways   E. Not at all
    C. In some ways

40. Would you like to be the kind of person your father is?
    A. In every way   D. In just a few ways
    B. In most ways   E. Not at all
    C. In some ways

41. Would your mother stick by you if you got into really bad trouble?
    A. Certainly   D. I doubt it
    B. Probably   E. Don't know
    C. Maybe

NOW GO TO ROW 42 ON THE UPPER RIGHT HAND
SIDE OF ANSWER SHEET 5.

42. Would your father stick by you if you got into really bad
    trouble?
    A. Certainly   D. I doubt it
    B. Probably   E. Don't know
    C. Maybe

43. How are most decisions made between you and your mother?
    A. She tells me what to do   D. We talk about it until we
    B. We talk about it, but   agree
       she decides   E. I do what I want, but she
    C. I decide, but I have to   wants me to consider her
       get her permission   opinion
                                  F. I do what I want

44. How are most decisions made between you and your father?
    A. He tells me what to do   D. We talk about it until we
    B. We talk about it, but   agree
       he decides   E. I do what I want, but he
    C. I decide, but I have to   wants me to consider his
       get his permission   opinion
                                  F. I do what I want

45. Which of your parents most often punishes you?
    A. Almost always my mother
    B. Usually my mother
    C. Both mother and father equally
    D. Usually my father
    E. Almost always my father
    F. I never get punished

46. How much influence do you have in making family decisions?
    A. A lot   C. Very little
    B. Some   D. None

At what age do you think your parents would approve of you
living away from home? Please write the age you think they would
approve in Box A on the lower left side of Answer Sheet 5.

47. When you go out in the evening on schoolnights, about what time do your parents want you to get home?
    A. Before 8 o'clock
    B. Before 9 o'clock
    C. Before 10 o'clock
    D. Before 11 o'clock
    E. Before 12 o'clock
    F. Midnight or later
    G. No set time
    H. I never go out

48. Has your mother met your friends?
    A. Most of them
    B. Some of them
    C. None of them
    D. I have no friends

49. In general, what do your parents think of your friends?
    A. Strongly approve
    B. Approve
    C. Disapprove
    D. Strongly disapprove
    E. They do not know them
    F. I have no friends

50. Which of your parents would make the final decision if they were deciding how the children should be punished?
    A. Father always
    B. Father usually
    C. Father & mother equally
    D. Mother usually
    E. Mother always
    F. Don't know

51. Which of your parents would make the final decision if they were deciding where to live?
    A. Father always
    B. Father usually
    C. Father & mother equally
    D. Mother usually
    E. Mother always
    F. Don't know

52. Did your mother read to you when you were little?
    A. No
    B. Once or twice
    C. Several times
    D. Many times, but not regularly
    E. Many times, and regularly
    F. I don't remember

53. Did your father read to you when you were little?
    A. No
    B. Once or twice
    C. Several times
    D. Many times, but not regularly
    E. Many times, and regularly
    F. I don't remember

54. On the average, how many hours a week does your mother spend reading books?

   A. About ½ hour or less   D. 4–5 hours
   B. About 1 hour   E. 6–7 hours
   C. 2–3 hours   F. 8 hours or more

55. On the average, how many hours a week does your father spend reading books?

   A. About ½ hour or less   D. 4–5 hours
   B. About 1 hour   E. 6–7 hours
   C. 2–3 hours   F. 8 hours or more

PART II. PARENTS' BACKGROUND

---

56. How old is your mother?

   A. Under 26   E. Age 46 to 55
   B. Age 26 to 30   F. Over age 55
   C. Age 31 to 35   G. Parent is not living
   D. Age 36 to 45   H. Don't know

57. How much education does your mother have?

   A. Some high school or less   D. Some college or
   B. Graduated from high   junior college
       school   E. Graduated from a
   C. Trade or business school   4-year college

58. How much education does your father have?

   A. Some high school or less   D. Some college or
   B. Graduated from high   junior college
       school   E. Graduated from a
   C. Trade or business school   4-year college

59. On the average, how often does your mother attend religious services?

   A. Once a week or more   D. Only on important holidays
   B. Two or three times a   E. Hardly ever
       month   F. Never
   C. Once a month

60. On the average, how often does your father attend religious services?

A. Once a week or more
B. Two or three times a month
C. Once a month
D. Only on important holidays
E. Hardly ever
F. Never

61. Where was your mother born?

A. RICHMOND, California
B. In the RICHMOND AREA, but not in Richmond
C. In CALIFORNIA, but not in this area
D. In the SOUTH (Texas, Oklahoma, Arkansas, Louisiana, Kentucky, Tennessee, Alabama, Mississippi, West Virginia, Virginia, North and South Carolina, Georgia, and Florida)
E. Elsewhere in the United States
F. Outside the United States
G. Don't know

62. Where was your father born?

A. RICHMOND, California
B. In the RICHMOND AREA, but not in Richmond
C. In CALIFORNIA, but not in this area
D. In the SOUTH (Texas, Oklahoma, Arkansas, Louisiana, Kentucky, Tennessee, Alabama, Mississippi, West Virginia, Virginia, North and South Carolina, Georgia, and Florida)
E. Elsewhere in the United States
F. Outside the United States
G. Don't know

63. About how long ago did your family come to the Richmond area?

A. Within the last 4 years
B. 5–9 years ago
C. 10–14 years ago
D. 15–19 years ago
E. 20–24 years ago
F. 25 or more years ago
G. Don't know

64. During the past three years, how many times has your family moved from one house to another?
    A. Not at all
    B. Once
    C. Twice
    D. Three times
    E. Four times
    F. Five times
    G. Six times or more

65. Do your parents now own their home, or do they rent?
    A. They own it
    B. They rent
    C. Don't know

66. Are your parents in good health?
    A. Both are
    B. My father is
    C. My mother is
    D. Neither parent is

67. Is your mother working?
    A. Working full-time
    B. Working part-time
    C. Looking for work
    D. Keeping house
    E. Not working because of illness or disability
    F. Retired
    G. Not working for other reasons
    H. Parent is not living

68. Is your father working?
    A. Working full-time
    B. Working part-time
    C. Looking for work
    D. Keeping house
    E. Not working because of illness or disability
    F. Retired
    G. Not working for other reasons
    H. Parent is not living

69. Is your father satisfied with the job he now has, or the one he usually has?
    A. Very satisfied
    B. Satisfied
    C. Dissatisfied
    D. Very dissatisfied
    E. Don't know
    F. Father is not living

70. Does your father spend much time with the family?
    A. Very much time
    B. Some
    C. Not much
    D. None

71. How much of the time during the past three years has your mother been out of work because she could not find a job?
    A. Not at all   D. 7 months to 1 year
    B. Less than one month   E. 1 to 2 years
    C. 1 to 6 months   F. 2 or more years

72. How much of the time during the past three years has your father been out of work because he could not find a job?
    A. Not at all   D. 7 months to 1 year
    B. Less than one month   E. 1 to 2 years
    C. 1 to 6 months   F. 2 or more years

73. Have your parents received welfare payments?
    A. No, never
    B. Not now, but they used to
    C. Yes, now

74. Do your parents belong to a trade union or labor union?
    A. No, neither does   D. Both do
    B. Father does   E. Don't know
    C. Mother does

Now we want to ask you one question on a different subject. If you could have one wish, what would it be? Please write what you think your one wish would be in Box B of answer sheet 5. Tell us as much about it as you can.

PART III. HUMAN RELATIONS

---

75. Do you think a person of your race would get paid as much as a person of other racial groups for doing the same kind of work?
    A. He would probably get paid more
    B. He would probably get paid the same
    C. He would probably get paid less
    D. Don't know

76. If a family of your racial group rented the same kind of house as a family of other racial groups, do you think they would have to pay the same amount of rent?

A. They would probably have to pay more
B. They would probably pay the same
C. They would probably have to pay less
D. Don't know

77. In the city where you live, do you think that Negroes are discriminated against when people are being hired for jobs?
A. Definitely   D. Definitely not
B. Probably   E. Don't know
C. Probably not

78. If you could choose, in what kind of neighborhood would you prefer to live?
A. One that is integrated
B. One with only Mexican families
C. One with only Negro families
D. One with only Oriental families
E. One with only White families
F. I don't care one way or the other
G. Undecided

79. How many of your friends are Mexican?
A. All   D. Only a few
B. Most   E. None
C. About half

80. How many of your friends are Negro?
A. All   D. Only a few
B. Most   E. None
C. About half

NOW TURN YOUR ANSWER SHEET OVER AND BEGIN WITH ROW 8 ON THE LEFT HAND SIDE OF ANSWER SHEET 6.

8. How many of your friends are White?
A. All   D. Only a few
B. Most   E. None
C. About half

USE THESE ANSWERS

9. Have you ever eaten at the same table with a Mexican?

10. Have you ever eaten at the same table with a Negro?

11. Have you ever eaten at the same table with a White?

A. Often
B. Sometimes
C. Never

12. Have you ever danced with a Mexican?

13. Have you ever danced with a Negro?

14. Have you ever danced with a White?

15. Have you ever gone to a party where most of the people were Mexican?

16. Have you ever gone to a party where most of the people were Negro?

17. Have you ever gone to a party where most of the people were White?

NOW USE THESE ANSWERS

18. How do you feel about Mexicans?

19. How do you feel about Negroes?

20. How do you feel about Whites?

A. Like them
B. Don't especially like or dislike them
C. Dislike them

21. How do your parents feel about Mexicans?

22. How do your parents feel about Negroes?

23. How do your parents feel about Whites?

How do you feel about these Negro organizations?

24. The Urban League

25. NAACP (National Association for the Advancement of Colored People)

26. CORE (Congress of Racial Equality)

27. SNCC (Student Non-Violent Coordinating Committee)

28. Southern Christian Leadership Conference

29. Afro-American Association

30. Muslims

31. ADVANCE (Negro Council for Community Improvement)

A. Have never heard of it
B. Strongly approve
C. Approve
D. Disapprove
E. Strongly disapprove

Here is a list of ways that have been suggested by some Negro groups to reach their goals. How do you feel about each of these?

32. Urging Negroes to strike back if attacked

33. Keeping all Whites out of Negro organizations

34. Having organizations led by Negroes, but allowing Whites to become members

35. Getting all Negroes to take the same stand on racial issues

36. Improving the attitudes and conditions that exist in the Negro community itself

37. Requiring Whites to accept Negroes into the white community

A. Strongly approve
B. Approve
C. Undecided
D. Disapprove
E. Strongly disapprove

When you hear the following names, do you think of someone in civil rights, an entertainer, a writer, or an historical person?

38. Martin Luther King

39. Ralph Ellison

40. Marcus Garvey

41. Ray Charles

A. Civil Rights
B. Entertainer
C. Writer
D. Historical Person
E. Don't know

NOW GO TO ROW 42 ON THE UPPER RIGHT HAND SIDE OF ANSWER SHEET 6.

42. Crispus Attucks

43. Langston Hughes

44. Roy Wilkins

45. Joseph Blood

46. Medgar Evers

47. Nat Turner

48. Richard Wright

49. Have you personally ever been treated badly because of your race?
   A. Often   C. Seldom
   B. Sometimes   D. Never

50. Would you say that your skin is
   A. Very dark   D. Light
   B. Dark   E. Very light
   C. Tan

51. If you could change would you like to be
   A. Lighter
   B. Darker
   C. The same

52. Do any of these men live at your home now?
   A. My real father   D. Guardian
   B. Step father   E. None of these
   C. Foster father

53. Do any of these women live at your home now?
    A. My real mother   D. Guardian
    B. Step mother   E. None of these
    C. Foster mother

Who is the most important person in your life? We don't want the person's name, but tell us a little bit about the person in Box A of Answer Sheet 6. Tell us such things as: is the person a man or a woman, old or young, related to you or not, and what he or she is like.

54. Do you spend any time taking care of your brothers and sisters?
    A. I have no brothers or sisters
    B. No, I don't take care of them
    C. Once in awhile
    D. Quite often
    E. Every day

55. Do you know about Neighborhood House in North Richmond?
    A. No, I've never heard of it
    B. I've heard of it, but I've never been there
    C. I've visited Neighborhood House
    D. I used to participate in a Neighborhood House program
    E. I participate in a Neighborhood House program now

If you have heard of Neighborhood House, or have been there, what have you heard or what do you think about it? Write your comment in Box B in the upper right hand corner of Answer Sheet 6.

PART IV. ATTITUDES AND OPINIONS

Do you agree or disagree with these statements?

56. Most of the people I know have more money than I have

57. The community should take care of those who cannot take care of themselves

A. Strongly agree
B. Agree
C. Undecided
D. Disagree
E. Strongly disagree

58. My ideas about what I want to be seem to change all the time

59. When you get right down to it, becoming a success in life is up to the individual

60. Getting a good education is harder than getting a good job

61. I don't approve of sports

62. On the whole, I am satisfied with myself

63. I sometimes feel that I have to be twice as good as other people to get ahead

64. I often feel that I would like to be someone else

65. If you don't watch yourself people will try to take advantage of you

66. Most people like me

67. Things are all mixed up in my life

68. An easy life is a happy life

69. Even when I get married my main loyalty will still be to my mother and father

70. There is a life beyond death

71. The Devil actually exists

72. I can't seem to stay out of trouble no matter how hard I try

73. I certainly feel worthless at times

A. Strongly agree
B. Agree
C. Undecided
D. Disagree
E. Strongly disagree

74. There is no sense looking ahead since no one knows what the future will be like

75. I wish my father had a better job

76. My parents want me to aim for goals which I think are of little value

77. Most people in government are not really interested in the problems of families like mine

78. I often have trouble deciding which are the right rules to follow

79. Suckers deserve to be taken advantage of

80. I'm always looking for something better than I've got

A. Strongly agree
B. Agree
C. Undecided
D. Disagree
E. Strongly disagree

THANK YOU VERY MUCH FOR YOUR COOPERATION.

Appendix C-2. Police Data Coding Form

The following information was collected on all boys in the original sample during October 1965 at the Richmond and San Pablo Police Departments, and at the Contra Costa County Sheriff's Office.

1. Age at first offense.
2. Date of most recent offense.
3. Total number of offenses since December 31, 1962. (Does not include complaints, "suspicion," "possible," or "questioned.")
4. Total number of offenses ever committed.
5. Total number of arrests/citations.
6. Has the boy ever been placed on formal or informal probation or made a ward of the court?

7. Has the boy ever been committed to the California Youth Authority?
8. Total number of petty or grand thefts (Penal Code numbers 484, 484a, 487, 488).
9. Total number of burglaries (Penal Code numbers 459, 460).
10. Total number of auto thefts (Penal Code number 10851).
11. Total number of offenses involving force and violence (Penal Code numbers 148, 211, 212, 242, 243, 245, 415, 417, 520).

Selected Bibliography

Becker, Howard S. *Outsiders*. New York: The Free Press, 1963.

Blake, Judith, and Kingsley Davis. "Norms, Values, and Sanctions," in Robert E. L. Faris, ed., *Handbook of Modern Sociology*. Chicago: Rand McNally, 1964.

Bordua, David J. "Sociological Perspectives," in William W. Wattenberg, ed., *Social Deviancy among Youth, The Sixty-Fifth Yearbook of the National Society for the Study of Education*. Chicago: University of Chicago Press, 1966. Pp. 78–102.

Bowlby, John. *Child Care and the Growth of Love*. Baltimore: Penguin Books, 1963.

Briar, Scott, and Irving Piliavin. "Delinquency, Situational Inducements, and Commitments to Conformity," *Social Problems*, XIII (1965), 35–45.

Clark, John P., and Larry L. Tifft. "Polygraph and Interview Validation of Self-Reported Deviant Behavior," *American Sociological Review*, XXXI (1966), 516–523.

Cloward, Richard A., and Lloyd E. Ohlin. *Delinquency and Opportunity*. New York: The Free Press, 1960.

Cohen, Albert K. *Delinquent Boys*. New York: The Free Press, 1955.

———. "The Study of Social Disorganization and Deviant Behavior," in Robert K. Merton et al., eds., *Sociology Today*. New York: Basic Books, 1959.

Cohen, Albert K., and James F. Short, Jr. "Juvenile Delinquency," in Robert K. Merton and Robert A. Nisbet, eds., *Contemporary Social Problems*. 2nd ed. New York: Harcourt, Brace and World, 1966.

Cohen, Albert K., et al., eds. *The Sutherland Papers*. Bloomington: Indiana University Press, 1956.

Coleman, James C. *The Adolescent Society*. New York: The Free Press, 1961.

Cressey, Donald R. *Other People's Money*. New York: The Free Press, 1953.

Dentler, Robert A., and Lawrence J. Monroe. "Social Correlates of Early Adolescent Theft," *American Sociological Review*, XXVI (1961), 733–743.

Durkheim, Emile. *Moral Education*, trans. Everett K. Wilson and Herman Schnurer. New York: The Free Press, 1961.

———. *Suicide*, trans. John A. Spaulding and George Simpson. New York: The Free Press, 1951.

Elkin, Frederick, and William A. Westley. "The Myth of Adolescent Culture," *American Sociological Review*, XX (1955), 680–684.

Glueck, Sheldon and Eleanor. *Unraveling Juvenile Delinquency*. Cambridge: Harvard University Press, 1950.

Gold, Martin. *Status Forces in Delinquent Boys*. Ann Arbor: Institute for Social Research, 1963.

Gordon, Robert A. "Social Level, Social Disability, and Gang Interaction," *American Journal of Sociology*, LXXIII (1967), 42–62.

Hirschi, Travis, and Hanan C. Selvin. *Delinquency Research*. New York: The Free Press, 1967.

Hobbes, Thomas. *Leviathan*. Oxford: Basil Blackwell, 1957.

Kitsuse, John I., and David C. Dietrick. "*Delinquent Boys: A Critique*," *American Sociological Review*, XXIV (1959), 208–215.

Kornhauser, Ruth. "Theoretical Issues in the Sociological Study of Juvenile Delinquency." Center for the Study of Law and Society, Berkeley, 1963. Mimeographed.

Kvaraceus, William C., and Walter B. Miller. *Delinquent Behavior: Culture and the Individual*. Washington: National Education Association, 1959.

MacIver, Robert M. *Social Causation*. Boston: Ginn, 1940.

Matza, David. *Delinquency and Drift*. New York: Wiley, 1964.

McCord, William, and Joan McCord. *Origins of Crime*. New York: Columbia University Press, 1959.

———. *The Psychopath*. Princeton: D. van Nostrand, 1964.

Merton, Robert K. *Social Theory and Social Structure*. New York: The Free Press, 1957.

Miller, Walter B. "Lower Class Culture as a Generating Milieu of Gang Delinquency," *The Journal of Social Issues*, XIV (1958), 5–19.

Myerhoff, Howard L. and Barbara G. "Field Observations of Middle Class 'Gangs,'" in Edmund W. Vaz, ed., *Middle-Class Juvenile Delinquency*. New York: Harper and Row, 1967. Pp. 117–130.

Nadel, S. F. "Social Control and Self-Regulation," *Social Forces*, XXXI (1953), 265–273.

Nye, F. Ivan. *Family Relationships and Delinquent Behavior*. New York: Wiley, 1958.

Palmore, Erdman B., and Phillip E. Hammond. "Interacting Factors in Juvenile Delinquency," *American Sociological Review*, XXIX (1964), 848–854.

Parsons, Talcott. "Age and Sex in the Social Structure of the United States," in *Essays in Sociology*. New York: The Free Press, 1954.

———. *The Social System*. New York: The Free Press, 1951.

Reckless, Walter C. *The Crime Problem*. 4th ed. New York: Appleton-Century-Crofts, 1967.

Reiss, Albert J., Jr. "Delinquency as the Failure of Personal and Social Controls," *American Sociological Review*, XVI (1951), 196–207.

Rothstein, Edward. "Attributes Related to High Social Status: A Comparison of the Perceptions of Delinquent and Non-Delinquent Boys," *Social Problems*, X (1962), 75–83.

Sherif, Muzafer and Carolyn W. *Reference Groups: Exploration into Conformity and Deviation of Adolescents.* New York: Harper and Row, 1964.

Short, James F., Jr. "Differential Association and Delinquency," *Social Problems*, IV (1957), 233–239.

Short, James F., Jr., and F. Ivan Nye. "Reported Behavior as a Criterion of Deviant Behavior," *Social Problems*, V (1957), 207–213.

Short, James F., Jr., and Fred L. Strodtbeck. *Group Process and Gang Delinquency.* Chicago: University of Chicago Press, 1965.

Stinchcombe, Arthur L. *Rebellion in a High School.* Chicago: Quadrangle, 1964.

Sutherland, Edwin H., and Donald R. Cressey. *Principles of Criminology.* 7th ed. Philadelphia: Lippincott, 1966.

Sykes, Gresham M., and David Matza. "Techniques of Neutralization: A Theory of Delinquency," *American Sociological Review*, XXII (1957), 664–670.

Toby, Jackson. "Social Disorganization and Stake in Conformity: Complementary Factors in the Predatory Behavior of Hoodlums," *Journal of Criminal Law, Criminology, and Police Science*, XLVIII (1957), 12–17.

Toby, Jackson, and Marcia L. Toby. "Low School Status as a Predisposing Factor in Subcultural Delinquency." Rutgers University, New Brunswick, N.J., about 1962. Mimeographed.

Werthman, Carl. "The Function of Social Definitions in the Development of Delinquent Careers," in *Juvenile Delinquency and Youth Crime.* Washington: USGPO, 1967. Pp. 155–170.

Wilson, Alan B. "Educational Consequences of Segregation in a California Community." Survey Research Center, Berkeley, 1966. Mimeographed.

Wolfgang, Marvin E., et al., eds. *The Sociology of Crime and Delinquency.* New York: Wiley, 1962.

Wootton, Barbara. *Social Science and Social Pathology.* New York: Macmillan, 1959.

Yablonsky, Lewis. *The Violent Gang.* New York: Macmillan, 1963.

Index

Abrahamson, Mark J., 95 n.
Academic competence, 79-80, 111-120, 132-134, 177; self-perceived ability, 117-120, 129-130; *see also* Education
Achievement motivation, 144, 156, 178-179
Adolescent culture theory. *See* Cultural deviance theory
Adult status, claims to, 162-170, 179, 196, 217
Affection. *See* Attachment
Age, 62, 235-237
Akers, Ronald L., 13 n.
Ambition. *See* Achievement motivation; Aspirations
Analytic induction, 14-15
Andry, Robert G., 100 n.
Anomie, 124, 172, 198, 202
Aspirations, 5-6, 8-9, 124-125, 126, 143-145, 227-228; and education, 165, 171-179, 182, 185, 186 n.; and parental pressure, 174-177; and income and occupation, 180-186
Attachment, 16-19, 27-28, 29-30, 200, 203, 229; to parents, 83-109, 128, 131-132, 139-140, 141-143, 149-150, 204; to conventional parents, 83, 88-94; to unconventional parents, 94-100; to mother, 86-87, 89-91, 100-107, 142, 143; to father, 91, 92-97, 99-105, 131-132; to peers, 84, 135-161; to delinquent friends, 98-100, 112, 135-141, 147-159; to teachers, 85, 123, 125-127, 130, 131-132, 204; to school, 120-134, 156, 164, 168
Automobile, importance of, 169, 194-196, 217-218

Balistrieri, James, 210 n.
Ball, Richard A., 212 n.
Barron, Milton L., 114 n., 187
Becker, Howard S., 14 n., 21, 49, 137 n.; quoted, 20, 32, 48, 231
Beliefs. *See* Values

Bendix, Reinhard, 27 n., 28
Blake, Judith, 18 n.
Blame, 183-184, 206-211, 227
Bond theory. *See* Control theory
Bordua, David J., 66 n., 81, 159, 180
Boredom, 192-196
Bowlby, John, 86, 87 n.
Briar, Scott, 11, 19, 68 n., 73; quoted, 33, 137
Broken homes, 68 n., 83, 86-87, 103, 242-243; *see also* Family
Burgess, Robert L., 13 n., 95 n.

Clark, John P., 59 n., 235 n.
Class theory. *See* Strain theory
Cloward, Richard A., 4 n., 13 n., 64 n., 86 n., 122 n.; and lower class, 6, 7 n., 8 n., 110-111, 120, 179-184; and definitions of delinquency, 47 n., 48, 52; and values, 86 n., 94, 197 n., 223; and heightened expectations, 117
Cohen, Albert K., 5 n., 7 n., 52 n., 190, 197 n., 225-226 n.; and conformity, 10 n., 17 n.; and social class, 27 n., 110, 125, 139, 140, 191 n.; quoted, 32, 47 n., 48; definitions of delinquency, 47 n., 122 n.; and attachment, 139, 140; and values, 223
Cohesiveness. *See* Gang membership and cohesiveness
Coleman, James C., 139-143
Commitment, 20-21, 27-29, 178, 179 n., 202; lack of, to education, 164-170; *see also* Aspirations; Attachment; Goals
Communication, intimacy of, 90, 105, 108; with father, 91, 93, 96, 99-100, 104, 131-132, 156; with mother, 103; *see also* Attachment
Companionship. *See* Peer relations
Configurational definitions, 49-51, 53; *see also* Role definitions; Typological definitions
Conformity, stakes in. *See* Peer relations, and stakes in conformity

Myerhoff, Barbara G., 217-218
Myerhoff, Howard L., 217-218

Negroes. See Race
Neutralization, techniques of, 24-25,
127, 199-200, 205-212; denial of
responsibility, 206-208; denial of
injury, 208-209; denial of the
victim, 209-211; condemnation of
condemners, 211
Nonresponse bias. See Questionnaire,
nonresponse bias
Norms. See International, of norms
Nye, F. Ivan, 3 n., 19, 58, 241 n.;
quoted, 11, 67; delinquency scale
of, 54-55; and social class, 67, 73;
and attachment, 87, 95 n., 240;
and importance of father, 100 n.,
101, 105 n.; and mother's employment, 237, 238 n.

Occupational goals, 180-186
Official reaction hypothesis, 68, 77-
79
Ohlin, Lloyd E., 4 n., 13 n., 64 n.,
122 n., 223; and lower class, 6,
7 n., 110-111, 120, 179-184; definitions of delinquency, 47 n., 48,
52; and values, 86 n., 94, 197 n.,
223; and heightened expectations,
117
Olson, Virgil J., 66 n.
Opportunity, 117-120, 158, 171 n.;
see also Discrimination; Peer relations, and stakes in conformity

Palmore, Erdman B., 158
Parents. See Family
Parsons, Talcott, 3 n., 4 n., 18 n.,
33 n., 100 n., 127 n., 169 n., 170 n.
Peer relations, 84, 135-161, 194-195;
and delinquent friends, 98-100,
112, 135-141, 147-159; and stakes
in conformity, 137-143, 151-161;
and individualistic aspirations, 140,
143-145; and attachment to parents, 140-143, 149-151; and self-
image as delinquent, 145-152
Piaget, Jean, 29-30
Piliavin, Irving, 11, 19, 33, 64 n.,
68 n., 73, 93 n., 137
Police, respect for. See Respect, for
police
Police records, 41-46 passim, 57, 60,
63-64, 68, 75-81, 99-100, 113, 114,
118, 119
Psychopathy, 17-18, 24, 84

Questionnaire, administration of, 39-
41; nonresponse bias, 41-46; delinquency scale, 54-57, 61; and self-
reporting, 56-64, 67, 69-72, 74-79,
114-119; other indexes used, 62-
64; quoted, 247-299

Race, 65, 68 n., 75-81, 97, 119-120,
182-184; see also Lower class
Recidivism, 87-88
Reckless, Walter C., 3 n., 84, 136
Recreation, 187, 189-190, 196
Reiss, Albert J., Jr., 3 n., 19, 42, 54,
87-88, 198 n.
Respect, 30, 127, 200, 209; for
police, 79, 201-202, 204, 211; for
friends' opinions, 146-152; for law,
199, 202-205, 214-215, 216; see
also Neutralization, techniques of
Rhodes, Albert Lewis, 42
Rivera, Ramon J., 109 n.
Roach, Jack L., 141
Role definitions, 48-49, 52-53, 145-
152 passim; see also Configurational definitions; Typological defi-
nitions

Sample, selection of, 35-37; weight-
ing procedures, 37-38; data sources,
39-46; see also Questionnaire
Schools. See Education
Selvin, Hanan C., 13-14 n., 50 n.,
136 n., 137 n., 153
Shaw, Clifford R., 11
Sherif, Carolyn W., 83 n., 139
Sherif, Muzafer, 83 n., 139
Short, James F., Jr., 9 n., 58, 108 n.,
132-133, 139 n., 141 n., 151-152,
160-161, 178 n., 179 n.; quoted,
32, 66; delinquency scale of, 54-55
Smartness. See Lower class, culture
Smoking, 128, 129, 156, 164, 165,
166-168
Social class, and strain theory, 6-10;
relation to delinquency, 66-75, 81-
82, 165 n.; and educational aspirations and expectations, 73, 82,
111, 173-179, 182; and lower-class
culture, 95-97, 141, 179, 212-223,
229-230; and attachment, 95-97,
107-108, 140, 142; and income
and occupational aspirations and
expectations, 180-186; see also
Family, socioeconomic status of;
Lower class
Social control theory. See Control
theory